# Understanding Linguistics: The Science of Language

## John McWhorter, Ph.D.

THE
GREAT
COURSES®

**PUBLISHED BY:**

**THE GREAT COURSES**
Corporate Headquarters
4840 Westfields Boulevard, Suite 500
Chantilly, Virginia 20151-2299
Phone: 1-800-832-2412
Fax: 703-378-3819
www.thegreatcourses.com

# John McWhorter, Ph.D.

Senior Fellow, Manhattan Institute

John McWhorter, Senior Fellow at the Manhattan Institute and weekly columnist for *The New York Sun*, earned his Ph.D. in Linguistics from Stanford University in 1993 and became Associate Professor of Linguistics at UC Berkeley after teaching at Cornell University. His academic specialty is language change and language contact. He is the author of *The Power of Babel: A Natural History of Language*, on how the world's languages arise, change, and mix, and *Doing Our Own Thing: The Degradation of Language and Music in America and Why We Should, Like, Care*. More recently, he is the author of *Our Magnificent Bastard Tongue: Untold Stories in the History of English*. He has also written a book on dialects and Black English, *The Word on the Street*; three books on Creole languages; and an academic linguistics book entitled *Language Interrupted: Signs of Non-Native Acquisition in Standard Language Grammars*.

The Teaching Company released his 36-lecture audiovisual course *The Story of Human Language* in 2004. Beyond his work in linguistics, Dr. McWhorter is the author of *Losing the Race*; an anthology of race writings called *Authentically Black*; *Winning the Race: Beyond the Crisis in Black America*; and *All About the Beat: Why Hip-Hop Can't Save Black America*. He has written on race and cultural issues for *The New Republic*, *The Wall Street Journal*, *The Washington Post*, *The New York Times*, *The Chronicle of Higher Education*, *National Review*, the *Los Angeles Times*, *The American Enterprise*, *Ebony*, *Vibe*, and *City Journal*. He provides commentaries for *All Things Considered* and previously appeared weekly on NPR's *News and Notes*; he has also appeared on *Meet the Press*, *Dateline NBC*, *Politically Incorrect*, *Talk of the Nation*, *Today*, *Good Morning America*, *The NewsHour with Jim Lehrer*, and *Fresh Air*.

# Table of Contents

# Understanding Linguistics: The Science of Language

# Understanding Linguistics: The Science of Language

**Scope:**

As an introduction to linguistic science, this course's main goal is to show that speaking is more than a matter of knowing words and putting them in order. Linguists have discovered that language is an intricate hierarchy of systems, ever changing in surface appearance but ever consistent in organizational essence.

We begin with sounds, of which any language has many more than what the writing system indicates, often even masked in the process (for example, in terms of sound the default English plural marker is not [s] but [z]). Above this level come not words but morphemes, units of meaning, be this *microphone*, *the*, *-ed* in *walked*, or even *-a-* in *came* versus *come*. Then above this is syntax, which as studied by followers of Noam Chomsky has revolutionized linguistics over the past 40 years. The hypothesis is that there is a single innate grammar configured in our brains, with assorted "on-off" switches (e.g., verb first or verb last). Which switches are on and which are off make the difference between, for example, Japanese and English.

Words are, of course, hardly irrelevant to language, and the study of semantics examines how meaning is managed in its journey from a thought to a sentence. Languages differ vastly, however, in how they translate meaning into words; for instance, what is a subject in English is marked in different ways in other languages, depending on whether the subject does something or just feels something. In the same way, languages differ in how they translate into words a speaker's feelings about the topic or which part a speaker wants to emphasize; linguists call this issue *pragmatics*.

Language always changes; thus Old English is a different language from modern English. We examine how 19th-century linguists first proposed that this change happens according to regular tendencies in how words change and then how this developed into a science that allows us to reconstruct ancient languages that were never written and are no longer spoken. We then examine how grammar itself emerges when concrete words like *mind* become abstract bits meaning *-ly*, such as *-ment* in French or *-mente* in Spanish.

Language change is gradual; languages are passed on to new generations of speakers, who can communicate with the older ones. How children learn languages, in all of their complexity, is much more than simply learning words one at a time. We will also examine how adults learn new languages if they have to and how well they manage the task.

The course also covers how social class, gender, and even race determine differences in how we speak a language and how these differences often even determine how the language changes over time (for example, working-class men are the prime changers of language, not Blue Americans, teenagers, or women). We also encounter a burgeoning area of study showing the various processes that result from widespread bilingualism, such as the simplification of a once more-challenging tongue (English is "easy" for this reason). Also, in a social vein, we discover how conversation is guided by rules we subconsciously internalize and how much of conversation consists of using sentences as commands and requests rather than as statements. We will also see that all of the above also differ vastly according to culture: In Malagasy-speaking villages, for example, one asks someone to wash something by saying that "the soap will be used to wash the clothes," without mentioning who will be wielding the soap.

In the final lectures, we meet founding philosophers of language, such as Ferdinand de Saussure, who pioneered the approach to languages as founded on structured interactions between sounds and morphemes, and Edward Sapir and Benjamin Lee Whorf, who proposed that the particularities of one's language channel the way one thinks. We also examine the tension between linguists, who simply describe the way language is used, and much of the general public, who feel that there are ways that language should and should not be used.

Subsequently, we visit how writing emerged in the Fertile Crescent and the proliferation of writing systems since, then the newly burgeoning study of how language began in the first place. For the following two lectures, you get to be a linguist as I show how linguists actually analyze an unknown language's grammar. The first is a Euro-African hybrid of Suriname, called Saramaccan, and the second is an obscure tongue of the Caucasus Mountains in Russia, called Kabardian. Finally, we will survey some of the leading theories about how the language faculty evolved in our species.

# Lecture One
# What Is Linguistics?

**Scope:** Linguistics is the study of human language, rather than an attempt
to learn languages or change how people express themselves
through language. It is a science that, in its current form, has
existed only for the past 200 years. A great many things about
language that seem apparent in fact are quite otherwise upon
examination, and this is what makes linguistics a fascinating field.

## Outline

**I.** People outside of the field of linguistics are often unclear on just what
linguistics is.

    **A.** People often suppose that a language is essentially just its words,
but you could know all of a language's words and still be unable to
communicate above the level of a one-year-old; linguists are
interested in the mechanisms via which we put the words together.

    **B.** It is also commonly supposed that grammar is a mere matter of
classifying words according to which of eight "official" parts of
speech they represent. This, however, is a highly approximate
representation of what grammar consists of.

        **1.** For example, take the sentence *She kept on popping in and out
of the office all afternoon.*

        **2.** What is the verb in that sentence, *kept* or *popping*? You may
have learned about auxiliary verbs, like *have* and *be*—is *kept*
one? What tense is this sentence in? In *kept on*, what part of
speech is *on*?

**II.** Linguistics is a *scientific* analysis of language, as opposed to
understandable but *impressionistic* analyses of language.

    **A.** There is a science of how sounds work in languages.

        **1.** *Singin'* is not a shorter word than *singing*. No "letter" has been
left off of *singin'*, because the final -*ng* of *singing* represents
not two sounds, *n* and *g*, but a single sound with no letter of its
own in the English alphabet.

        **2.** Writing is as approximate a representation of speech as the
drawing style of *The Simpsons* is an approximation of how
human beings actually look.

3

**B.** There is a science of what concepts are the core of language as opposed to incidental frills.

  **1.** English is a much stranger language, as languages go, than we are aware.

   **a.** In the vast majority of the world's languages, there is no word for *the* or *a*. In the vast majority of the world's languages, there is no verb *have*; instead you say that things are "to you."

   **b.** In all of the world, the only languages that have to use *do* in negative sentences and questions ("You do not knit," "Do you knit?") are English, Welsh, Breton (spoken across the English Channel, in France), and a small number of tiny Italian dialects.

  **2.** Linguists have found that a great many aspects of language that feel essential to humans depending on what language they speak are actually incidentals, that certain incidental features tend to appear in a language only if other ones do, and that orderings like this may well be a result of how our brains are configured to learn language as infants.

  **3.** Consider this analogy: There are basic principles as to how ingredients in food preparation interact in combination and according to conditions such as temperature and aging. Peoples of some regions have access to certain ingredients unavailable in other areas, but all peoples cook according to certain fundamental chemical principles. Linguists are interested in those principles, rather than assuming that the human ability to cook is something as local as the cuisine of Italy or Thailand.

**C.** From this scientific perspective, much of what we naturally feel as "wrong" renditions of our language are simply random variations not analyzable as "mistakes." In the 1800s, many grammarians considered the following extremely déclassé: *all the time*, *born in*, *lit*, *washtub*, *standpoint*, *have a look at, the first two*, and *the house is being built*, as well as saying "stacked" instead of "stackèd."

**III.** Linguists are not translators.

**A.** The word *linguist* is occasionally used that way but not to refer to practitioners in the field of linguistics.

**B.** Linguists are also not language police. The attitude of Henry Higgins in George Bernard Shaw's *Pygmalion* toward vernacular English is not one that any modern linguist would share.

**C.** We study language, rather than teach it or fix it.

**IV.** In this course, we will experience how linguists study language.

**A.** We will first examine how linguists analyze the basic building blocks of language. The main areas will be the study of sounds, the construction of words, the structure of sentences, and how sentences express meaning through all of these factors.

**B.** These basic tools of analysis are used by researchers in several subfields of linguistics, which we will examine in turn. These will be how languages change over time (*historical linguistics*), how children learn to speak (language acquisition), how the use of language varies according to social and sociological factors (*sociolinguistics*), noted perspectives on the nature of human language (*philosophy of language*), and how writing emerged.

**C.** In two lectures near the end, you will encounter two languages that you have never encountered before and will experience analyzing them as a linguist would.

**D.** We will finish with a look at modern theories on how the language faculty evolved in humans.

**E.** You may have taken my previous Teaching Company course on language, *The Story of Human Language*.

**1.** That was a course about one aspect of how language has existed since it evolved—namely, that one original language became several, which overgrew with "incidentals" while mixing madly with one another, with brand new languages often emerging in the process.

**2.** Within the framework of this course, *The Story of Human Language* was about certain aspects of historical linguistics, with some sociolinguistics mixed in. This course will introduce you to the larger scientific principles that the perspective of that course was based on.

**V.** Modern linguistics is new.

**A.** Linguistics in the modern sense has existed only since the early 19$^{\text{th}}$ century.

1. Before this there was a rich tradition of the study of language, but not in the sense of what is today considered linguistics. Socrates, Plato, and Aristotle examined the relationship between speech and the thoughts that it communicated, terming humans' gift of language *logos*.
2. Today such inquiry is classified as philosophy of language.

B. The first grammatical descriptions of individual languages date back two millennia, with the Indian grammarian Panini's description of Sanskrit around the 4th century B.C.E. and Dionysius the Thracian's *Techne Grammatike* from the 2nd century B.C.E. However, because travel was so limited in the ancient world, Greek analysts of language thought of Greek as the quintessence of language and even thought of Latin as a strange kind of Greek (because there were so many words in common).

C. As Europeans started encountering other peoples while exploring the world, missionaries and others wrote descriptions of the languages of the people they encountered.

D. Yet most of these people were hampered by an understandable assumption that "language" was, essentially, the way European languages worked.
1. For example, Bishop John Wilkins (1614–1672) devised a writing system designed to express human thought irrespective of the differences between languages.
2. However, he was unaware how different languages can be. For example, in Japanese, a normal way to say "I like Pam" is "*Pam ga suki*"—"Pam likeableness."
3. Wilkins's system looked pretty much like English sentences written word by word in pictures.
4. From a modern linguist's perspective, the utterance "I like Pam" contains three concepts: the *I* who is speaking, the issue of liking, and *Pam*.
5. It is a core feature of language to have a subject, but depending on the language either *I* or *Pam* can be the subject. In Japanese, *Pam* is. The *like* aspect can be expressed as a verb but also as another "part of speech," such as in Japanese, where it is a noun.
6. A language might also have a word or prefix or suffix that shows that the subject is a subject—like Japanese's *ga*—or it might not, as in English.

**7.** Even the *I* can be left to context, as in Japanese; languages differ on what gets left to context and what must be said, and some have even hypothesized that this affects how a language's speaker processes the world.

**E.** When we are finished, you will find yourself looking at and listening to language in ways that likely never occurred to you before. Certainly you will understand that there is more to a language than a collection of words and what parts of speech they classify as.

**Essential Reading:**

Crystal, *The Cambridge Encyclopedia of Language.*

Sapir, *Language: An Introduction.*

**Supplemental Reading:**

Harris, and Taylor, eds., *Landmarks in Linguistic Thought I.*

Joseph, Love, and Taylor, *Landmarks in Linguistic Thought II.*

**Questions to Consider:**

**1.** Part of what makes language such a fascinating subject of scientific inquiry is that something as complex as a language is learned by small children so quickly. Think of how children start by learning just single words at a time and then advance to using two and then three at a time—and then, in the blink of an eye, there is a "phase shift" and they are using complete sentences. There is a "break" between *Put me down* and *I think we should have broccoli tonight, don't you, Mommy?* Has it ever occurred to you that there is something magical about the fact that all mentally normal human beings pull this off without even trying?

**2.** We often think of speaking as a matter of stringing words together in a certain order and being careful to observe certain "rules," such as not saying "Billy and me went to the store." But have you ever noticed that people who are under the influence of alcohol, or even mentally unwell, nevertheless easily command fluent speech? Someone passed out in a gutter could quite plausibly say "He never even thought about coming up with a single reason why." That sentence requires using an irregular past marking for *think*, using the gerund form of *come*, saying *a* rather than *the* (the way, for example, a Slavic foreigner might), and using *even* in a way that, if you think about it, no one ever taught you explicitly. Once again, isn't language magic?

# Lecture One—Transcript
## What Is Linguistics?

My name is John McWhorter, and welcome to my course. This is a course on linguistics, and the fact of the matter is that it's not unusual to not really know exactly what linguistics is. By the time you're finished with this course, you will very much know what it is. But just to start you off, I think that what we should realize—and something we're going to see in this course again and again—is that the fundamental thing that linguistics is about is that language is more than just a big bunch of words. It's easy to think that what we're doing when we're speaking is producing words that we learned when we were kids—and now we know them, and we string them together in some sort of way, and that maybe there's some wrong ways to string them together that you learn in school and you get your knuckles rapped for—but that basically what we're doing is just using a big bunch of words.

If you really think about it, words alone can't be even most of what using a language—in terms of what would be interesting about using a language—is. That's because if you think about it, imagine if you inhaled a Russian dictionary. Let's say that you, for all intents and purposes, knew every single word in the language. If you think about it, really, even then you would be unable to have any kind of meaningful conversation in the language, and three- and four-year-olds would be light years ahead of you. That's because, obviously, there is also the issue of how you put the words together in order to convey meaning.

There's also a sense that if a language is more than just a big bucket of words, then as far as grammar is concerned, it's a matter of deciding whether words fit into one of eight parts of speech. The idea is that once you've got these parts of speech, then you've got what there is besides just the big collection of words. Actually, the parts of speech that you learned in school constitute a very approximate sense of what a language's actual structural system is. For example, take a sentence like this one: *She kept on popping in and out of the office all afternoon*. That's a perfectly ordinary sentence; nothing strange about that. *She kept on popping in and out of the office all afternoon*. First of all, if it's really just all about the parts of speech, what's the verb in that sentence? Is it *kept*? Because, you know, *popping* is a verb. What's the verb? You know a sentence has a verb; you learn how to parse that. Well, what's the verb? Is it *kept* or is it *popping*? Or you may have learned that *have* and *be* are used as auxiliary verbs often. Is *kept on* auxiliary here? Were you ever taught that *kept/keep* is an auxiliary? It seems like one. We didn't learn about that in grammar school. Or we talk about, *kept on popping in and out of the office*. OK, *on*. What part of speech is *on* in this case? Is it a preposition? Are we talking about something being *on* the table? *Kept it on the table so that it would melt* or something like that? Obviously it's a different kind of *on*. Clearly the parts of speech—the wonderful *Schoolhouse Rock* segments on TV in the '70s if you're of a certain age like mine and remember—those things will only take us so far.

Linguistics shows that there is more than that. Namely, linguistics is a scientific analysis of language, as opposed to the more impressionistic analysis of language that all of us spontaneously make because we all use language all the time. The idea is to find system in what appears to be either chaos or just randomness, such as the fact that the big bucket of words is a part of what a language is.

What do I mean by scientific? I will tell you. For example, here's one example of how linguistics is scientific: There is a science of how words work in languages. For example, we can say "singin'," or we can say "singing." We're often told that *singin'* is shorter than *singing*, that a *g* has been dropped. But if you think about it—and I'm always saying, "If you think about it," because these things become obvious if you just pause for a second and smell some roses and think about it—if you think about it, actually, there is nothing dropped at all in *singin'*. Nothing has been left off, because the final sound of *singing* is not two sounds—even though it's written that way with an *-ng*. It's just one sound.

Here's how you know. Here are two words: There's *singer*, and we know how that's spelled, and then there's *finger*. Notice that those two words only differ in terms of the initial consonant. But one of them is *finger*, and the other one is *singer*. You don't say "finner"—that doesn't work—and you don't say "sing-ger." I once knew a professor; he was this kind of gouty, rather aged professor. It was a course on music, and he kept on talking about "sing-gers." I didn't know why, and it was like somebody jabbing their finger in my eye every time he said it, because that's not the way it's pronounced. You have a "singer" and a "fing-ger." The difference is that in one of those cases you are actually enunciating an *n* and a *g*, and so a "fing-ger." They're right there. But with *singer*, you don't say "sing-ger." It's really just "singer." In other words, if you isolate what's in the middle, it's this "nguh" thing—not "nnn-guh," but "nguh." That "nguh" is a separate sound in English, and that's the sound at the end of *singing*. It's

9

"singing," not "singing-guh," which is not something anybody would say. There's a system. There is a sound system of language, which is very different from the way language happens to be spelled. One thing that we're going to learn again and again is that we have to get past letters. Language is about sound.

In fact, the way that language is represented on the page is very similar to how people are drawn on *The Simpsons*. For example, if Stephen Jay Gould guests on *The Simpsons*, then he's going to have big eyes and this kind of blobby drawing style. That's the way everybody looks on *The Simpsons*. There could be no *Homo sapiens* that actually look like that. We're just used to that kind of refraction of what people look like on *The Simpsons*. Letters are to spoken language as Simpsons are to real life and the way it actually looks. There's a science of sound, which is very different from the alphabet that we diligently learned and now think of as something sacrosanct.

Or there is a science—there is a scientific perspective—on what concepts are core to language as opposed to ones that are incidental frills. The things that are incidental frills are often ones that seem very meat-and-potatoes and central and vital to us within the particular language that we speak. For example, in the vast majority of the world's languages, there are no words for *the* and *a*. We kind of think that it's necessary to distinguish *the* soap that we slipped on this morning from *a* turtle that mysteriously popped up in the living room and that we're mentioning right now. Actually, that is a very fine shade of meaning that many languages completely do without in any fashion, and it's not something that is typical of a language, to have two words with those meanings. English is odd in that way.

Most languages in the world do not have a verb *to have*. We think of it as the most ordinary thing in the world to say, like as I do, "I have a cat." But why would you put it that way? It's interesting. If you talk about verbs, it could be "I own a cat," and then there is this financial arrangement. I think mine cost a hundred dollars; it's funny how you forget those things. Or it can be "I grasp a cat," or it can be "I possess a cat." But to say "I have a cat," what am I doing? I'm really specifying a kind of relationship between me and my cat, not something that I do. I don't walk around "having"; it's really kind of a state. Actually, in a great many languages, the way that you say you have something is to say that thing is "to you." Those of you who happen to know Russian will be familiar with this, and this is very common around the world. To say "have," it's kind of a European fetish for the most part. Most of the languages in the world have some other way of dealing with *have* when using neutral sentences.

Or there's this business of *do* in English. We use *do* funny. You say, "I do not walk quickly." What's the *do*? Can't you just say, "I walk not quickly?" If you've learned any other language, then you'll notice that's the way it's said. It's either "I not walk quickly" or "I walk not quickly," but what's this "I do not walk quickly"? We just kind of get used to it, but it's there. When you ask a question, "Do you walk quickly?" *Do* what? What's the *do* doing? If you're an English speaker, that just seems like the most natural thing, but notice that you don't find that in pretty much any other language that you may happen to have learned. Why don't you just say, "Walk you?" That's the way it would be in many languages. What's *do* doing there? In fact, if you look at the languages of the whole world—and I mean really, if you get in a little plane, and it's like in an old black and white movie where the plane flies all around the globe, and you actually look everywhere— then as far as this kind of little *do* usage, that is in (1), English; that is in (2), some Celtic languages like Welsh and Breton. Then, as far as I know—and I haven't checked every language in the world, and I'm not going to—but I have reason to believe that one of the only other places where *do* is used in that way is way up in some mountains in Italy in these villages where like six and a half people live. There are few of these dialects where they use *do* of that kind only in questions. That's way up there, in God-Knows-What-Might-Happen way up there. Those are the only languages in the world— and in this case they're just dialects of Italian—that use it in that way.

Linguists have actually found that a lot of aspects of language that might feel essential to the speaker of one of them are actually incidentals, that the incidental features tend to appear in a language only if other ones do in certain orders, and that the orders that these things appear in just might have something to do with how our brains are configured to learn language when we are infants. When it comes to language, the proper analogy could be seen to be food preparation. There are all sorts of ways of preparing food around the world, but when you really think about it, all food preparation is based on certain basic principles involving temperature and whether or not and how you age the food in question. There's no such thing as a cuisine that is not based on those fundamental elements. Of course in some regions some items are more easily available than others. There are traditions that have set in as to what you eat and what you don't eat. But all cooking is ultimately based on certain fundamental chemical principles. A Martian could be taught those and come up with a kind of food that would make a certain basic sense almost anywhere in the world. We're looking for—in a way, as linguists—what the universals of, say, cooking mechanisms are, except as applied to language. Thai food's great, but we wouldn't want to say that the essentials of cooking are lime juice and chili and the particular things that they do. Those are variations on something much more general. In linguistics, we are looking for the general.

Another example of science versus impression: There is a natural sense that anybody has when they are speaking a language that some things are wrong—or they're not as right as other things in terms of how you might put things. As a result, we—and this is most people, thoroughly reasonable people—have a sense that, for example, English is a language where people are walking around making mistakes in it all the time. There's this way of speaking it that is pristine and proper, and you learned it in school. And then there are all these people running around making errors. I knew a wonderful person—who was not a man—years ago, and she talked to me about how she had had to end a liaison with a fellow, and that one of the main reasons was that he was just walking around making too many grammatical errors. I thought, "That's so sad." The fact of the matter is that, looked at in broader view—looked at in terms of a perspective on language as something that happens and it's fine the way it is—we see that a lot of the things, in fact really most or even all of the things, that are considered wrong or errors are really just issues of aesthetics and that we're really dealing with a kind of fashion that changes, very much like clothes do.

For example, it used to be that if I wanted to talk about where I was born, I would have said that I was born "at Philadelphia." That's what I was supposed to say, and not if I were a person who's pretentious enough to talk like that, just ordinary people. I wasn't born "in Philadelphia"; I was born "at Philadelphia." If I said that I was born "in Philadelphia," that sounded a little déclassé. That seems utterly arbitrary to us now, but the fact of the matter is that the things that bother us now will seem just as silly to people later. It used to be that you would talk about how you "lighted" something; you didn't "lit" it. "I lit the candle." Oh, vulgar! That's like Oliver Twist running around in the street untutored or something. You have to say "lighted," people were told. Now if you said "lighted," somebody would probably take you to the hospital, or, you know, they might dump you for making a grammatical error. That's because these things change in a very arbitrary way. It used to be you were supposed to say "stackèd" instead of "stacked some books." It was considered a little vulgar to leave out the *e*, so to speak. These things change, and these things are not based on a scientific perspective of language.

It's not that we aren't all human. There are things I don't like, too. There's one that probably I have to hear about once a day: "Can I get a … ?" That's what people say in a restaurant: "Can I get a Coke?" What? It's like, what do you mean, "Can I get a … ?" It's not about "can you get" it; it's about whether they're going to give it to you, and so you should say, "May I have a …" or "I would like a …"; but "Can I get a hamburger?" just rubs me the wrong way for all sorts of reasons that are purely aesthetic. It's like I also don't like the color scarlet, and I think that almonds are overrated. I just don't happen to like it. It's the same thing with a lot of the things that we are taught are wrong, which are really just there.

Linguistics is not about translation; that is not something that we do. The word *linguist* is occasionally used to indicate a translator, but that's not what an academic linguist is. We are also not language police. The view of language that Henry Higgins has in *Pygmalion* is very amusing, even more so when set to music. But that is not something that any linguist would agree with. We study language rather than teaching it or fixing it, and I'd like to show you how to do the same.

First, we're going to look at how linguists analyze the building blocks of language. We're going to start with the study of sounds, and then we're going to go on to how words are formed—and that is quite counterintuitively different in many languages than the way we do it here in English. There are many Native American languages, for example, where many of the sentences I have said so far in this lecture would all actually be one word. *What is a word?* is a richer question than you might think.

Then we're going to talk about the structure of sentences, and that is more than the grand old parsing diagrams. In fact, the person who has really set the tune in terms of how that kind of sentence analysis is done in linguistics today has been Noam Chomsky, who is known, I think, to most people as a political thinker. But he is also the grandfather of how modern linguists analyze sentence structure as well. And then, of course, we also express meaning. And there is a different sense of meaning than just what happens when you put a sentence together. There is many a slip between the sentence construction and what we mean. How a language does that is something which can be seen as universal across all languages. But then there are the peculiarities, so we're going to look at the basic building blocks of how you go from seeing something and wanting to say something about it, thinking about something and wanting to say something about it, and how it will actually come out. In other words, we're going to look at *semantics* and *pragmatics*, and you'll see what those mean when we get to them.

We'll look at those things. Then we're going to look at how these basic tools are used by people in various subfields of linguistics. And so we're going to look at how language changes over time. For example, Latin is not a dead language. Latin is spoken today all over Europe. Latin is being spoken in a tiny little village up on top of a mountain in Italy. Those dialects are Latin. There was no time when everybody woke up in the morning and said, "My God, we speak Italian." Really, Latin just kind of gradually morphed into the Romance languages, including those Italian dialects. They are speaking today's version, up in those mountains, of the language that Julius Caesar spoke. There's no difference; it's just that all languages are changing all the time. So we're going to study *historical linguistics*, as it is called. We're going to look at how children learn to speak; we're going to look at what is called *language acquisition* because there are things there that are worth noticing other than, "Oh look, Justin learned a new word today." As always, language is about more than words; there is also grammar, and grammar can be quite keen as well.

Then we are going to look at what's called *sociolinguistics*. That is about how language varies—not just in terms of what vocabulary you use, but the structure of your language varies in systematic ways according to race, according to class, according to gender, and according to education level. Some of those things involve dealing with subjects that Americans are sometimes a little ticklish about dealing with, especially class. But these things have been shown to have interesting interactions with people's speech, and these patterns hold worldwide. So we're going to look at that.

Then we're going to pull the camera back and look at what's called the *philosophy of language*. That is looking at the nature of human language, what it is in terms of psychology and philosophy, and what it is that is different in us as opposed to the way language is used by other beings. We're going to take a look at some of the theories along those lines. Then we are going to take a look, a brief look, at the evolution of writing.

Then, in the two lectures near the end, I'm going to let you be the linguist in a way. We're going to look at two languages that you are vanishingly unlikely to have grown up speaking if you're taking this course. One of them is going to be a language spoken in the rainforest of Suriname, which is only a few hundred years old and is a hybrid of English and Portuguese and Dutch and two African languages. Then we're going to look at a very different language spoken in the Caucasus Mountains. If any of you have been around as long as me or longer, you might remember those Dannon yogurt commercials where the idea was that Dannon had something in it that made people live a long time. They went to a village in the Caucasus Mountains, and they had a person who was like 500 years old being patted on the back by his mother. I mean the guy literally was about 100, and you could tell. He couldn't have been; he must have been 90, and then there's his mother who's like 105. Anyway, that's the Caucasus Mountains, and we're going to look at a language there called Kabardian. We're going to pretend that we're just flying into, say, Yogurt Village or something and trying to figure out the language from the ground up. Then we will end by looking at current theories about how language evolved in us as a species in the first place.

In any case, you may remember my course in 2004, *The Story of Human Language*. (That was a very sad attempt to imitate Troy McClure on *The Simpsons*. I won't do that again.) But *The Story of Human Language* was a very different course than this one. That one was, in a sense, based on a subset of what we're going to look at in this more general treatment of linguistics. *The Story of Human Language* was about how one original language became several, and how all of them mixed deliriously together, and how too many of them are now dying. That was a story that fit into roughly what is being treated as historical linguistics with a little bit of sociolinguistics here. This is a more scientific course. This is based on showing how we identify the system amidst the chaos and randomness of language on the surface.

This way of looking at language—this scientific approach to language—has really only existed since the early 19th century. Before that there was a rather rich tradition of the study of language, but not in the sense of what we call linguistics today. Socrates, Plato, and Aristotle did examine the relationship between speech and the thoughts that it communicated. They had a term for language: *logos*. All of this was very interesting, but it was more the kind of thing that today classifies as philosophy of language. It wasn't about the intricacies of grammar, per se.

That sort of thing—such as grammatical descriptions of languages—is something that goes back about two millennia, someone sitting down and describing the rules of their language. Not exactly the most intuitive thing to do, if you think about it. There aren't a whole bunch of other ones as models. Just why would you sit down and write down the rules of a language that you speak and everybody you know speaks it, so it doesn't seem like it's such a big deal? Nevertheless, when people started writing grammars like these was about 2,000 years ago. One of the earliest masterpieces is one by an Indian grammarian named Panini. Nothing's really known about him except that he wrote a magisterial description of Sanskrit—4th century B.C.E., this is. Then there is the *Techne Grammatike* by Dionysius the Thracian, and that's a description of Greek. But the problem with, for example, the *Techne Grammatike* is that if you are a Greek person in the ancient world, then because travel was so difficult and in many cases impossible, there was a sense among Greek thinkers that Greek was the quintessence of language and that other languages were just something else and often variations on Greek. For example, many Greek thinkers thought that Latin was just a strange kind of Greek, because since the languages are related they have a lot of words in common. Their idea was that here's a Greek dialect that sure has a lot of funny stuff in it. That's the best that you could do with the limited purview that these very brilliant people had.

As Europeans started encountering other people in the world and messing things up and bothering them, they started noticing—especially the missionaries among them—that there were all of these other languages and that they were quite different from what you might think language is if you spend your entire life around the Mediterranean Sea. There's a language head in every crowd, and so there would always be somebody—often a missionary, maybe not—who would write a description of the local language that was encountered. But in this era, still, people were hampered by an understandable assumption that basically the way language is supposed to go is like a European language. You find what are now rather quaint mistakes.

For example, there was a bishop in England in the 1600s, John Wilkins; he made a very noble effort to devise a writing system that would express human thought irrespective of the differences between the languages, and so he had this code. But its problem was that he didn't understand how different languages could be. For example, in Japanese to say a sentence like "I like Pam," what you say—the ordinary thing that you would say—is "*Pam ga suki.*" Here's that sentence. What that means, basically, is *Pam likeableness*; that's what's in it. That's how they indicate that. You could get the *I* part in; you could say, "As for me, Pam likeableness." But in Japanese, you can leave that *I* to context. That's how different languages get. I say, "I like Pam," and a Japanese person will say, "Pam likeableness." That's ordinary Japanese. Wilkins didn't know things like this, and so his version of, for example, the Lord's Prayer was pretty much like the English sentence written word by word in pictures.

That, of course, is something more likely of someone in the 1600s than of today. Wilkins did not have the linguist's mind-set in the modern sense. For example, from a modern linguist's perspective, *I like Pam* has three concepts. There's the *I* who is speaking, there's the issue of the liking, and then there's *Pam*. It is a core feature of language to have a subject, so you're going to have a subject. But in some languages, the subject of the concept you're expressing when you say "I like Pam" will be *I*. But then notice that in Japanese the subject—*Pam ga suki*—is *Pam*. We're talking about the fact that I have this affection for Pamela, but the way that that sentence comes out might not have me as the subject at all.

Then, as far as liking, we think, "Oh, of course *like* is going to be a verb." But no, not necessarily, because, as we see in Japanese, it's a noun. You talk about likability, and of course that gets in the concept just as well. It does not have to be a verb. A language might have a prefix or a suffix or a little bit of stuff to show that something is the subject, to keep the traffic going nice and smoothly. Japanese has that; English does not. Then even the *I* can be left to context, like in Japanese, because if you're sitting there saying it, chances are that you are talking about yourself. Who else would you be talking about—somebody on the other side of the world, on the other side of the room? Probably, it's you; you don't have to fill that in, especially if you're tired. We have to say "I," but the Japanese can just leave it out, and that's not uncommon. Languages differ in terms of what they have to put in, and what they can leave out, and what they have to leave out, and some people have even hypothesized that this channels the way people think about the world. We will look at that in a couple of our lectures.

In any case, I'm hoping that when we're finished you'll find yourself looking at and listening to language in ways that never occurred to you before. Most importantly, I want you to come away understanding that the conception of a language as the words and the way they're spelled and little things that you shouldn't do with the words in terms of putting them in order on the pain of getting your knuckles rapped, I hope that that conception of language will be one that will play less of a role in how you think about language. That's because really, for me, linguistics, in all of its facets—to be perfectly frank—it's neat. This stuff turns me on, and it turns a whole lot of other people on. For me, the kind of bucket of words conception of language is kind of like the first 15 minutes of the film *The Wizard of Oz*, and I'm going to assume you've seen it. It starts out black and white. There are these scenes where it's black and white, and there's a tornado. And you've got Uncle Henry and Aunt Em. (The actress who played Aunt Em—Clara Blandick—killed herself, which is something I always think about watching those first 15 minutes.) It's just gray. You wouldn't like the movie if it stayed that way. Then Dorothy walks into Oz, and there's this big beautiful set with the painting in the back of it. There's all of this color, and there's some effect in the orchestra, and you're happy that for the rest of the movie you get to be in this color part. That is where linguistics is. For me, that is the journey from just thinking of it as a bunch of words and some persnickety grammar rules you learned on the blackboard a long time ago and the wonder of what human language really is and the way it works. Come down the Yellow Brick Road with me, and let's learn about linguistics.

# Lecture Two

## The Sounds of Language—Consonants

**Scope:** The English alphabet gives a very approximate sense of what the actual sounds of the language are. There are 26 letters but 44 sounds. For this reason, linguists transcribe the sounds of languages with a special alphabet that represents sounds as they actually are, the International Phonetic Alphabet, inspired in part by the linguist on whom *Pygmalion*'s Henry Higgins was based. This lecture presents the consonant sounds.

## Outline

**I.** The problem: The alphabet gives the appearance that there are 26 sounds in the English language. In fact, there are quite a few more: English has 44 different sounds. The alphabet only reflects the reality of English sounds approximately.

  **A.** *Cough*, *tough*, *bough*, *through*, and *though* demonstrate five different pronunciations of the sequence of letters *-ough*. In English, the relationship between spelling and pronunciation is inconsistent, sometimes even arbitrary.

  **B.** Because linguists are engaged in analyzing language as it actually is, they transcribe languages according to the actual sounds in them, rather than approximations. English—and all languages—as transcribed in this way can be counterintuitively different from the way we are used to writing.

  **C.** Yet to think as a linguist is to conceive of language as transcribed as it actually is, and this way of "seeing" language will be basic to all of the schools of thought and concepts we will engage in this course.

  **D.** In this lecture, I will introduce you to what consonants look like to a linguist.

**II.** Linguists have come up with a way of looking at the sounds of language that is more honest to the sounds we make and hear by emphasizing the place and manner of articulation.

  **A.** We will start with *p*. A *p* requires stopping an airflow by putting your lips together. Now notice that *b* is actually a lot like *p*; *b* is, basically, an *s* with a hum in it, and you may feel as if making a *b* requires more of a push.

**B.** Now think about *t*. A *t*, like *p*, requires stopping an airflow, only here you stop it by putting your tongue on the ridge behind your upper teeth, the alveolar ridge. Then, just as *b* is a kind of *p*, *d* is a kind of *t*. Thus we have another pair of related consonants, even though the alphabet makes them look unrelated.

**C.** You can also stop an airflow further back in the mouth. That creates a *k* sound, and the humming/pushy equivalent is a *g*. This time, you stop the airflow with the soft palate, called the *velum*.

**D.** We now have the beginnings of a chart of how consonants are actually produced in a human mouth. Imagine a cross section of a human head, facing left; *p* and *b* are produced by the lips at the front of the mouth, *t* and *d* in the middle, and *k* and *g* in the back.

**E.** Now try *m* and notice that you use your lips to produce it just as you do with *p* and *b*. Then you produce *n* on the alveolar ridge just like *t* and *d*.

**F.** However, when we get to the soft palate, we meet the first sound that English has no written letter for. That sound is the one written as *ng* in *singer*. It may seem that *ng* actually is a sequence of an *n* and a *g*, but it is actually a single sound. We know this because there are words where we actually do produce a sequence of *n* and *g*, such as *finger*. The one in *singer* is a sound in its own right and is called *engma*.

**G.** At this point we can see that consonants pattern in a way that the sequence of the alphabet obscures. The sounds that halt an airflow are called *stops*. The buzzing ones are called *nasals*. The ones produced with the lips are called *bilabials*, the ones on the alveolar ridge are called *alveolars*, and the ones on the soft palate are called *velars*.

**H.** Among the stops, the ones that have a hum or a push in them are called *voiced*, while the others are called *voiceless*.

**I.** Thus there are three features that consonants can have. Where in the mouth they are produced—lips, alveolar ridge, palate—is called the *place of articulation*. How they are produced—such as a stop or a nasal hum—is called the *manner of articulation*. Then there is the *voicing*. Thus linguists refer to *b* as a *voiced bilabial stop*.

**III.** Linguists use a different kind of alphabet called the International Phonetic Alphabet (IPA). Note: In the IPA, sounds and transcriptions of words and sentences are indicated in brackets, like so: [b], [ð], [æ].

    **A.** The first person to develop an alphabet of this kind was linguist Henry Sweet (1845–1912), who wrote in 1876 that "We must learn to regard language solely as consisting of groups of sounds, independently of the written symbols."

    **B.** In 1886, today's IPA was invented by a French professor of English, Paul Édouard Passy.

**IV.** Now we can fill in the grid with other consonants.

    **A.** Some of the remaining consonants are produced not by stopping the airflow but by obstructing it, making a hissing sound.

        **1.** Take [s]; notice that you produce it where you produce [t], [d], and [n]. It is an alveolar sound. Then [z] is its voiced counterpart. Hissy sounds are called *fricatives*. [s], then, is a voiceless alveolar fricative.

        **2.** Another hissing sound is [f]. It is produced with the lips, but also with the teeth. This happens somewhat further back in the mouth than bilabially but further forward than the alveolar ridge. [f], then, is a voiceless *labiodental* fricative. Its voiced counterpart is [v].

        **3.** You can also make a fricative by putting your tongue between your teeth. These are the *interdental* fricatives. In English, an interdental fricative is rendered with *th*. However, *th* is pronounced differently in *thin* than in *weather*. That difference is one of voicing. Thus we have two interdental fricative sounds, a voiceless one, [θ], and a voiced one, [ð].

        **4.** In the same way, you can make a fricative between the alveolar ridge and the palate—an *alveopalatial* fricative— which leads to what is usually written as *sh*. However, there are two *sh* sounds—the one in *show* and the one in *pleasure*. Linguists transcribe the first, voiceless, as [ʃ] and the other, voiced, as [ʒ].

    **B.** The sound indicated in English by *ch* is actually a stop followed by a fricative. Linguists indicate it as [tʃ], and its voiced counterpart, the *j* in *judge*, is [dʒ]. These two are called *affricates*.

**C.** The sounds indicated by *l* and *r* are called *liquids*. Both are produced on the alveolar ridge. In terms of manner of articulation, [l] is called *lateral* and [r] is called *rhotic*.

**D.** Finally, in English there are two sounds called *glides*. They are the first sounds in *wash* and *yard*. [w] is a bilabial sound, so it is a bilabial glide. What is written as *y* in English is rendered by linguists as [j]. It is an alveolar sound and thus an alveolar glide.

**E.** [h] is a fricative but is produced further back than the soft palate, in the glottis. It is, therefore, a *glottal* fricative.

**F.** English has another sound that the alphabet lacks. The first sound in *uh-oh* is not a vowel but a catch in the throat. Thus it is called a *glottal stop*; it is indicated with [ʔ].

**G.** Notice that there is no symbol for the English letter *x*, which is just a sequence of [k] and [s]. Meanwhile, there are two symbols for consonants the alphabet lacks: the engma, [ŋ], and the above-mentioned glottal stop, [ʔ].

**V.** There are consonants beyond those in English.

   **A.** Each language fills in only part of this "grid." Other languages have consonants that fill in places in this grid that are empty in English. For example, the *ch* sound in *Bach* is a velar fricative, indicated with [x].

   **B.** Japanese people pronounce *Fuji* in a fashion that sounds, to us, as if they simply "have an accent." However, their sound is not an [f] at all but a bilabial fricative, indicated with [ɸ].

   **C.** The throaty *r* we learn in French classes is, in terms of place of articulation, *uvular*—it is a voiced uvular fricative, indicated with capital *r* written upside down: [ʁ].

**Essential Reading:**
Pullum and Ladusaw, *Phonetic Symbol Guide*.

**Supplemental Reading:**
Ladefoged and Maddieson. *Sounds of the World's Languages*.

**Questions to Consider:**

1.  Another consonant that English does not have is a variant of the *r* sound, the trilled version familiar from Spanish words like *perro* ("dog"). In fact, although there is an informal tradition of representing the English *r* sound as [r], in the IPA the English *r* sound is technically represented by [ɹ]. An [r] represents the trilled *r* sound of *perro*. Given that trill sounds are part of the IPA, think of the sound we can make by flapping our lips to express that it's cold ("Brrrr!") or the more raucous sound known as the Bronx cheer. After this lecture, where would you place each of these sounds in our grid? What is the place of articulation, manner of articulation, and voicing? There are, in fact, languages in New Guinea where the Bronx cheer is not an expressive interjection but as normal as [t] and [m]!

2.  English spelling has *ng* in the words *hangar*, *linger*, *longer*, *headbanger*, *hunger*, and *ringer*. How would you render what is spelled as *ng* in each of these words? The lesson here is that English spelling is deceptive; The IPA transcribes the actual sounds, which are what linguists study.

# Lecture Two—Transcript
## The Sounds of Language—Consonants

Welcome back. In this lecture, we're going to examine the sounds of language in what may be a new way to you. Here's what confronts us: We have 26 letters in the alphabet—that beautiful alphabet that we can all recite with the little song—and yet, in fact, there are by most counts 44 different sounds in the English language. That means that the alphabet only reflects the reality of the sounds of English in a very approximate way. In terms of doing linguistics, as we say, that is something that simply will not do.

For example, think about our crazy spelling—and that we're all aware of on some level. *Cough*, *tough*, *bough*, *through*, and *though* are five different pronunciations of the sequence of letters -*ough*. That's annoying, arbitrary, and also makes "system" hard to talk about when you're talking about, for example, how words change over time or how we enunciate a word, especially if we were coming at English from another language and just analyzing it as a scientific object. That won't do. Or more to the point, when you say the word *through*, you can count the letters—and there are seven letters—but you're surely aware that you're not uttering seven sounds; under no conception. A lot of you may think you're uttering four sounds; it would be something like *thru*. Even that happens to be not quite right, but it certainly isn't seven. Spelling won't really take us very far; this just will not help us. What we need to do is come up with a way of looking at the sounds of language in a way that's more honest to what we're actually pushing out of our mouths and what we're actually hearing. This is something that's very basic to linguistic analysis; it's something very basic to a lot of the other sub-subjects that we'll see in this course. That's what we're going to do here.

This is the basic lesson: If you are going to be a junior linguist or dip into this crazy world of linguistics, you must realize that the ABCs have nothing to do with what we're doing—no ABCs, no alphabet. The idea that the sounds come in that order is a complete artifice. We all view it warmly—I like the "Twinkle, Twinkle" melody myself, etc.—but no ABCs. In order to show you what I mean, we're going to start in this lecture with the consonants.

How do consonants actually work? They do not begin with *b*; the last one is not *z*; it's something completely different. For example, let's start with *p*, just *p*. The way you utter a *p* is you stop the airflow by putting your lips together: "puh" (rendered in the International Phonetic alphabet, or IPA, this would be [p]); simple enough. What's kind of like [p]? If you notice, *b*—what we think of as *b*—is a lot like [p]. You're putting your lips together, and you're stopping the airflow; it's just that *b* is really kind of a [p] that has a little bit of a hum in it. Actually, the way I find it easier to think of it is that if you are going to pronounce a *b* in an explicit way, you'd put a little bit of your belly into it. There's "puh" and there's "buh" (IPA: [b]). Now, *b* and *p* are completely separate in that alphabetical sequence, so you don't think of [b] and [p] as having anything to do with each other. But listen to how similar they sound, and that is actually crucial to the insight that they belong together in terms of a scheme of how the sounds of our language actually work independently of the ABCs. Let's imagine [p] and [b]; there they are on the screen.

Let's think about another letter. As we'll see, "letter" is not a good concept for us, but we're still in the world of letters; I understand. Another letter: *t*. *T* is another one of these sounds where you end up stopping an airflow just like with [p], but you're doing it in a different place. For most of us, you are putting your tongue on the ridge behind your upper teeth. You're not stopping it here: "puh"; you're stopping it up there: "tuh" ([t]). If there's a relationship between [p] and [b]—"puh"/"buh"; kind of the belly one—then [t] actually has something similar. The consonant that's most like [t] is not *s* because *s* comes before it in the alphabet but "puh"/"buh," "tuh"/"duh" ([d]). Those things are related, so [t] and [d], although quite separate in the alphabet, actually are related sounds. It's another pair of related consonants. We can add them in. So far we've got our "puh," "buh," "tuh," and "duh."

This airflow stoppage, you can do it here: "puh"; you can do it here: "tuh"; or you can go further back. If you go further back, you might even be able to do it without me telling you. What might that letter be? "Puh," "tuh," now go further back and you get a "kuh," and so that's a "kuh." We're not going to indicate that with a *c*; that's letters, and that's this kind of nasty, mucky little world. We're going to indicate it instead with a [k]. That's what linguists do; and so "kuh" is with a [k]. If you can go "puh buh" and "tuh duh," you can go "kuh guh" ([g]); [k] and [g] are related sounds.

Here we have this little grid of these sounds. These are how these sounds are actually produced. You might be thinking: What significance does that grid have? Actually, what that represents in a schematic way is where these sounds are actually pronounced in our mouths. In order to understand that, you have look at it as we see here. You can see the lips and alveolar ridge—

which is that ridge up there behind your upper teeth—and then you've got further back, and we can put these sounds in the mouth here. For example, let's put [p] up here between the lips, and then let's have [t] here right by this alveolar ridge. Then, let's have "kuh," which is further back. This is how the sounds are actually represented in the mouth. Just keep that image with you; we're going to fill that mouth with a whole lot of other stuff.

Let's try this: Take what you might think of as the letter *m*—so "mmm" ([m])—but where is [m]? It's the two lips—again, I'm not talking about the flowers; tulips—and so that's where you have your [m]. You use it and pronounce it with your lips, just like with [p] and [b]. Then let's take this trip backward again. If you were going to go "mmm," but instead you were going to have the sound flowing around the alveolar ridge, then you get "nnn" ([n]); [m] and [n] have a relationship. That happens to be obvious by chance because of what the order of the alphabet happens to be. That's just an accident, however, but if it helps you remember, then good; and so we have [m] and [n].

Things in life tend to pattern—deaths come in threes, etc.—and you can imagine that if you have the "puh tuh kuh" (and remember that goes backward in the mouth) or the "buh duh guh" (those going backward in the mouth), then you're going to have "mmm nnn," and then if you put this buzzing sound somewhere else further back, you get "ng." Of course, you're thinking to yourself that there is no such sound as the "ng"; we don't do that. But, in fact, we do; it actually is a sound.

Here's what I mean: We in English write *ng*. For example, we'll write something like *finger*. You think, well, yeah, there's an *n* and a *g*. Think about *finger*, and now think about the word *singer*. You don't say "sing-ger"—I actually knew one person who would always say "sing-ger"; I wanted to pull his legs out from under him—but clearly, that's not the way the word is pronounced. He was trying to make it sound like it was on the page. There's *finger*, and there's *singer*. What's that sound in *singer*? It's not just an *n*, because that's a *sinner*. It's not just a *g*, because that's a *sigger*, which doesn't really exist. We don't say "sing-ger," we say "singer" and so there's this "ng." That is a sound, and there's a symbol for that in this alphabet that we're learning. It's actually called an *engma* ([ŋ]), but you don't have to remember that; just remember that there is a symbol for it. Think about it: You've got a *finger*, but then if you could *fing* something— if that were an ordinary verb, *fing*—then you wouldn't be the "fing-ger," you'd be the "fing-er." There's a difference between *finger* and *singer*. That little sound is one that isn't indicated as a special sound in our alphabet, but it is very much a sound. You don't happen to ever find it at the beginning of a word in English—there's no such thing as an "ngog" or something like that—but you do find it in the middles. You also find it at the end; that is what *singing* is. It's not "singing-g" like we saw in the last lecture.

You have a pattern: You have "puh tuh kuh," "buh duh guh," and then "mmm nnn ng." All of these things are patterning together; you can see from this pattern that there's something systematic going on. Of course, these concepts have names. It's less important that you memorize all the names than that you see that these things are systematic entities, systematic correspondences. We call the sounds that halt an airflow *stops*: "Puh," "tuh," and "kuh" are stops; "buh," "duh," and "guh" are also called stops. Sometimes you see them called *plosives*, but I'm going to call them stops. Then the buzzing sounds—the "mmm," "nnn," and "ng"—are called *nasals*; I think the reason is obvious.

You also have terminology for where in the mouth these things are produced. If something is produced between the lips, then it's called a *bilabial* sound, and it's clear why. If something is pronounced on the alveolar ridge, then it has the very counterintuitive name of being an *alveolar* sound. If you go further back in the mouth, it's called a *velar* sound because the scientific word for the soft palate is the *velum*. You've got terminology for these things.

In addition, you notice that among the stops, you've got the little pairs: "puh"/"buh," "tuh"/"duh," etc. There's a difference. The ones that we started with—"puh," "tuh," and "kuh"—are called *voiceless*, in contrast to the ones where you've got a bit of a buzz in them or you use a bit of the belly in them; those are called the *voiced* stops. You have your voiceless stops and your voiced stops. The convention is that the voiceless stops are indicated above the voiced stops. That really is just arbitrary, but that is the way these things go.

This means that, in terms of consonants, we're seeing that there are three features that they can have. For one thing, there is what's called their *place of articulation*. The place of articulation is where in the mouth they are produced in terms of in the front in various ways or in the back. The place of articulation might be alveolar, velar, or bilabial. Then, on the other hand, we have what's called *manner of articulation*. So far, we have seen two manners. There is the stop; one manner is to stop the air completely, and then let it out in a little explosion. Then, on the other hand, there is this humming; that's another manner of articulating. Something with a certain manner of articulation, such as humming, also has a place of articulation. If it's alveolar, then it's in the middle, back there behind the teeth, and it's what we think of as an *n*. Then there's also the voicing. What this means is that a [b] is, for one thing, a stop. Then it's also a stop with a place of articulation in the mouth, and that's between the two lips, so it's bilabial stop. Then, as far as whether it's voiceless or voiced, [p] is the bilabial stop that's voiceless, and [b] is the one that's voiced. The pointy-head term for [b] is that it's a voiced bilabial stop. Don't worry; I will not spend this lecture set only referring to sounds in that way, only when it's necessary. But that's how we think about these things, because this is the terminology of the International Phonetic Alphabet; I'm giving you the famous IPA. In my experience, actors are taught it for some reason. Here we're not being actors, we're being linguists, and this is the International Phonetic Alphabet. This is how linguists transcribe the sounds of speech because spelling is an arbitrary collection of historical accidents and only represents language too approximately for us to actually have normal conversations and normal exchange without constantly having to backtrack and stipulate, etc. This is how we transcribe.

The first person actually to develop an alphabet of this kind was Henry Sweet, who lived from 1845 to 1912. He was a phonetician, and he was partly the model for Henry Higgins in *Pygmalion*. He wrote in 1876, "We must learn to regard language solely as consisting of groups of sounds, independently of the written symbols." That is exactly what we're trying to get across here. That's what he did. In German, if you are doing a production of *My Fair Lady* and you're doing "Why Can't the English," it starts as "*Kann keiner lehren uns warum Kinder wie man spricht?*" Isn't that cute? I have a record of that. Anyway: Henry Sweet. The actual International Phonetic Alphabet was formulated in 1886 by a man named Paul Édouard Passy. It hit the ground running for the most part, and it's still being used today in order to talk about the sounds of language in a coherent and accurate way.

We have a grid that we're filling. Obviously, these nine consonants we've got are not all of what there is in English. One of the most important groups is that sometimes when you're making a consonant, you don't stop the airflow and you don't buzz. You just obstruct it but let the air keep going through, kind of like when you put a very small hole in a balloon. For example, take what we think of as *s*; there's "sss" just like the balloon. Where are you pronouncing the *s*? There is some variation among people— I'm one of them who apparently say it in a strange way—but most English speakers pronounce the *s* at that alveolar ridge, and so here is an alveolar sound. It's this alveolar hissy sound. Then it's the same sort of thing as with "puh"/"buh" and "tuh"/"duh." There's "suh," and then you can "zuh"— there's a little buzz in it; there's a little belly in it—"suh"/"zuh." Those two sounds have a relationship, and now you know that the relationship is that "suh" ([s]) is voiceless and "zuh" ([z]) is voiced. These are hissy sounds. Obviously, that is not what they're called—they're called *fricatives*; [s], for example, is a voiceless alveolar fricative. It's a fricative, pronounced on the alveolar ridge, and deprived of a voice. It is a voiceless alveolar fricative: "suh"/"zuh."

There are other hissing sounds, for example what we think of as *f*: "fuh" ([f]). That involves both the teeth and lips. As a result, it's called *labiodental*. That's a labiodental fricative: "fuh." Then the voiced counterpart is "vuh" ([v]). We can put this into our grid: Stops come on top, the fricatives come below them, and then conventionally the nasals come below them. Fricative is a new manner of articulation for us. You can be a stop, a nasal, or a fricative.

Here's something that we have to be careful of. Another way you can make a fricative is that you can put your tongue between your teeth, and so you get "thuh" like that. Here's where the alphabet trips us up, because we have this *th* and we think, well, that's two letters. But if you think about it, it's one sound. When you say "thuh," you're certainly not saying "tuh-huh," and you're not really saying two of anything. "Thuh." How do you subdivide it? Is it like "huh-hyuh-huh"? It's one sound: "thuh." However, if you think about it again, there are actually two *th*'s. You can have *thin*, that's one; but then you have *weather*. If you think about it, you don't say (voiceless *th*) "weh-ther"; that's somebody who learned English last week. It's (voiced *th*) "weather." In the same way, you wouldn't say what a (voiced *th*) "thin" person; it's a (voiceless *th*) "thin" person. Our alphabet doesn't indicate that difference; however, the International Phonetic Alphabet must, and it does. Noticing the differences between things like "puh," "buh," "tuh," and "duh"—get it—it's "thuh" and "the." It's *thick* and *this*. Those are different sounds. One—"thuh"—is voiceless. The other one—as in *this*, *weather*, etc.—is a voiced sound. Those are our *interdental* fricatives, and they come in a nice little voiceless-voiced pair. We can put them in the chart here. Notice that they have symbols. The voiceless one is called a *theta* ([θ]), and the voiced one is called an *eth* ([ð]). You don't have to know that, but they have names.

In the same way, we have something that is indicated as *sh* in our writing system. Again, though, it's pronounced "shuh." Where are the two sounds? It certainly isn't "suh huh"; it's not *s* and *h*. The alphabet, we're going to pick that up and we're going to go like this—"Gulp!"; that's gone. We're going to think about what it really is. It's really just one sound, and it is "shuh." I probably don't need to tell you that there's also a voiced version, so there's "shuh" and "zhuh." There's *should* and then there's *pleasure*. It's not "plessure"; you don't say that. You certainly don't say "zhould" instead of "should." Really, what we have in the alphabet is covering two different sounds, "shuh" and "zhuh." Those things are pronounced between the alveolar ridge and the palate, and therefore, they are called *alveopalatal* sounds; those are alveopalatal fricatives. They come in a voiceless-voiced pair. In our chart, they go here. They have cute symbols as well: That big kind of slinky *s* ([ʃ]) is not just an *s* that's trying to look like a 1950s fashion model. That is a different kind of sound completely: that's "shuh," and then you have your "zhuh" sound ([ʒ]).

In the same way, there's one other confusing part, which is *ch*. Again, it certainly isn't "kuh huh." It's two sounds, but it basically comes together as one sound. It's not *c* and *h*; it's actually a stop followed by a fricative. When they are this closely knit, then we are dealing with a whole new different kind of sound. We call this an *affricate*. Affricate is a new manner of articulation for us, and we put them below the fricatives. As you can imagine, there's a voiceless "chuh" ([tʃ]) and then there's a voiced "juh" ([dʒ]) Here comes the "judge." That's a voiced sound; you wouldn't say here comes the "chudge." On the other hand, there's "chalk" on a blackboard; it's not "jalk." We have these two sounds, and those are placed on our chart in this way. You can see that they're indicated as combinations of stops and fricatives; however, they are considered sounds in their own right.

We can actually see at this point that we've got quite a few sounds arranged. We can see that we have our stops above on a line, and then we've got our fricatives—a whole bunch of fricatives; English is a "fricativey" language. Many are not, but ours is. Then, you've got your affricates under there. You've got your nasals. All of this is about the way these things are pronounced in the mouth—in the oral cavity—rather than this alphabet business.

We can finish it off; we're almost there. *L* and *r* are called *liquids*. These are sounds that are produced in a particular way, mostly having to do with positioning the tongue in a certain way. There's no obstruction; they're queer sounds in that way. Both *l* and *r* in English are pronounced on the alveolar ridge. In terms of manner of articulation, *l* is called *lateral* ([l]) and *r* is called *rhotic* ([r]), but we'll just stick them in here so you can see them on the chart.

There are a couple of sounds that are called *glides*, and it's because they glide. They are what we think of as *w* and *y* in terms of letters. *W* is—if you think about it—bilabial, and so we put *w* here: "wuh" ([w]). The *y* sound is indicated in the International Phonetic Alphabet as what we think of as *j* ([j]). It's an alveolar sound, and so we put that one here, like that.

We are almost there. We have left out *h*. What is *h*? We think of *h* as just some letter that comes after *g* and before *i*. I always think that if you could eat an *h*, it would taste like wood. I don't know why I feel that way; it's called synesthesia. Anyway, what is an *h*? *H*, if you think about it, is a fricative. This is one of these things where there's a partial obstruction: "huh" ([h]), like that. It's way back there; we need something other than this velar place of articulation. We've got a place that's further back; a more distant place. In this case, it's what's called the *glottal* region, because the glottis is back there in our throats; [h] is a glottal fricative; that goes there.

While we're in this glottal region—these things that go on back there—think about another sound. This is one that is not indicated in our alphabet in any way. It's not indicated in our alphabet misleadingly or wrong; it's just not there. It is the glottal stop. This is a sound in our language: "uh"; that's a sound. What I mean by that is imagine that you take an alphabet, drop it on the floor, watch it shatter into pieces, and then you sweep it away. When it first hit the floor, you would say, "Uh-oh!" Think about how you really said it. You didn't say "uoh." That sounds like somebody with some sort of problem; you have to say "uh-oh." What's the "uh"? It isn't just part of the vowel. There's no vowel *uh*; the vowel sound is "aah." The "uh" is a glottal stop. We don't write that in our alphabet—we don't miss it—but in terms of transcribing what we actually say, and especially in terms of transcribing what is said in a lot of languages where it's much more prominent in determining different meanings of words, we need our "uh." That's a glottal stop, and you get this question mark thing ([ʔ]). We have a glottal fricative where you're back there and you're partially obstructing: "huh." Then, if you stop things—"uh"—you've got the glottal stop, and so that's our "uh-oh" sound.

We've got the grid filled in, and notice there are certain things that don't happen. For example, there's a letter *x*, but why would you need a letter *x*? It's really just "kuh suh" ([ks]). In the International Phonetic Alphabet, you don't need that. Then, there are two sounds for consonants that our alphabet doesn't indicate in a special way at all. That's a "ng" and an "uh"—a glottal stop and the velar nasal—so that's how it goes.

English's filling in of this grid is, of course, only the way English does it. As you can see on the grid, there are all sorts of other places that English doesn't happen to fill in that some other language just might. For example, in English, we don't have a velar fricative. We've got the stop there; we've got the nasal; that's all very nice, but why couldn't you have a velar fricative? Why couldn't you have a sound like "chh"? Of course, many languages do. That is the sound that German has as the final consonant in *Bach*. That is a velar fricative; one can do that. That happens to be indicated with the [x] symbol in the International Phonetic Alphabet, as you can see here.

Or, we talk about a mountain in Japan called Mount "Foojee"; I'm going to climb Mount "Foojee." That's not the way the Japanese say it; they say "Fhuji." We listen to them saying it and we think, well, they just have an accent or Japanese is different. Their *f* is weird or something like that. But, in fact, they're not using an [f]; they're not using a labiodental fricative at all. What they actually have is what we can now classify as not just a crummy, peculiar, or quaint way of making an *f*; they have a bilabial fricative ([ɸ]). Of course, there could be such a thing. We don't do it, but many languages do, as does Spanish. In Japanese, if you're saying "Fuji," then what they're saying is "fff." It's a partial obstruction. You make a hiss like with the balloon and you do it with your bilabes—you do it with your two lips—and so it's "Fhuji."

Or, if you've ever suffered in a French class and you've got that *r*—the *r* that's in the back of the throat, *Pierre*, that thing—it's easy to think, well, it's French and there's something romantic about that, or they just have a rather odd *r*. But it's not as simple as that; it's that they have a whole different sound. In fact, there's a different place of articulation that one needs to indicate it. That *r* is actually pronounced by wobbling the uvula. If you're looking at a Looney Tune and you go into somebody's mouth and there's that thing hanging from the back, that is the uvula and you can vibrate it. That's what the native pronunciation of that *r* is. It's not a uvular stop because air is getting through; it is a uvular fricative. It has a symbol, like everything in the IPA does: It's a little upside-down capital *r* ([ʁ]). If we were going to be doing French, we would add that sound. Of course, English doesn't have that sound.

What we're seeing is that all of these consonants are not just in alphabetical sequence, but they can be organized in such a way that we can see where they're actually pronounced in the mouth. We can see what the actual sounds of the language are, such as that there's a "thuh" and a "the," and that there is a "ng," or that there is a glottal stop, rather than what the alphabet indicates. That's how the IPA works. Of course, consonants are not the only sounds in the language; there also vowels. Blissfully, there are fewer of them than there are of these consonants. In the next lecture, we'll see how it works with the vowels. We'll take a look at how a language looks when transcribed according to the way it really is, rather than the charming artifice of alphabet.

# Lecture Three
## The Other Sounds—Vowels

**Scope:** The actual vowel sounds in English vastly outnumber the five
vowels in the alphabet—*a*, *e*, *i*, *o*, and *u*—and include one that is
not distinguished in the alphabet at all. The way the vowels are
produced in the mouth also explains just why the way we spell
vowels in English is so different from the way they are
pronounced. At the end of this lecture, we will be able to transcribe
entire words and sentences in the IPA.

## Outline

I.   In the English alphabet, there are five vowels: *a*, *e*, *i*, *o*, and *u*.

    **A.**   In school we learn that there are actually "long" and "short"
versions of vowels, e.g., "short *a*" in *cat* and "long *a*" in *father*.

    **B.**   The reality of English vowels is, in fact, even richer, as we can see
from how vowels are rendered in the IPA.

II.  There are five "basic vowels" (especially if you've had Spanish
or Italian).

    **A.**   Like consonants, the vowels are produced in the mouth in ways
that have nothing to do with the order *a*, *e*, *i*, *o*, *u*.

    **B.**   Make the sound "ee" and notice that you make it high in the mouth
and near the front. Now notice that the sound "oo" is just as high
but requires shifting to the back.

        **1.**   Those two sounds are [i] and [u] in the IPA (which will be
familiar to those who have studied many other languages).
The [u] sound is produced behind the [i] one, and so we will
place [i] in the front and [u] in the back.

        **2.**   The sounds "ay" and "oh," on the other hand, are produced
lower in the mouth. Their symbols are [e] and [o]. The [e]
sound is produced in the front, like [i], while the [o] sound is
produced in the back, like [u]. We place them below [i] and
[u], respectively. This represents where these sounds are
produced in the mouth.

3. Finally, the sound "ah" is produced even lower than [e] and [o], and in the back like [u] and [o]. When we place it on our grid, we have a fundamental representation of vowels in human languages. Most languages have at least these five vowels. Some have just these; most have many more.

**III.** Three kinds of additional vowels bring us to the sound of English itself.

**A.** Most of the "basic" vowels have what are called *lax* alternates, as opposed to the *tense* ones we have seen. For example, the vowel sound in *hit* is not [i]—in which case the word would be *heat*—but a different one in the IPA: [ɪ]. It is pronounced somewhat less frontward than [i].

**B.** In the same way, the vowel in *bed* is not the same one as the one in *made*. It is "eh" rather than "ay," and in IPA it is [ɛ], again less frontward than [e].

**C.** The lax alternative to [o] is "aw": [ɔ]. It is produced somewhat less toward the back than [o]. In the same way, the lax alternative to [u] is the "uuh" sound in *foot* and *soot* (not *boot* or *coot*). It is [ʊ] in the IPA.

**D.** A characteristically English vowel is the *a* in *cat*. This is not the "ah" sound in *father*, and it has its own symbol: [æ]. It is produced as low in the mouth as [a] but in the front rather than the back.

**IV.** Vowels are determined by three parameters: *height*, *frontness*, and *roundedness*.

**A.** [i], for example, is *high* and *front*. [o] is *mid* and *back*. [æ] is *low* and *front*.

**B.** All of the back vowels except [a] involve rounding the mouth. Thus we specify whether a vowel is *rounded* or not.

   **1.** [o] is a mid back rounded vowel; [i] is a high front unrounded vowel.

   **2.** Roundedness is important because front vowels can be rounded as well, while back ones can be unrounded even when they are not [a]. The vowel in French *lune* ("moon") or German *Schlüssel* ("key") is a high front rounded vowel, [y] in the IPA.

3. Japanese people pronounce what is written in Roman transcription as *u* as a sound that is transcribed as [ɯ] in the IPA, a kind of "ih" pronounced further back, "ueh," which is a high back unrounded vowel.

**V.** Vowels in between the front and back vowels are called the central vowels. The last two English vowels occur in the central region.

    **A.** One is the "uh" sound. It is transcribed with a symbol called a *caret*, [ʌ], and pronounced in the mid region.

    **B.** The final sound is one that the alphabet does not distinguish at all: *schwa*. This is the sound of *a* in *about* or *o* in *lemon*. It is very common in English, especially in unaccented syllables, and is written [ə]. It occurs slightly higher than [ʌ] but still in the mid zone.

    **C.** One of the hardest sounds for an English speaker to master in Russian is the vowel ы in words like those for "was" (был) or for "mouse" (мышь), which is a high central vowel, indicated in the IPA with what is called a *barred i*, which is written [ɨ].

**VI.** Combinations of vowels and glides are called *diphthongs*. In English, they are [aj] (*rice*), [aw] (*house*), and [ɔj] (*boil*).

**VII.** The Great Vowel Shift.

    **A.** The gulf between spelling and pronunciation in English is due to changes that occurred in the 1400s affecting where vowels are placed in the mouth. *Made* was once pronounced "mah-duh" ([madə]) but the vowel shifted from its low position, [a], to the mid position, [e].

    **B.** At the same time, *feed* was once pronounced "fade" ([fed]), but the vowel [e] moved upward to be pronounced [i]. In the same way, *food* was once pronounced "fode" ([fod]) but the vowel [o] shifted upward to [u].

**VIII.** How a linguist transcribes a word and how we are used to seeing it spelled can differ considerably.

    **A.** For example, many people use *a* not only before consonants but also before words that in writing begin with a vowel.

    **B.** In fact, such people are using the "proper" rule, because words that we think of as beginning with a vowel are often pronounced with an initial glottal stop—a consonant: [ʔʌʔæpl̩], "a apple."

**IX.** There are a great many ways that a language can fill up its grid, with English about the middle in terms of the extremes.

**A.** Rotokas, spoken in Melanesia, is notorious among linguists for having startlingly few sounds, including only six consonants.

**B.** Polynesian languages such as Hawaiian and Samoan have unusually few sounds—though more than Rotokas.

**C.** The !Kung [!xũ] language, a click language spoken in the southern part of Africa, has one of the biggest consonant inventories of any language in the world.

## Essential Reading:

Pullum and Ladusaw, *Phonetic Symbol Guide*.

## Supplemental Reading:

Ladefoged and Maddieson, *Sounds of the World's Languages*.

O'Grady, Archibald, Aronoff, and Rees-Miller, eds. *Contemporary Linguistics*. I have given only a basic characterization of the IPA for the purposes of these lectures. For a fuller command, I suggest the presentation in this textbook.

## Questions to Consider:

**1.** The goal of the past two lectures has been to wean you off of a natural tendency to think of words as composed of "letters," as opposed to sounds. In order to reinforce this, figure out what sentences the following transcriptions represent. Note: We do not pause between words when we speak, and thus neither does the IPA!

[ʃigaʔlɪdəl]

[gɛdæwdəðɛr]

[sʌʔmzʌp]

**2.** There have been many proposals over the years to write English "phonetically" due to our clumsy, arbitrary spelling system. Do you feel that it would be better if English (and maybe all languages) were written in the IPA? Or perhaps do you feel that this would be problematic or inappropriate in some fashion? Opinions differ considerably on this point.

# Lecture Three—Transcript
## The Other Sounds—Vowels

We're back to the wonderful world of the International Phonetic Alphabet. This time, we're going to do the vowels. The vowels are interesting. I remember when I was really little, I read kind of early. I remember when the other kids were being taught to read from the ground up in class, I was watching them learn to read with a kind of an anthropological fascination. I was interested to see how one learned to do this, because I didn't remember learning how to do it. I remember coming home one day—it was probably in like 1970—and telling Mom, "You know what they were teaching us in class today? There are long vowels and short vowels. There's *a*, and if you pronounce it "ay," then it's long; if you pronounce it "ah," then it's short. Isn't that neat, Mom?" I thought that was this interesting way of looking at it. It's funny: As time went by, I realized that it really didn't seem to describe how vowels actually work. I couldn't have put it in so many words, but I realized that when you're reading, this business of there being a long one and a short one didn't seem to quite work. I asked my mother at some point—not when I was five; somewhat older than that—I remember saying, "Why aren't there enough vowels?" What I meant is, "Why aren't there enough vocalic letters?" I don't remember what Mom said—it was something like "life is hard," or something like that—but I was not given a coherent answer, because who knows? Unless you happen to be a linguist, in which case you have a way of dealing with this.

We want to look at the vowels. The way that vowels are represented in our alphabet with just those five little symbols is vastly inadequate. It just won't do, because we have many more vowel sounds than that. Let's see how vowels work in the International Phonetic Alphabet. There are these five basic ones, especially if you've had Spanish or Italian. Even just by looking at what we write, you can have a sense that there is "ah, ay, ee, oh, oo" when you say *a*, *e*, *i*, *o*, and *u*. Especially if you go to many other languages, then you've got this sort of basic set of five: "ah, ay, ee, oh, oo." Those are there, but let's get away from that order—*a*, *e*, *i*, *o*, *u*—which has no meaning at all in terms of what these vowels actually are in our mouths. Let's actually pronounce them. Let's start with what we think of as *i*, and let's use this sort of basic pronunciation: "ee." You're pronouncing it, and you've got this "ee" up there. Notice that it's high—"ee"—you have your tongue tensed up, and it's in the front: "ee"; that's where the action is. It's a high front sound.

Let's do *u*, and let's go "oo." You go "oo"; so "ee, oo": Notice that you pull back to say "oo." "Ee" is in the front; "oo" is in the back. There's a difference between them. "Oo" is just as high; you still have this sort of pushing upward—"ee, oo"—it's just that one of them is front and one of them is back. The way we transcribe those sounds—and just those sounds, not the vast other loads that the written symbols *i* and *u* take care of, but just "ee" and "oo"—those are transcribed in the International Phonetic Alphabet as the symbols for a lowercase *i* and a lowercase *u* ([i] and [u]). That's how that works, and we can kind of look at this here.

In the same way, it's just like with the consonants; these things tend to pattern. You can make the "ee" ([i]) sound as in the letter e. The basic one would be "ay"—for example, if we were speaking Spanish or something like that—you can go "ay," and then you can pull back and go "oh"; they're in the same place. "ay" ([e]) is lower than [i]; [i] is up high, [e] is kind of here, lower, and then "oh" ([o]) is what happens when you pull back; [o] is still below [u], and so there's a relationship between these two things. We place [e] and [o] below the [i] and the [u] sounds, respectively.

"Ah" is even below [o]. You can go [u] and [o], and then "ah" ([a]). There's something that you're doing even more than you were doing when you did [o] and [u]; that means that [a] is in the back here as well. But we're going to stick it below the [o]. You can look at that now, and you see where those basic kinds of vanilla vowels fit. You have [i]/[u] up on the top, [e]/[o] in the middle, and then you've got [a], and that one is down in the back. This is the representation of those vowels in terms of the IPA and in terms of where they are. Now we can put the vowels where they are. The [i] is high in front, the [u] is high in back, and so on. That's where they are.

There are many languages that have only those five vowels or something very close. Some languages have even fewer, and then there are many, many languages that have many more vowels than that. But as you can see, English is a language where [a], [e], [i], [o], [u]—in whatever order you put them in—does not represent the vowels that we use. Listen to me talking right now: There's something going on way beyond [i], [u], [e], [o], [a], and that's because we have many more vowel sounds. Something like the [i], [u], [e], [o], [a] is closer to the way, for example, Italian works. Italians have some more, too; but still, if you have a language that depends to a much larger degree on those vowels than English, then you have something quite different. If you think about a language where the vowels are [i], [u], [e], [o], [a], it sounds like somebody conducting a gondola in Venice in tight pants, singing in a high tenor voice. That sounds like a very tight language. The reason for that is because what I have given you in terms of the top four of these sounds is what's called *tense vowels*; they are pronounced in a tense way. Compared to what, you think? Compared to what is that there are a series of *lax vowels*. Those are the ones that make this something like the English language. For example, if you think about it, you look at the word *hit*. There's an *i* in it, but it's not pronounced "heat." It would be in a certain kind of foreign accent, but in our language, that would be a whole different word, and it's pronounced "hit." That's actually a sound, and we have to have a way of getting it down, and we do. There is an IPA symbol for "ih" ([ɪ]) which is different from the one for "ee" ([i]). [ɪ] is what's called a lax vowel. It's also pronounced somewhat less frontly than [i]. You've got [i] way up there; [ɪ]—you can feel it—is a little further back. This is the way that we represent "ih," and so here we have a high front, but lax, vowel: [ɪ]. We put it there.

In the same way, let's go down to [e], here. There's another sound that *e* represents in the English language, and that is "eh." We don't talk about going to "bayd"; we talk about going to "bed." There's a difference between [e] and "eh." As you can see, if you actually roll these sounds around in your mouth, "eh" is laxer than [e]; [e] is tense compared to "eh." "Eh" means pulling a little bit more in than [e]. This is another lax vowel, and we place it analogously to the way we place the [ɪ]. There that is right there: [ɛ].

We can keep going with this. We can also see how spelling can be a problem. If we have our lax alternative to [o] over here in the back, if you make [o] a little bit laxer and pull it a little closer to—in this case not backwards, but it's a little bit closer to—the front, you go "oh, aw," and that's a lax sound. We spell that *aw*, but that won't really do because if you look at what *aw* literally would mean, for example, in the International Phonetic Alphabet, that would be "ow" and that's not what we're trying to say. We're trying to say "aw." "Aw" is a sound of its own, and we represent that with an *o* with a bite out of it ([ɔ]), which is what I think of as and many people call the "backward c"; whichever. That sound is indicated a little bit below and a little bit inward from [o], and so that is our lax sound; a little bit lower, and a little bit further in.

Let's look at [u] up here. We also have a lax slightly inward alternative to [u]. That is the sound in, for example, *foot*. We might look at it, and you can imagine a foreigner new to English thinking that it was "fooot," but it isn't; it's "foot." As ugly as we might find that sound "uuh"—it's my least favorite sound in the language for very arbitrary reasons; it's like, can I get a hot dog—despite the fact that "uuh" could be considered ugly, it is a legitimate sound and is not just some kind of [u]. It has a symbol of its own, and that is this [u] that has kind of feet and is upside down. That is this symbol, [ʊ]; and so we place that here.

At this point, we're getting to what English actually is, but if you notice there's a hole in the system. There is this slot down here on the bottom in the front where you would expect something to be, and mysteriously there isn't. These grids of sounds in languages are rarely perfect, but this particular hole is still something that kind of leaps out. You'd think that, especially with everything so lovely so far, there must be something. You can almost come up with it yourself. Let's say that you've got this low back sound and it's [a]. Let's say you're going to pull it forward: "ahhhh … aaaah" That sounds funny; but then again, think about it: "aah," that's like the English sound extraordinaire. I mean, if you are learning any other language, the chance that that language had an "aah" in it is rather small; however, in English, of course you have "cat," "that," down to the "mat." That is a standard sound; it's not just [a], but with a twist; it's a sound of its own, and it's indicated in the IPA with this symbol here: [æ]. We've got everything nice and tidy, and that is a large part of what we've got in this language.

Let's deal with a little bit of thoroughly nonthreatening terminology, which is—and I've actually kind of slipped some of this in for you, and none of it is particularly difficult when it comes to the vowels—we see that vowels are determined by three main parameters. For example, take the i, this [i] sound. For one thing, it's *high*, and for another thing, it's *front*. On the other hand, [o] is in the middle—we see that it falls in between [u] and [a]—and we call it just mid in linguistics. It's not front, and therefore we call it— three guesses—*back*; and so that's where it's placed. Then [æ] is *low*—it's not high, it's not in the middle; therefore, it must be low—and [æ] is front, so you talk about a low front vowel. You can talk about "an æ sound," but linguists will talk about a low front vowel, and that is [æ]. You have that which is the *height*, and then what's called the *frontness*—it's just a matter of these scientific descriptions—then there's something that is called *roundedness*. That's because [o] and [u] in the back there have rounding.

It's not true that everything in the back has to have rounding—because [a] doesn't have the rounding—but with [u] and [o], you have to make the kind of kiss gesture with your mouth in order to enunciate them. We call [o] a *mid* back rounded vowel, because it's all of those things. It's got the rounding, it's in the back, and mid it is. What we call *i*, but "ee"—is a high front unrounded vowel; that's what we call these things. The roundedness may seem like we're just sort of being obsessive butterfly-collecting types of people and mentioning this roundedness, but the fact is that front vowels can be rounded as well, and back vowels can be unrounded even when they're not [a] as far as languages go.

For example, in English, the rounded vowels happen to be back ones—[u], [o], the kind of cute Clara-Bow-lips kind of vowels. (Clara Bow was a silent film star.) However, for example in French, there is the very cute French *u*. If you pronounce French badly and you're talking about the moon, then you'll say "la loon"—and I imagine the French are used to that. But really, you're supposed to say something like "la leune"; that's how they say it. To us, we think they say *u* in a cute and kind of fetching way, but actually what they're doing is they're pronouncing a high front vowel, which has the Clara-Bow-lips roundedness that in English is only present on the [u] and [o]. Instead of saying "leen," they'd say "leune," and so that's what they're doing. They've got not only the sound [i]—they've got their high front unrounded—but they also have their high front rounded vowel: [y]. If we were going to put this in our chart, then we would put it here, like so. So, that can happen.

Then, on the other hand, you can also have back vowels that are unrounded, and they are not all just [a] like in English. Take the Japanese again—the ever phonetically misrepresented Japanese. We say I'm going to "Mount Foojee," and then they say "Fhuji." You think they sound like there's something wrong with them, but in fact they are using different vowels. They're not saying [u]; they're saying "ueh." "Ueh" is what happens when you've got a high back vowel, but you're not doing the kiss. Instead of "oo," it's "ueh"; and so: "Fhuji." The bilabial fricative ([ɸ]) is the "f," and their "oo" is actually an "ueh." It has a completely different symbol—one that we're not used to—and here it is: [ɯ]. It's this *m* that's on its back as if it were a dead cicada at the end of whatever month it is that cicadas live and die in. That's how you do that in the IPA. Roundedness is important. In terms of looking at what a vowel is across languages, we have to specify that [o] and [u] are rounded back vowels, because a back vowel does not have to be rounded.

We're at a point where we've got almost all the vowels in English, but then there are some others. For example, you can say "root," and we have our [u] sound for that. You could say—as some people do—"ruuht," and then there's foot, book, etc. We have a symbol that looks like a *u* for that: the *u* with the serifs; the feet ([ʊ]). That still does leave something else, though; what about the sound in "cut" or "but"? It's not "boot"; it's not "buuht"; it's "but." [u] has already been used for "oo," and then we've even got something that looks like a *u* for "uuh," so what do you for "but," which is very much a sound of the language? It's part of speaking English. We don't just have "oo" like the Italian; we have "uh." That's what there is in English. The way that you transcribe that sound is with this symbol: [ʌ]. It's called a *caret*—caret as in "c-a-r-e-t," not the vegetable that is very hard to grow on your own in a garden. (We did 23 vegetables last year, and the only one where nothing ever happened was the carrots!) Anyway, there is this thing that is called a caret, and that's "uh." This is one that is neither front nor back; it's in the middle. We can't call it mid because we already have that for the height, and so we call this central—nothing difficult about that—and we place it right here. It's in the mid region in terms of height; it's central in terms of frontness. That's how we do "uh."

Finally, what's the sound in "lemon"? Not the "eh"; what's the other vowel? It's this kind of "uh." What's the sound in *about*? Or what's the sound in, "Oh, look, it's a *photographer*"? What's the sound in between the [f] and the [t] at the beginning? It's this rather indistinct sound. If you could eat it, it would taste like dirty dishwater, but nobody ever eats it. It's indicated with an upside-down *e*, and you may know it's called a *schwa*: [ə]. Schwa is one of our sounds, and it's placed close to the [ʌ] symbol. We can put it like so; we can put it right there.

This whole central region is not something that's just made up in order to account for English; lots of things go on in the center. For example, in Russian, one of the weirdest vowels to master is the one in their word for *was*. Their word is был (*byl*); or *mouse* is мышь (*myŝ'*); that's the best I can do. That is not just basically a screwed up or weird sound or something like that. It is what linguists often call the *barred i*: [ɨ]. It is central—it's in this [ʌ]/[ə] region—and it's high, because of course, you can have that. We don't have it—thank God—but if you have this high central vowel, then it comes out as [ɨ]: "That's a *myŝ'*." That's how it works.

To cross the *t* and dot the *i*, so to speak, we do have a few other things. We have what are called *diphthongs*—not "dip thongs," which is easy to say—

but diphthongs, and that is combinations of vowels and glides. The ones that are central in English are "eye" ([aj]), indicated with the *a* and *j* that is an indication of the "yuh" sound in the IPA—as in "rice"; and then [aw], which is for "house." Then, for "boil," the "oy" sound; we have our "backward c" for "aw," followed by the glide "yuh": [ɔj]. This is where those fit into the chart. That's how English vowels work.

Now you've got pretty much the whole set. This is how linguists spell, so to speak. We pride ourselves on spelling close to the way language is actually produced—the way we actually produce sounds. This is how linguists spell. As a matter of fact, when you are able to conceive of the vowels in this way—when it is spontaneous to you to imagine the vowels actually in the mouth or in these relationships to each other with the highness, the frontness, the centrality, the mid, the backness, and the rounding—then something about English spelling makes a lot more sense. For example, in English there are these huge gulfs between spelling and the way we pronounce things. It's easy to just think, well, good Lord, it just—you know—it's no fair, and that's just a quirk of dealing with English written down, but there is system to it. It's not just a series of complete accidents.

For example, take a look at the word *feed*, and look at the way it's spelled. As literate English speakers, we immediately know that it's pronounced "feed" ([fid]) But then it looks like it should be possibly pronounced "fade" ([fed]). What are those *e*'s doing there? In fact, that is the way that it used to be pronounced: That was a "long *e*," and that's why there are two of them. The idea at the time was to make the spelling at least approximate the way people spoke, i.e., what any sensible people would do. It's what you would expect. But, unfortunately, that was a very, very long time ago. After a while, there was something which is called the Great Vowel Shift. It happened mostly in the 1400s. What happened in the Great Vowel Shift was that, for example, [fed] raised. That means that it went upward, and so we talked about how [e] is a mid sound that became a high sound. What's the high sound right up above [e]? It's [i], and therefore [fid]; it made sense. Things pattern, and so let's think about the word *food* ([fud]). If you've got those two *o*'s, shouldn't it be "fode" ([fod])? It was [fod], and it had this raising process. It wasn't just that raising happened to one thing randomly like lightning striking, it was just this general process; and [fod] raised. What's up there above? [fud]; and so that's why it's that way.

Something that's a little bit less predictable but actually makes sense if you watched the steps, step by step, which we will not, is that look at a word like *made*. There's a reason why it looks like it was pronounced "mah-duh" ([madə]); it was. But there was a raising. You have what used to be pronounced as [fed] rising up into the region of [i] and becoming [fid]. You've got an empty slot, so to speak. [madə] moved up to where the [e] used to be in that mid and front region, so it went from back to front. But it went upward into the mid region, and became pronounced [med]; that's how those things work. Those things happened according to where the vowels actually sit in the mouth, certainly not according to spelling and not according to pure serendipity. This is the way vowels shift. They shift according to a "pah-un," as certain people from Great Britain say it; I have no idea why I just said it that way.

What this means is that how a linguist will transcribe a word and how we're used to seeing it spelled can differ considerably. For example, we talked about the word *through*; now we're in a position to see how *through* works. It's not that it's four sounds because th is two sounds. *Th* is not two sounds; it's one sound: It's "thuh"; it's our theta ([θ]); it's our voiceless interdental fricative. That's interdental and voiceless, and therefore it's a voiceless interdental fricative. It's our [θ], and then there are only two more: [r] and [u]. So, that's [θru]. That's the way it looks in the International Phonetic Alphabet. Or, try something like somebody says, "Somethin's up." One way to deal with that is to write *something is up*. But that's not what anybody would say in any situation in English. But then, on the other hand, if you write *somethin's up* and you have an apostrophe where the *g* is supposed to be, none of that really represents what's going on in the mouth. If you wrote it in the International Phonetic Alphabet, we've got that caret again. It's [sʌʔmzʌp], and it goes right there. There's a glottal stop—[sʌʔ] … [mz] … [ʌp]; that's what you actually say—so there it is in the International Phonetic Alphabet.

This also explains why many people will say "a apple" and yet actually be following a rule. We think of the rule as being that you say *a* before a consonant and *an* before a vowel. There are so many people walking around talking about *a animal*, *a apple*, and you think, "Ignorant, heathen, breaking the rules of their own language!" But, actually, listen to the way they say it. They don't say "uhaapple" or, if they do, then they're just about to die; I mean, only then would somebody say that. They say, "uh apple." What's the "uh"? It is a consonant, and so somebody is not saying, "aapples"; they're saying, "apple," and "uh" is real: [ʔ], So if they say, "uh apple" ([ʔʌʔæpl̩]), they are obeying the same rule as somebody who says, "a father" or "a bible" or "a wall." It's "a apple" because there's a consonant ([ʔ]) there. People often make more sense than it seems like they do.

In any case, there are a great many ways that a language can fill up its grid. We're seeing the English one, but English is actually in about the middle in terms of the extremes that we see. For example, take a look at the English grid in terms of the things that in English are basic in terms of the places of articulation—bilabial, alveolar, velar, etc.—and in manners of articulation—Is it a stop? Is it a fricative? Is it a nasal?—just looking at what space can be from the English perspective.

Then here's a language called Rotokas; it's spoken in Melanesia, a very small community. Rotokas is notorious among linguists for just having startlingly few sounds, and this would include consonants. Here are Rotokas's consonants: [p], [t], [k], [g], [β], [ɾ]. There they are. You've got a little of this, a little of that, very little and nothing else; none of this bric-a-brac that we were talking about. Rotokas is a legitimate language with a complex grammar, but sounds are just not what they're terribly interested in. That is also true of the Polynesian languages. Hawaiian has unusually few sounds—not this few—but Hawaiian, Samoan, these are languages where the proliferation of sounds that we see in a language like English just hasn't happened. It's interesting.

Then, on the other hand, you can look at a language like, for example, this one spoken in the southern part of Africa. Here's a click language. This one is called something like [!xũ], but it's a completely different language. Look at the consonants in this language, because it's got clicks. It's got lots of clicks. It's not just one click. It's not just two clicks. It is a whole bunch of clicks. Remember, they're not what you use to call the cat; these are consonants just like [b], [d], [f], and [g] are to us. Just imagine being able to hear a language like this actually spoken; but these are the languages spoken. Often in the media they've termed what's written down as the "Kung"; that is transcription for we handicapped people of what is actually "CLICK!-kung"—something like that.

Now you are at a point where you can understand that when linguists talk about sounds, they're talking about something quite different from the ABCs. The ABCs are for our reading pleasure when we're sitting in a chair with brandy or, of course, we have to teach our children the ABCs to get along in this world. But when we're looking at language, we have to realize that things like that transcription of *through* and *somethin's up* are our reality, and that the ABCs are just clothes.

# Lecture Four
## In the Head versus On the Lips

**Scope:** A fundamental insight about language's sounds has been that some are "real" sounds that distinguish meaning, like *b* and *p* in *pat* and *bat*, while some are just variations on other sounds, like the *p* that makes a puff of air on your hand in *pot* as opposed to the *p* that does not when you say, "spot." What is just a variation in one language is a "real sound" in others: In Korean, one can utter the *p* in *pul* either with a puff or without, and with the puff *pul* means *grass* while without the puff *pul* means *fire*. Languages differ in which sounds are phonemes ("real sounds") and which are allophones (variations of "real sounds").

## Outline

I. You now understand that the actual sounds of a language are something quite different from what is indicated by its alphabet and that the sounds of a language are related to each other in ways that the alphabet gives no hint of, such that [p] and [b] are variations on the same operation (bilabial stop).

II. Armed with this, you are now in a position to understand one of the most basic, frequent, significant differences between the apparent and the actual in language. Namely, in this lecture we will see that we generate words on two levels, according to a basic contrast that linguists have studied over the past hundred years: the *phonemic* versus the *phonetic*.

III. The basic insight is that what comes out on the surface is often quite different from the way the brain originally generates it.

    A. In English, the words *bat* and *pat* are obviously different. What makes the difference is that *bat* begins with [b] while *pat* begins with [p].

    B. However, in Korean there are no words that begin with [b] nor any that end with it. To a Korean, there is no [b]. The sound does occur, but only as something that happens to [p] in a certain position.

**C.** That is, [p] turns into [b] when [p] is between two vowels. So, the word [pəp] means *law*. To make that word into *lawlessness*, you add a prefix *mu-*. So the result should be [mu-pəp].

**D.** But it isn't. Just like in English there is a rule that *a* is used before nouns starting with a consonant and *an* before nouns starting with a vowel (*a pig, an apple*), in Korean there is a rule that [p] turns into [b] between vowels. So instead of [mu-pəp], the word for *lawlessness* is [mu-bəp].

**E.** So [b] is just something that comes from a [p] sometimes. There is no such thing as a word [bəp]. That is, to a Korean, [b] is not a "real sound." The writing system indicates no *b* sound; where a *b* sound occurs like in [mu-bəp], Korean writing shows a *p*.

**F.** In the same way, say "pot" and then "spot." Notice that when you say the [p] in *pot*, there is a puff of air when you put your hand in front of your face. Then note that there is not that puff of air when you say "spot." The sound pronounced with the puff of air is called *aspirated*.

**G.** There is a rule in English: Stops occurring at the beginning of a word (or a syllable with the accent on it, like in *capacity*) are aspirated, but not when they are somewhere else in the word. Aspiration is written in the IPA with a superscripted h, and thus [p$^h$].

**H.** But we don't think of [p] and [p$^h$] as different sounds. We think of [p$^h$] as simply something that happens to [p] under certain conditions. This is because the difference between [p] and [p$^h$] cannot make the difference between two words' meanings. It's not that [p$^h$at] means something you cook with while [pat] means, say, to shiver.

**I.** But that's exactly how it is in Korean. [pul], for example, means *fire*. But [p$^h$ul] means *grass*. The difference between an unaspirated stop and its aspirated equivalent does make the difference between words in Korean. To them, [p$^h$] is indeed a "real sound" in a way that it isn't to us.

**IV.** What this means is that there is more to a language's collection of sounds than just the fact that they are all there.

**A.** In each language, some sounds are "real sounds," making the difference between words' meanings, while other sounds are just the product of something happening to a real sound depending on where it comes in the word and what kind of sounds are near it.

**B.** In linguistic terms, "real sounds" are *phonemes*. The other sounds are *allophones* of a phoneme. In English, [b] and [p] are phonemes; [pʰ] is merely an allophone of [p]. In Korean, [p] and [pʰ] are phonemes, while [b] is just an allophone of [p].

**C.** In transcription, linguists put phonemes in slashes (/p/) and allophones in brackets ([pʰ]).

**D.** On the phonemic level, then, *spot* is /spat/ and *pot* is /pat/; with the original phonemes, before anything has happened to them based on what they are near or where they are in the word. This is the *underlying form*.

1. On the phonetic level, however, *spot* is [spat] while *pot* is now [pʰat]. Now, the *p* in *pot* is rendered as the aspirated *allophone* of phoneme /p/. This is the word's *surface form*.

2. In the same way, on the phonemic level, Korean for *lawlessness* is /mu-pəp/. On the phonetic level, /p/ is changed into its [b] allophone, and the result is how the word is actually pronounced, [mu-bəp].

**E.** The distinction between something going on underneath (phonemic) and something that happens on the surface (phonetic) occurs throughout linguistics, to the point that some linguists talk about just *emic* and *etic*.

**V.** Another example of underlying versus surface is the English plural.

**A.** Allophones—minor variations on a phoneme's basic nature—are not the only thing that happens in surface forms. Phonemes can also come up on the surface as sounds that themselves are "real sounds" in the language in general.

**B.** Another example of the difference between underlying and surface forms of words is the plural in English. Because of how we spell, we suppose that we make a plural by adding s. But note that, usually, the sound we actually make is [z]. *Cards, pigs, fans, hams, houses.*

**C.** In fact, the sound we make is [s] only with a small set of sounds: *caps, cats, hacks, coughs, moths.* From Lecture Two, you know that these sounds share a feature: They are *voiceless*.

**D.** This means that there is a rule: The actual *underlying* plural marker *for all words* is a [z] sound. There is a rule that if the [z] sound ends up after a voiceless sound, then it becomes voiceless as well. The voiceless equivalent (alveolar fricative) to [z] is [s].

**E.** The phonemic form of the plural marker, then, is /z/. *Pots*, underlyingly, begins as /pat/ + /z/. But in the surface form, /z/ becomes an [s] because the *t* in *pot* is voiceless. The result is the surface form [pʰats].

**VI.** The study of how speakers generate words by working from underlying to surface forms is called *phonology*; the study of how speakers produce sound itself is called *phonetics*.

**A.** Allophones, although often represented by one letter of the alphabet, are quite central to how we express sounds.

**B.** For example, because there are many allophones of the phoneme /l/, the word *oil* actually sounds virtually identical when played backward.

**Essential Reading:**

Sapir, *Language*. Pages 42–56 on language sounds remains one of the most lucid introductions to the phonemic versus phonetic distinction ever written.

**Supplemental Reading:**

O'Grady, Archibald, Aronoff, and Rees-Miller, eds., *Contemporary Linguistics*. The chapter on phonology in this textbook gives more detail on the differences between words in phonemic transcription versus phonetic transcription.

**Questions to Consider:**

1. In Japanese, there is something quirky about the [s] sound. [s] never comes before the [i] sound. So, to use words familiar to Americans, there is *sake* wine, the karate *sensei*, the delicious *soba* noodles, and *sushi*. But then, there is the Shinto religion [ʃinto] rather than [sinto], there is sashimi ([saʃimi]) rather than [sasimi], and even when you feel like there "should" be a [si], it is a [ʃi] instead—*cigarette* is *shigaretto*. Based on what you have learned about underlying phonemic form and surface phonetic form, what rule do we see operating in Japanese regarding the [s] sound before the [i] sound? What is the phonemic, underlying form of the word *sushi*?

**2.** When we say "prove" (/pruv/), the [u] is longer than when we say "proof" (/pruf/). If we said *proof* with the vowel sound as long as in *prove*—"proo-oof"—we would still be saying "proof," just in an odd way. But in the language of people on the island of Yap near Guam, [pul] means *gather*, but if you make the vowel long like the one in English's *prove*, then it is a different word, *moon*. In English, the [u] sound gets long based on a certain rule—look at how the [i] in *dweeb* is longer than in *deep*, or how the [o] in *doze* is longer than the [o] in *dope*. We are dealing with what is termed *vowel length*. In which language, English or Yapese, is vowel length *phonemic*, and in which is it merely a surface phenomenon, *phonetic*?

# Lecture Four—Transcript
## In the Head versus On the Lips

In this lecture, we're going to spend some more time with sounds. What we're going to see is based on the fact that now you understand that the actual sounds of language are quite different from the way we transcribe or print them on paper. Now that you understand that the sounds in a language are related in ways that the arbitrary sequence of the alphabet cannot and does not indicate, armed with that, you're in a position to understand that one of the most basic aspects of the way we generate language—today, we're going to see this on the level of sound; we'll see it in other ways later—is that there is what's called an *underlying form*, and then there's a *surface form*. There are two levels: an original foundational level and then there's what happens when we actually present what we want to say to the world. This is called, in linguistics, the difference between the *phonemic* and the *phonetic*.

Let me give you a sense of what I mean. The basic insight here is that what comes out on the surface is often quite different from the way the brain originally generates it. Let's take the words in English *bat* and *pat*. They're obviously different words. What makes the difference is that *bat* begins with [b] and *pat* begins with [p]; but that is not the relationship between [b] and [p] in all languages. Let's take a language which is not English, such as Korean. In Korean, there are no words that begin with [b], there are no words that end with [b], and in fact, in the mind of a Korean speaker, there is no "letter *b*." That's not there. If you listen to a Korean talking, you would hear "buhs" ([b]) here and there; however, it's a different kind of [b] than our [b]. In Korean, [b] is just something that happens to "puh" ([p]), depending on where [p] happens to be in the word. To be more specific, [b] is something that happens to [p] when [p] happens to fall between two vowels.

Here's what I mean: There is a word in Korean—[pəp]—that means *law*. Notice if you see [pəp] on the screen that the vowel is a schwa. If we were just using ordinary spelling, how in the world would we write [p However we chose to write it—with a *u* or something else—we'd have to explain it to whomever we were writing this for; there'd have to be an informal agreement. One of the uses of the IPA is that we can have this sound, which in Korean plays a different role than it does in English. We can just write [pəp], and there it is. There'd be no way to write it in English where everybody would understand. In any case, the word *law* is [pəp]. Just like in English, there are prefixes and suffixes in Korean that will change the—if we will—part of speech of a word. The word for *law* is [pəp], then the word for *lawlessness* involves putting a prefix on the word, and it happens to be [mu]. You don't have to worry about the details, but you say "law," and then if you want to say "lawlessness," then you would think you would say [mu-pəp], like this. However, in fact, the word is not [mu-pəp]. That's because there is this rule in Korean that whenever a [p] winds up between two vowels, then it becomes a [b].

That's not so counterintuitive—we know now—because it used to be that in this primordial era we thought of *b* and *p* as where they are in the alphabet, but now we know [p] and [b] are both bilabial stops. They are only different in terms of the fact that [p] is voiceless and [b] is voiced. These sounds are like two peas in a pod; [p] changes when it's between two vowels, and what it changes to—rather predictably—is its voiced counterpart. You've got this [b] in there. What this means is that, in Korean, [b] is just something that happens to [p] sometimes; it's just something that happens kind of later in the process. There's no word [bəp]. That would never happen; it would be [pəp]. The [p] only changes to [b] when there's a vowel before it, and so: [mu-bəp]. That means that in Korean, [b] is not a "real sound." [p] is a real sound; [b] is just something that happens to [p] sometimes. Even when Korean writes [mu-bəp], it writes the [b] sound with a [p] because the real word under there is [p]. To them, [mu -bəp] is just the way that you pronounce [mu-pəp]; [b] is just something that happens to [p]; there is no real [b].

Take that from Korean, and mentally put that aside. Now we're going to look at a different case which complements it, and then I'll bring these things together to give you a sense of what I'm talking about. Let's use English. Say "pot," and then say "spot." In both cases, you've got a [p]. But when you say "pot," if you put your hand in front of your face, you feel a puff: "pot." If you say "spot," you don't feel that puff, or you feel much less of one. Don't be too explicit with the way you really say it: "pot," "spot." There are two different ways of saying [p]. When you say it with the puff, as in "pot," what you're doing actually has a term: It's called *aspiration*. So that's an *aspirated* version of a [p]. That kind of [p]—the kind of puffy [p]—only happens when the [p] is at the beginning of a word or at the beginning of a syllable like in *capacity*; that's where that occurs. There are actually two kinds of [p]'s: There's "puh" ([pʰ]), and there's "peh" ([p]). We don't usually say it in isolation, but there's the [p] that's in "spat";

"spat" doesn't have a puff. There's puffy [pʰ] and puffless [p]: "puh" and "peh." We don't think of [pʰ] and [p] as different sounds; rather, [pʰ] and [p] are two different ways of saying *p*. It's not as if we could have [pʰ] and [p] making the difference in meaning between two words, like "puh" and "buh"—[pʰ] and [b]—do with *pat* and *bat*. It's not as if a [bæt] is something that you hit a ball with, and a [pʰæt] is something you get on the head, and a [pæt] is something that you scramble with your eggs. There's no such thing as a [pæt]; that wouldn't happen. Rather, [pʰ] is just something that happens to [p] when it comes at the beginning of a word or syllable.

However, this is the thing: In Korean, [pʰ] and [p] are real sounds. What I mean by that is they make the difference in the meanings of a word. For example, in Korean, [pʰul] means *grass*. That's a puffy [pʰ], but it's not puffy because it's at the beginning of a word; [pʰul] means *grass*, but [pul] means *fire*. Watch that again and listen to it: [pʰul] means *grass*; [pul] means *fire*—completely different words. That means that both [pʰ] and [p] are different, real sounds in Korean. Remember, we saw that [b] is not a real sound; [b] is just what happens when [p] gets caught between two vowels. They don't even use it in their alphabet. But then we do not have any indication of the puffiness of *p* in our alphabet. It's just that you sometimes say "puh" and sometimes you say "peh"; it depends on where the *p* happens to be. You can be pardoned for probably never having thought about that before.

But in Korean, they'll think about it. They'll tell you. People who are not linguists know that there is [pʰ] and there's [p]. They have to know because when they say a word like [pʰul], they mean *grass*. Then if somebody says [pul], that means something completely different: *fire*. If you've ever had any experience with Korean and noticed that it's very hard to get things across to native speakers without either being laughed at, getting things wrong, or having to making many repetitions, a lot of it is because of these aspects of the consonants. We think of [pʰ] and [p] as the same thing; in my head, they certainly are. But to them, if you say [pʰul], it's one thing and if you say [pul], it's another. They are real sounds.

What this means is that in a language, as we've seen, there is a grid of sounds, but there's more to a language's collection of sounds than just that they're all in there. There's a certain relationship. In each language, some sounds are real sounds, and that means that they can make the difference between words' meanings. [bæt] and [pæt]—[b] and [p]—are real sounds for us; [pʰul] and [pul]—"puh" and "peh"—are real sounds in Korean, whereas there are other sounds that just arise as the product of some other sound, depending on where that sound happens to be in a word. In linguist terms, the real sounds are called *phonemes*. (Note: Phonemes are placed between slashes instead of brackets: /p/.] Phoneme is not just a synonym for a sound; phoneme is the "real sound." In Korean, there is no phoneme /b/, because [b] is just something that happens to /p/ when it gets caught between two vowels. It's a regular process, but it's not thought of as a real sound; it's not a phoneme. In English, [p] as opposed to [pʰ] is not a phoneme; it's a sound. [p] and [pʰ] are both sounds, but the phonemes are /p/ and /b/.

Any phoneme has variations. For example, in English, there is what we can think of as the grand concept of *p*: There's something that you could call "p-itude." It's the grand conception of *p*. I was once trying to explain this to a class and made up a word by accident that really got me in a little trouble: p-itude. We have two kinds of p-itude. You have puffy [pʰ], and then you've got kind of boring *p*; non-puffy *p*: [p]. You've got "pot p" and "spot p"; those are variations on /p/. Those two kinds of /p/—the "pot p" ([pʰ]) and the "spot p" ([p])—what we call them are *allophones* of the phoneme /p/. /p/ is a phoneme: It's a real sound but comes in variations, and those are called *allophones*; it has allophones. That's how it works in English.

Over in Korean, things are different. /pʰ/ and /p/ are phonemes: They make the difference in the meaning of a word, but there is no such thing, for example, as [bəp]. You have [pəp] and that's *law*, but there is no [bəp]. [b] only happens when it gets caught between two vowels. There is a phoneme in Korean: /pəp/; that's the "spot p" for us. It's the "non-puffy *p*." It comes in two variations. You either have [p], and that's, for example, at the beginning of the word [pəp] : *law*. Then you've got [b], and that's what happens when this phoneme /p/—not aspirated /pʰ/, but /p/—happens to come between two vowels. [b] in Korean is just a type of /p/; [b] is just one of two allophones I'm showing you of "non-puffy *p*." Then over here, you've got "puffy *p*," and that is a whole different phoneme: /pʰ/. Here you can see on the screen what this relationship is.

There are different things that a language can do with its "b-ness," so to speak. There are different things that a language can do with its p-itude. There is a grand concept of *p*—and you might think of it is a capital letter P—and it has allophones. There are types of P. In English, [pʰ] and [p] are variations of P. In Korean, those same two variations are actually separate sounds. You can think of a capital P, and then a capital aspirated Pʰ, and we don't have to worry about the allophones of aspirated /pʰ/. But with capital P, there are two variations: Just ordinary [p]—which is non-aspirated, "non-puffy *p*"—and then [pʰ]; and so that's how that works. There are phonemes, and there are allophones.

To give you a little bit of transcriptional detail in terms of phonemes, we put phonemes in slashes in linguistics. If we're talking about the phoneme /p/—if we're talking about grand poobah p-itude—then we put the *p* in slashes. Allophones go in brackets. If we're talking about, for example, "puffy *p*" in English—which is really just one kind of p-itude—then we put that in brackets: [pʰ]. You can do transcription. On the phonemic level in terms of what the succession of grand, real sounds are, then if you are going to transcribe the word *pot*, it's just good old *p*, *a*, *t*; in slashes, you just have /pat/, like so. However, if you're going to talk about the phonetic transcription—that is, not what is the first thing that you put together in your mind but how you happen to pronounce it—then you indicate that that *p*, because it's the beginning of the word, is pronounced as a certain allophone of p-itude. In this case, because it's at the beginning of the word, it gets what we call aspirated—you can call it puffified—but therefore you have [pʰat]. When you put that in brackets, that's the way the word is actually pronounced. We think of the phonemic transcription as the way the word is generated initially, and so there is this level of the phonemic versus the phonetic.

The phonemic form is called the *underlying form* because it is the original; that's thought of as the substrate. The phonetic form is called the *surface form*. That's what happens when you actually produce the word when you, as it were, put it out to the surface. In the same way, the word for *lawlessness* on the phonemic or underlying level is /mu-pəp/; and so you have the /p/ there, because the /p/ at first is just put there on some level, mentally. The phonetic or surface form is—and this is what you put in brackets—[mu-bəp]. That's where you show that when a nice unsuspecting /p/ happens to be between two vowels, it has a voice put into it. I can put it that way; it becomes a voiced bilabial stop ([b]). That's what happens because vowels—if you think about it, to take you into this a little further—are voiced. When the vowel has a voice, that is a voiced thing. There's no, for our purposes, voiceless vowels. The /p/ ends up being a little bit more like what it's surrounded by, it takes on a voice, and it becomes [mu-bəp]. That's something that you indicate as having happened as the word was generated—as we put it—from underlying to surface. You've got underlying form and surface form.

That's how language works. There's something going on underneath, and then there's something that actually happens on the surface. There can be differences between them. There's the phonemic level and the phonetic level. This is something that happens throughout grammar, on different levels as we'll see, to the point where there are linguists who talk about just *emic* and *etic*. Those are words that have been derived from the original concepts of phonemic and phonetic. Emic is underlying; etic is what happens to the underlying material when it is pummeled about by things such as sounds wanting to be more like each other or any number of things. This emic-versus-etic issue also ties into how language changes, as we'll see. But, you understand now—I hope—that there is a basic conception, which is that there is a grand concept of, for example, P. That's your phoneme; the real sound (/p/). Then there are ways that the /p/ can be pronounced, and that varies. The way that sort of thing varies with each sound in a language means that there's a difference between what /pʰ/ versus /p/ means in a language; there is a difference between what /b/ versus /p/ will mean in a language. It varies with the sound sets of each language.

Let me show you another example of how what's going on on the bottom can be different from what's going on on the top. Let's think about the English plural: We have these various words, and we're told, based on writing, that the plural marker in English is s. That's because that's what we see on the page, and it's perfectly natural to think that's what's going on. But have you ever noticed that actually—not just some of the time, but most of the time—this supposed *s* is pronounced as [z]? Think about it. You've got *cards*, *pigs*, *fans*, *hams*, and *hogs*. There's no way you would say "hogsss"; that's not what the plural marker is. You have one *ham*. That's, you know, nice. If you have more than one *ham*, do you say "hamsss"? That's not even a word of English; you say "hamz." It's a [z] really; it's a [z] most of the time. You've got a *house*, and then you have "housesss"? No, you have "housez." In fact, you only pronounce the plural marker with an [s] in a certain case. For example, think about it: *caps*, *cats*, *hacks*, *coughs*, and *moths*. You would not say, for example, *cats* like "catz." That doesn't make any sense. You wouldn't say for *hacks*, "hackz"; you can't, really. You say "hacks." This is giving you a hint as to what's actually going on.

The plural marker in English is not /s/. Whatever determined that it was written that way in writing a very, very long time ago when the language was actually at a different stage. In English, as we speak it now, the plural marker in the real sense is /z/. That's what it is most of the time after vowels. For example: I have an *auto*. If you think about it, *auto* is barely a valid word in modern English. Let's choose something else. I have a *chimpanzee*—I hate them! They wear diapers; they throw things. I was on a TV show once with a chimpanzee; I was very, very uncomfortable. It was *Dennis Miller*; the show was awful—anyway, the word is *chimpanzee*. You would never say "chimpanzeessss"; you would say "chimpanzeez." If you think about it, that's after all vowels. You go to many "venuez"; you don't go to "venuessss," etc. That's the way that works. Really, it's only just a few consonants. If you look at, say, *caps*, *cats*, *hacks*, *coughs*, it is what we now know as our voiceless consonants. The plural marker in English is a nice lovely /z/; it is a lovely voiced alveolar fricative. In certain cases, it becomes "suh" ([s]). That is when it happens to come after a voiceless consonant such as *caps*, *cats*, or *hacks*. In those three words, I'm giving you our original, classic, top-three voiceless consonants: [p], [t], and [k]. Those should be imprinted in your head one day, because they have that kind of relationship. Those are our bilabial, alveolar, and velar voiceless stops. *Cap*, *cat*, *hacks*; you say "caps." The /z/ becomes a voiceless alveolar fricative— remember [s] and [z] are in that relationship—because the /z/ ends up being more like the consonant that comes before it. That's something that happens all the time in the way we produce language and the way language changes; so, underlyingly, it's /z/. In terms of cases where the plural marker comes out as [s], that's after; that's something that's kind of *ex post facto*. That's something that only happened as the result of a process after the plural marker was put on.

Think of it this way: You're in your head—as if we aren't always—but you're in someone else's head; and you're watching a word being generated. You can imagine what our thoughts might be. You've got a cap; you're somebody who runs around wearing a cap. Then for some reason, you want to talk about the concept of *cap* in the plural—which I think is rare—but let's imagine that you wanted to talk about more than one cap. The plural marker is /z/. You've got /kæp/ and /z/, and you're going to put them together. The fact is that [kæp] and [z] don't go together gracefully, because you'd have to say "cap-zuh." They don't fit because [p] is voiceless and [z] is voiced; those two things don't go together. What happens is that at one point there's /kæp/ and /z/; there's /kæp/ stored in your brain somewhere, and there's /z/ stored in your brain somewhere. When you bring them together, you have to do something to make it a legitimate word in English: You have to make that lovely voiced sound voiceless because it's going to be coming right after one. You start with /kæp/; it's in your hand. You've got the /z/; imagine it in your hand. Think—for those of you who have been around a certain amount of time—remember back to *Sesame Street*. Actually, depending, you may be watching it with your kids.

Imagine these physical objects. You're going to put /kæp/ and /z/ together, but that doesn't work. /z/ has to be fixed, and so it becomes this [s] sound: [kæps] That means that there's an underlying form of the plural marker, which is /z/. Then—now and then—you have this surface form of it, which is [s], which only happens because of where it happens to be, what kind of sound it happens to be next to. In the same way, *pots* begins as /patz/. That's hopeless in English, and so it comes out on the surface as [pʰats]. There's this difference between underlying and surface.

The study of how speakers generate words in this way—in terms of how speakers generate sounds in this way—is called *phonology*. Careers are made on it. The basic assumption in phonology is that the underlying form is different from the surface form—often very different. Charting what the rule is, as to how you get from the underlying to the surface, can be much more difficult than figuring out that a voiceless consonant gets a voice when it's between two voices or vowels. Or even something a little trickier: The real plural marker must be /z/ because it appears everywhere else, and then it becomes a [s]. Sometimes these things get much more complex, and that's what phonologists do.

To give you a sense—I think this is really fun, and I want to share this with you—of how allophones work, and the fact that *allophony*, so to speak, is really central to how we express sounds (i.e., these things that are often represented by one letter of the alphabet). I want to show you something with the word *oil*. What is *oil*? Before we started this set, we thought of *oil* as something that's spelled with letters: *o, i, l*. Now we know that there are actually only three symbols that we need—or depending on what you want to call it, two, if you call the diphthong one. What we have is our sound for "aw"—this is the "backward *c*", /ɔ/—and we have a diphthong. So we have the *j* symbol which is the glide—and so /ɔj/—and then we have an /l/; and so there you go. That really is just the underlying—the phonemic—representation of how an English speaker actually says *oil*: /ɔjl/. That's because actually there are allophones of /l/.

For example, take the word *lateral*. I think I'm saying *lateral* the way most American English speakers say *lateral*. But really, there's a difference between the first *l* and the final *l*, because if there weren't—if you think about it—what I'd be saying is "lateral-luh" because I'm saying "luh." Let's isolate it—"luh"—so I'm doing this nice clean *l*. This *l* that flips gracefully into the "uh"; that's what we all do: "luh luh luh luh luh." "Lateral-luh"; I'm not doing that. Of course I'm exaggerating this little come off, but even so: "lateral-luh"; no, that's not what I'm doing. The *l* at the end is actually rather different. In fact, the *l* at the end of *lateral*—the way we really say it—is actually pretty much a vowel. It's "laterulll …"; do you hear that? In the same way, the *l* in *oil* is not what we think of as an *l*. Nobody, after all, says "oi-l," "oi-l." It's not the same *l* as at the beginning of, say, *liquid*. They're allophones of "l-ness" of "l-itude." There's the one that you use at the beginning of a word or a syllable: That's the "luh" one. I think in all of our heads, that's "real l" probably because it's at the beginning, etc. But when *l* happens in other places, then you're really getting a different kind of thing. That includes at the end of a word.

I will tell you that if you run the word *oil*—uttered the right way, uttered in a very ordinary way—backwards on a tape, then it sounds exactly like "oil." It's actually bizarre. Let's start with the spelling: You'd think that *oil* run backwards would sound like "lio" because that's the spelling, but obviously not. But even if we allow that *oil* is the diphthong [ɔj] and then [l], you might think that if you ran it backwards it would be something like "llliyo" or something like that. It isn't; it really isn't. I'm going to prove that to you: We're going to listen right now to the word *oil* said by a perfectly normal person, and he's saying it forward. Then we're going to run it backwards. I swear to you that this is not a trick; this is really the way it came out. Here is the word *oil* said by a standard American English speaker, un-intoxicated, not very long ago. Here's how he said it. He said it repeated times. Now, listen to the same guy at the same time saying the word, but run backwards. The tape is run backwards; this isn't him saying it backwards, this is the tape run backwards.

It's quite remarkable—or not, because actually the way you say *l* at the end of the word—"lll …"—is really more or less "aw." *Oil*, if we can get the peskiness of letters out of our heads, is really rather like saying "oyaw"; that's what you're saying. There's a slight difference, but the difference is so slight that if you run somebody saying *oil* backwards, it comes out as "oyaw," sounding not particularly like a Martian or somebody with brain damage. That's because there's an allophone of /l/ at the end of words. With that demonstration—that is remarkable, isn't it? I know it's quite jarring at first; I've gotten over it—now that we have seen that, we understand that there's a difference between the underlying and the surface, and that's a theme that we'll see again. Thank you for coming with me through the world of sounds.

# Lecture Five
# How to Make a Word

**Scope:** Sounds are the most basic element of language. Sounds come together to render morphemes, units of meaning. Words can consist of one morpheme (*dog*) or several (*un-think-ing-ly*). Morphemes can be either free (able to stand alone, like *dog*) or bound (requiring something to be attached to, like *-ed*), and languages vary from ones with no bound morphemes to ones where entire sentences consist of a single word made up of a string of bound morphemes. A street myth has it that bound morphemes—prefixes and suffixes—make a language more sophisticated, but this is untrue.

## Outline

**I.** Just as the actual sounds in a language only correspond partially to the alphabet, what conveys a unit of meaning in a language may be a word but just as often is something else.

  **A.** As true sounds are termed phonemes, actual units of meaning are termed *morphemes*. The most basic elements in a language are its sounds. The next level upward is the morpheme.

  **B.** Morpheme is not merely a technical term for *word*.
    **1.** A word may contain just one morpheme, such as *dog*.
    **2.** However, a word may contain several morphemes. *Hunter* has two units of meaning: *hunt* and the suffix *-er* that indicates someone performing an action. Thus *hunter* is one word, but it contains two morphemes. *Hunters* contains three. *Unthinkingly* contains four.

  **C.** Just as phonemes occur in allophones, morphemes have *allomorphs*.
    **1.** Often a morpheme that serves a grammatical function has more than one form, depending on things like what kinds of sound it occurs near.
    **2.** *A* and *an* are allomorphs of the indefinite article morpheme.
    **3.** In addition to [z] and [s] being allophones of the plural /z/ marker, [z] and [s] are also allomorphs of the /z/ plural marker morpheme.

4. In a language like Spanish where verbs are conjugated according to classes, the different tense endings across each class are allomorphs of the underlying person and tense. For example, the *-as* in *hablas* ("you talk") and the *-es* in *comes* ("you eat") are allomorphs of the second-person singular present-tense ending.

D. A morpheme that can occur by itself is a *free* morpheme, such as *hunt*, *dog*, *green*, and *run*. A morpheme that only occurs attached to another morpheme is a *bound* morpheme, such as the *-er* in *hunter*, the *-ed* that marks the past tense, or the plural marker. Prefixes and suffixes are bound morphemes.

II. Languages differ in the extent to which morphemes are bound or free.

A. They are bound often in European languages like English but never at all in other languages.

B. In Vietnamese, like in many languages spoken in East and Southeast Asia, morphemes are almost always free. There is no such thing as a prefix or suffix. Linguists call these *analytic* (or *isolating*) *languages*.

C. Then there are languages called *agglutinative languages*, where there are bound morphemes and each has a separate meaning, such as Swahili.

D. It may seem that English and other European languages would be agglutinative languages, but they are actually of a different type, called *fusional*.

1. Bound morphemes in English, for example, often carry more than one meaning at a time. The *-s* in *he wants*, for example, conveys not only third-person singular but present tense as well.

2. This is why languages with bound morphemes of this type are called fusional languages.

E. Finally, there are languages in which entire sentences consist of a single word composed completely of bound morphemes.

1. Here is a sentence in the Native American language Chinook, once spoken in Washington and Oregon: "*Inialudam.*" This means *I came to give it to her*. Even the word for *give* is a prefix that cannot stand alone.

2. This kind of language is called *polysynthetic*.

**III.** These types of strategies of using bound morphemes (or not using them) are called *typologies*. Chinook, for example, is a language with a polysynthetic typology.

   **A.** Wilhelm von Humboldt (1767–1835) was a Prussian diplomat and education minister who was also a scholar of languages. He was the first to classify languages in this fashion.

      **1.** He believed that fusional languages—like his native German—were "the best" kind of language in mirroring thought most accurately: "Such languages earnestly endeavor to unite every particular into the sentence, or to present the latter all in one piece."

      **2.** He thought agglutinative languages were just failed attempts at fusional ones: "Their obscure endeavor in the same direction is more or less of a failure."

   **B.** However, subsequent research has revealed no correlation between mental or societal advancement and how a language handles bound morphemes.

      **1.** As anthropologist and linguist Edward Sapir memorably put it in his 1921 classic *Language*, "When it comes to linguistic form, Plato walks with the Macedonian swineherd, Confucius with the head-hunting savage of Assam."

      **2.** He meant that Macedonian has as complex a system of affixes as Greek, while both Chinese and many tribal languages of Southeastern Asia have virtually no affixes.

   **C.** Important to note is that a language with no bound morphology can still be awesomely complex.

      **1.** Here is a sentence ("I gave him one fruit") of Akha, an analytic language of Southeast Asia:

           ŋà **nɛ** àjɔ̀q **áŋ** áshì thì **shì** bìq **ma**.
           I       him         fruit  one     give.

      **2.** The four words in bold do not translate into English. The first specifies that I did something that affected something or someone; the second specifies that the "him" was affected by someone; the third is used whenever something is described with a number and has different allomorphs depending on what kind of something it is; and the fourth means that I'm certain of what I'm saying!

**IV.** Affixation is not the only way to make a word from two morphemes.

    **A.** Compounding: Two free morphemes can come together and create a new word, called a *compound*. Compounds in English include *blackbird* and *steamboat*.

    **B.** There is a rule in English that we use subconsciously when we create compounds: The accent is always on the first syllable. If we say "black BIRD," then we could be referring to any bird that happens to be black. Only when we say "BLACKbird" do we mean blackbirds specifically.

    **C.** Accent shift: Often in English, to change a word's part of speech, we add a suffix: *happy, happiness*; *love, loveable*; *pressure, pressurize*; *establish, establishment*. However, another way to make a verb into a noun is to shift the accent from the second to the first syllable. The person who reBELS is a REbel.

    **D.** Finally, in English a morpheme can consist of a changed vowel. Many English verbs form their past tense not with an ending but with a vowel change: *come, came*. This has the same function with these verbs as the suffix *-ed*.

    **E.** The study of how morphemes come together to make words is called *morphology*.

        **1.** In practice, morphology focuses most upon morphemes that serve as tools of grammar—i.e., marking tense, changing words of one part of speech into another, or changing the meaning of words—rather than the morphemes that just describe an action or a person, place, or thing.

        **2.** Etymology—which is how laymen might expect words to be studied—is actually a matter of how words' meanings change over time. To the extent that etymology is studied by modern linguists, it would fall under the rubric of the study of language change: historical linguistics (which is discussed in Lectures Eleven and Twelve).

**Esseential Reading:**

Pinker, *Word and Rules*.

**Supplemental Reading:**

Payne, *Describing Morphosyntax*.

**Questions to Consider:**

1. "An endless string of unpredictable circumstances forced me to reconsider the plausibility of my intentions regarding pursuing a career in acting." There are 21 words in that sentence. How many morphemes are there? (If you want to really delve into playing a linguist on TV, also try transcribing the sentence into the IPA!)

2. Someone once recounted to me that she had been in a production of a play called *Last Summer at Bluefish Cove*. She pronounced it "blue FISH cove." Its standard pronunciation is, actually, "BLUEfish COVE." To myself, I surmised that she did not happen to be familiar with the variety of fish known as bluefish. How did her pronunciation of the play's title give away that she wasn't a bluefish eater, given what we have learned about compounds in English?

# Lecture Five—Transcript
## How to Make a Word

We have seen how the actual sounds in a language only correspond partially to the alphabet. In the same way, what we write as words corresponds only partially to actual units of meaning in terms of how we express ourselves. As true sounds are called *phonemes*—as we've seen—in linguistics, actual units of meaning are called *morphemes*. The most basic element in a language is its sounds, and then morphemes are the next level up.

This is what's important about morphemes. Morpheme is not just another way of saying "word"; for example, a word might contain just one morpheme. For example, *dog* is both a word and a morpheme, because *dog* is a single unit of meaning. However, a word could contain several morphemes. For example, take *hunter*. There are two units of meaning in *hunter*: There is *hunt*, and then there is the *-er* suffix, which means there's something doing the hunting. Both of those are units of meaning, so *hunter* can be subdivided into those two units; *hunter* is a word that has two morphemes in it. Or, for example, if you take *hunters*, then you've got three morphemes, because you've got *hunt*, *-er*, and then the plural marker. That means that you've got three units of meaning within that one word. Morpheme and word are not the same thing; morpheme is more specific. The word *unthinkingly* contains four morphemes: You've got the *un-*, *think*, *-ing*—because the word *think* is different from the word *thinking*; *think* is a verb, and *thinking* is a noun—and then the *-ly*, which makes it into an adverb. All of those things are separate entities that come together into a word, but there are four units of meaning—that is, morphemes—within the word.

Just as we saw that with phonemes, phonemes come in allophones—the allophones being variations on that basic sound (for example, with /p/ there would be your aspirated *p*, [pʰ], and then your unaspirated *p*, kind of like "peh," [p]) and those are allophones, varieties of the phoneme—morphemes can come in pairs, trios, or great big bunches of *allomorphs*. For example, often there will be a morpheme that serves a particular function in grammar. It will come in different forms, depending on things like what sounds it occurs around, just like what allophone occurs depends on what other sounds are in the context. For example, our definite article in English can be either *a* or *an*. Generally, we're taught that the issue is that it's *an* before a vowel, and *a* before a consonant. *A* and *an* are allomorphs of our definite article. Another example is that we saw how our plural marker in English underlyingly is actually /z/, not /s/, and that you can have either [z] or [s] on the surface. [z] and [s] can be termed allomorphs of the plural morpheme. They're different flavors that it can come in.

Or if you have ever suffered through learning a language like Spanish, where you have the long tables of verb conjugations—"I speak," *hablo*; "you speak," *hablas*; "he/she/it speaks," *habla*; etc.—you also remember that the verbs come in three conjugational classes. For example, if you want to say "you speak," then it's "*hablas*." If you want to say "you eat," the verb is "*comer*." To say "you eat," and it's a singular, it's "*comes*." It's *-as* in one conjugational class; it's *-es* in another conjugational class in the second-person singular in the present tense. Those are allomorphs of the second-person singular present-tense morpheme.

We have this kind of patterning. To get a sense of what an allomorph is, you might think about an old friend of mine's sneakers. There is this guy I knew a long time ago who had a pair of sneakers that otherwise looked the same but were a different color, and he would peg them to his outfits. This was in a linguistics department, so people starting joking that he had "alloshoes." What they meant by that was that all of these shoes were basically the same thing, but depending on—in a sense—what sound they occurred next to, or what clothes he happened to be wearing that day, he would wear them in a different color. So *a/an*, *-as/-es*, and then purple shoes one day when he was wearing lavender pants, and then yellow shoes if he was wearing his yellow pants or what have you: "alloshoes"; allomorphs. That is the basic way that morphemes work.

Getting a sense of how to look at a language in terms of its morphemes rather than its words—which to a large extent is a matter of graphic convention rather than what's actually going on—we have to think about the difference between free morphemes and bound morphemes, because some morphemes can occur all by themselves. That's—for example—*hunt*, *dog*, *green*, or *run*. Then there are other morphemes that only occur as bound to another word. For example: the *-er* in *hunter*. There's no such thing as saying, "Oh, look, there goes an er." You can't hold an "er" in your hand. The *-er* is something that's only appended to, for example, a verb. You have a *hunter*.

Or, for example, the past marker—which we think of graphically as *-ed*—is something that cannot occur alone. When you're thinking about something going on in the past, you wouldn't say that you're "thinking about ed" or something like that. It's only something that can be appended to a verb, so that you get *hunted*, *walked*, and things like that. This is the difference between free and bound.

One way that you know that a morpheme is bound is when nothing can come between it and the root that it applies to. For example, in English, we use a free morpheme to indicate the future, and that's *will*. You can say, "I will shiver." Then you can separate *will* and *shiver* by saying, "I will certainly shiver," if you ever wanted to say that. Then, on the other hand, if you were talking about *shivering* in the past, you could not say, "I shiver certainlyed." You could say, "I certainly shivered," but you can't put the *certain* between the *shiver* and the *-ed*, because the *-ed* is bound.

The fact is that if you look at languages around the world, you find that they differ in terms of to what extent their morphemes—especially the ones that just serve grammatical functions—are bound versus whether they are free. Often a language will have morphemes, many of which are bound—like in English and other European languages—but then there are also languages where morphemes are not bound at all. For example, in Vietnamese—and this is similar in many languages of East and Southeast Asia—morphemes are free to a much greater extent than anything that we consider intuitive. As a result, you have a language that chops things up much more. You can look at this Vietnamese example, and you can see that even the way that Vietnamese indicates *we* is with two morphemes: one word for *I* (*tôi*), and then a separate morpheme—free, not bound—that indicates the plural (*chúng*). This is because if you think about it, *we* is two *I*'s. In Vietnamese, that's played out right there (as *chúng tôi*). Or even this "take start" that you see—which is for "to begin"—divides up the concept of beginning in a way that is different from what would be done in English.

Linguists call languages like Vietnamese *analytic languages*. Perhaps a more memory-friendly rendition of that is *isolating language*, the idea being that it tends to express its morphemes in isolation. That's one type of language that there is, and it's by no means unusual. That kind of language is actually quite common in particularly the upper leftward half of Africa and very common in East and Southeast Asia. That is one way that a language might be very, very chary of prefixes and suffixes.

Then there are languages that are called *agglutinative languages*. As you could guess, that's because they agglutinate their morphemes. Swahili is one of these. You can see that there's a morpheme that indicates the third-person singular in the same way that we would have a separate pronoun for that, such as *he, she,* or *it*. Then you have a morpheme that indicates the present tense, and then you've got your verb right there: *anataka*. All of that is one word; the morphemes are agglutinated together, rather than being expressed separately.

Swahili looks familiar to us because, since we're used to morphemes being kluged together, we might think that English is an agglutinative language (or Spanish or another language that we might be familiar with). But actually, English and the European languages are a different type. We call them *fusional*, and this is why: Although it's not always apparent, when you think about it, a lot of our morphemes—our bound morphemes—actually mean two things at the same time. For example, in *wants*—so *he wants, she wants,* or *it wants*—the *-s* signifies first the third-person singular—and I think that's pretty apparent—but also it signifies the present, because if we're talking about *he/she/it wanted* in the past, then the past is indicated by *-ed*. The *-s* also indicates that we're dealing with the present tense as well as the third-person singular. This morpheme covers both of those things at the same time. That kind of double function is common in, for example, European languages. Languages like that are called fusional languages. They bring things together to an even greater extent than agglutinative languages, which, compared to fusional languages, are kind of like the sort of person who doesn't want their meat to touch their peas, or their rice to touch their corn, or something like that. Swahili is very tidy; it's easy to see where the lines between morphemes are. In a language like English, many morphemes actually have two functions, and so things have come together even more from what we can think of as an initial state such as Vietnamese, where everything is not only nicely subdividable but actually separate; so, we have that.

As you can imagine, there's no reason why English would necessarily be an extreme. It's actually that English is one intermediate step. The most extreme example—actually, English is but an intermediate step upon what can be seen as a continuum of manifestations of morphemes—there are languages, and a lot of them, where a word is what we think of as a sentence. What this means is that morphemes are crammed together into massive packages; you can think of these as very sticky languages. For example, take a look at this sentence from Chinook. Chinook is a Native American language—Washington and Oregon are its states, or I should say were; it is one of the great many that are no longer with us being passed on—however, a magnificent thing it was. Here, look at one word in it: just "*Inialudam*"; there it is. That word means *I came to give it to her*—to give some object to a person who was not a man. If you look at *Inialudam*, you can see that it packs into this one word a number of morphemes, which we would think of as something to go into a sentence with various words. You can see, for example, that *-u-* near the middle is something that indicates that there's been some sort of movement away in this "coming to give." Or look at how *give* is indicated: *Give* is just one of the many prefixes; *give* is just that *-d-*, as opposed to being the core aspect, what you think would be maybe the one thing that would stand alone because this is all about an act of giving. Here, it just has to stand in line with the other prefixes. This is a way of functioning that is by no means exotic; it's quite common. If linguistics had been founded by Mohawk Native Americans, then they would see fusional languages as some sort of exotic step. This is very common among Native American languages, for example, and there are other places in the world where languages like this occur. These are called *polysynthetic languages*, and that's our fourth type of language.

You can see that there are these four kinds: You've got the analytic or isolating languages; then you have agglutinative languages, like Swahili and Turkish; then fusional, which is our familiar sort of English, Spanish, or German; then you have polysynthetic languages, such as Chinook and many others. The person who subdivided languages into that typology—into that classificational system—was Wilhelm von Humboldt. He was Prussian, and he did this work during his life, which straddled the 18th and 19th centuries. He was one of those polymaths, so typical in that era when there wasn't quite as much to know as there is for us now. He was a diplomat, and then he was an education minister, and he meant it: There were people who knew him mostly for his work in that area. He was also a linguist—and a serious one—who did very important and wide-ranging work. He came up with this typology, noticing that morphemes were handled differently in different kinds of languages and that you can classify how this worked. He saw that you could see a clinal relationship between the four. Of course, naturally you might imagine that there are free morphemes and then, as time goes by, they start being run together as things tend to be—as we'll see in some later lectures about how languages develop, called historical linguistics—and that, in terms of how a polysynthetic language arises in the first place, is almost certainly true.

But von Humboldt had a propensity for looking at things like this as a matter of human mental sophistication. Of course, this was not uncommon in his era. This was a time when subjective and often rather aristocratic judgments—ethnocentric judgments—of those kinds were more common in scientific work than they are now. Of course we do not do our scientific work today with no biases, but here was a time when, for example, Carl Linnaeus, when he was formulating how we classify animals and plants with Latin names, would often give something a name that meant—as if he were doing it in English—"ugliest," just because he found it an unpleasant-looking creature. As if somehow in the eyes of a higher being these creatures are undesirable because they don't fall well upon his eye. In the same way, von Humboldt had the idea that fusional languages were the best kind—and wouldn't you know that German is a fusional language. His idea was that fusional language is the best because "such languages earnestly endeavor to unite every particular into the sentence, or to present the latter all in one piece."

I'm not exactly sure what he meant by that, but that's what he considered to be very important about languages like German and English—what he considered to be a respectable language. For him, I suppose, a polysynthetic language was seen as just kind of cramming things too closely together to be perceived clearly or something. That would mean that Eskimo and Inuit people don't really ever quite know what they're saying or what they talk about. But even agglutinative languages, which if you think about it don't seem all that different in spirit from fusional languages—agglutinative languages, which still are a matter of prefixes, suffixes, and words with many morphemes in them—for him, even that just wasn't quite good enough. He seemed to think of them as lesser fusional languages. He said, "Their obscure endeavor in the same direction"—that is of what fusional languages do—"is more or less of a failure." What that means is that German succeeds but somehow Turkish—which is an agglutinative language *par excellence*—is somehow a failure. That was the sort of thing that he said.

The fact is that subsequent research has shown that there is no correlation between mental or societal advancement and how a language handles its bound morphemes. This was put most beautifully by Edward Sapir. He put it in his 1921 classic book, *Language*, that, "When it comes to linguistic form, Plato walks with the Macedonian swineherd, Confucius with the head-hunting savage of Assam." By Plato—this is always hard—I don't mean that kind of salty-tasting goop that children play with, I mean Plato the philosopher, the one who we had to read in college. "When it comes to linguistic form, Plato walks with the Macedonian swineherd, Confucius with the head-hunting savage of Assam." What he meant by that was that Plato had his Greek, and Greek is a language that is just festooned with morphemes crammed into a word. It has many, many, many lists of conjugational endings, and the nouns decline, etc. But then, on the other hand, there is Macedonia. Macedonia is a Balkan country where there are many people who herd swine. Those who do that—living in the hills doing that—are not what we would call cosmopolitan people, but Macedonian is as massively complex in terms of bound morphology as Greek is. Macedonian is part of a kind of a group of closely related Slavic languages; Bulgarian, Macedonian, and Serbo-Croatian kind of slide into each other. Once when I was at a party, there was a Bulgarian on one side of me and a Bulgarian on the other side of me, and I said, "What's Macedonian?" They both said in unison, "It's a dialect of Bulgarian." Apparently, Macedonian is very close to Bulgarian.

Then, on the other hand: "Confucius and the head-hunting savage of Assam." Apologies for the terminology *savage*, but this was a very a long time ago. But as far as somebody who was living in Assam—and is not in a tall building, in therapy, and all the things that are so wonderful about our first-world lives—the fact is that both the language of that person and the Chinese language of Confucius are ones where bound morphology is sparse or even nonexistent. There's no correlation. It might be easy to think because when we're taught grammar that—grammar is so often a matter of learning a whole bunch of endings in some language or even being told about the endings in our own—that the endings are what grammar is and that if you don't have that, then you don't have any grammar. But that's actually not the case.

You can look at a language like Akha. Akha is spoken in Southeast Asia in Burma. Akha is a highly analytic—that is, isolating—language. Yet, it encodes all sorts of concepts, which we don't even have to express in our mighty and sophisticated English. If you look at Akha, look at the words in bold: *ŋà **nɛ** àjɔ̀q **áŋ** áshì thì **shì** bìq **ma*** (I gave him one fruit). The first one, this "*nɛ*," expresses that I did something that affected someone else. If you sleep, presumably it's not affecting someone else directly. But if you're giving something to someone, then they are going to come out having been given that thing. In Akha, you have to mark that with this morpheme. Then you have this second morpheme, "*áŋ*," and that indicates that you are the person who was affected and that happens to be used. Then you have this "*shì*" here, and that is something that is used whenever you use a number. You use a number, and then you have to add this little bit of stuff. That bit of stuff differs depending on what sort of thing you gave someone. If it was round, then you have to use a certain bit of stuff. If it had some other shape, it's a different bit of stuff. If it was an animate being, then you use a different little bit of stuff. That's the sort of thing that we barely have in English. We just talk about one banana. We don't have to say, one—long thing—banana. This is the sort of language where that happens. Then, this fourth thing, this "*ma*," just means that you're certain of what you've said. In English, we can say something like, "Well, you know, this is the rainiest day down here this year. I'm sure of that." You could say that, but you don't have to say that. In Akha, as in many languages, you have to tack on something indicating that you're sure or unsure or that it's only something that you heard, etc. There are all those things in this language where there would be no long tables of endings that are presented to you or anything like that.

In any case, I am showing you morphemes, and I'm trying to start from the familiar. In this case, that means talking about endings and prefixes—in other words, talking about affixes, prefixes, and suffixes—but the fact is that a morpheme can be more than just a bit of stuff. A morpheme can also combine with another morpheme to create a word without either of the morphemes being little bound morphemes. For example, you can make a word from two morphemes by putting two free words together, and you create what's called a *compound*. For example, *blackbird* is one word; you would write it as one word. It is one word—it refers to one thing—but of course, it comes from two other words: *black* and *bird*. *Steamboat* would be the same thing.

There's a rule in English that we use subconsciously when we create a compound: The accent is on the first syllable. If you think about it, a "black BIRD" is some bird that's black, and presumably quite a few of them are. A "BLACKbird" is that particular type of bird that there's that old song about. "Look, Mom, a black BIRD." It could be any number of things. "Look, Mom, a BLACKbird." That's a very particular kind of black bird. "Look, Mom, a black BIRD"—*black bird*; that's two words—"Look, Mom, a BLACKbird"—*blackbird* is one word; it's made from two, but now it's one. That's a compound. The way that we know is because of that accent pattern. This means that, for one reason or another, the two concepts have come to be associated so much that there is now one unitary concept such as the *blackbird*. It's interesting. There is an early episode of *Mary Tyler Moore*— it's the very early '70s. The American palate is still kind of bland—and Mary and her date are eating something they're calling "Chinese FOOD." "Oh, darling, why don't we order some Chinese FOOD?" Today, we would say "ChiNESE food." She says "Chinese FOOD" because, to Mary

Richards, eating this "Chinese FOOD" was kind of new. For her, it's kind of like "Look, Mom, it's Chinese FOOD." We say, "Look, it's ChiNESE food" because to us, really, it's a compound. It's one word in its way. That's something that's done just with the accent.

Accent also can change a word's part of speech. On the one hand, we can do that kind of thing with an affix. *Happy* is an adjective. *Happiness* is a noun; we did it with the *-ness*. You can have *pressure*, and that's a noun; you can *pressurize* something, and that makes it into a verb with the *-ize*. That's not the only way that we do this sort of thing, however. You can take a verb that has the accent on the second syllable, and if you then put the accent on the first syllable, you have created a noun. Think about this: I'm going to "outLAW" that practice. Anybody who does that from now on is an "OUTlaw." You wouldn't say "anyone who does that from now on is an outLAW"; frankly, that person had a stroke. It's an "OUTlaw." That's not only with *outlaw*. I'm going to "reBEL" against this rule, and therefore I'm going to become a "reBEL." No, I'm going to become a "REbel." Or, for example, I'm going to "reCORD" this lecture, and then I'll have a "reCORD" of it. No, I'll have a "REcord" of it. That *stress shift* is a way of making a word into a different part of speech—if you will—and what that means is that accent shift is a morpheme. A morpheme can be many things. It's unit of meaning; it can change a verb into a noun. That means it's a new word, so there's clearly a new morpheme. That's something that you can do in a morphemic way that's different from just the affixes.

Finally, a morpheme can just be a changed vowel. I *come* to the zoo; I *came* to the zoo. You didn't "comed" to the zoo; you can't do that. Where's the morpheme? It was that change from the *-o-* to the *-a-*; so *come* and then *came*. That's the way that works. A morpheme can be an affix, it can be an accent shift, or it can be just a change of vowel. The crucial aspect of it is that a morpheme is a unit of meaning. Of course, the vast majority of units of meaning in any language are things like nouns and verbs that can stand alone, not to mention your prepositions, adverbs, conjunctions, and everything else. But then there's also a large class of morphemes that are—in our language—bound, and they are the various affixes. Then there are morphemes that are just a matter of changing a vowel. There are morphemes that are a matter of changing accent. All of these things are units of meaning, and the overlap between the concept of "unit of meaning" and "word"—as you can see—is highly approximate.

People study this. When they study it, it is called *morphology*; the study of how morphemes work is called morphology. In practice, morphology focuses more on the morphemes that help grammar along, rather than the morphemes that just describe an action or a person, place, or thing. Morphology is much more about the past marker, the accent shift, and things like that than it is about *hunt*, *fish*, *chair*, *dog*, or *ring*. That's morphology. In shorthand, you can think of it as the study of endings and prefixes: affixes. But really, that's kind of a Eurocentric way of looking at it, because in many languages what's done with affixes is done with free morphemes and, nevertheless, the same sorts of functions are being carried out with the same sorts of processes, exceptions, and things like that.

Etymology—which is the way we might as laymen think of how you would study words—is actually a matter of how words' meanings change over time. To the extent that etymology is studied by modern linguists, it would fall under the rubric of the study of language change: historical linguistics. When we're studying words from the point of view of the modern theoretical linguist, what we're looking at is morphemes and how they interact with one another. Now that we've taken a look at that, let's take it to the next level.

# Lecture Six
## The Chomskyan Revolution

**Scope:** The linguistics field is dominated today by Noam Chomsky, who proposed in the 1950s that the capacity to learn and use language is innate and is driven by a neurological configuration that generates words in a hierarchical branching "tree" format, termed "phrase structure." This lecture introduces Chomsky's justification of this hypothesis and introduces the basics of phrase-structure tree diagrams.

## Outline

I. In this lecture, we will proceed to the next level of language structure, *syntax*. Sounds make up morphemes, morphemes make up words, and words come together in sentences; in linguistics, the study of how words come together in sentences is called *syntax*.

   **A.** The crucial insight is that forming sentences is not a mere matter of placing words in order one at a time.

   **B.** Rather, just as the phonemic/phonetic distinction underlies the mere assemblage of sounds, and just as conglomerations of morphemes underlie the surface rendition of words, in syntax there is what lies beneath and what is on the surface.

II. The history of studying syntax is relatively new.

   **A.** The study of phonology and morphology was well established by the 1920s. However, the leading scholars assumed that each language was an independent growth, rooted partly in its speakers' culture and partly in chance.

      1. This was in part because anthropologists had played a large role in setting the terms of the new discipline.

         **a.** Edward Sapir (1884–1939) and Franz Boas (1858–1942), for example, were ardent proponents of the validity of all human cultures, rejecting earlier conceptions of the world's peoples as rankable on a scale of "development."

         **b.** Because language is related to culture, this conditioned an approach to languages as cultural features, learned via the same cognitive processes as all other human activities.

2. This was also in part because psychology at the time was dominated by behaviorism, which stipulated that human behavior is all learned.

**B.** Language was thought to be just a matter of an arbitrary, chance conglomeration that one picked up, not a matter of any kind of underlying system. Therefore, linguistic analysis focused on describing the phonemes and morphemes of a language and described how they were placed in order.

**C.** However, starting with his work as an undergraduate at the University of Pennsylvania in the 1940s, Noam Chomsky (1928–) began to develop a theory under which all languages have a basic syntactic configuration that we are mentally hardwired to learn and use.

1. To support this theory, the task of the linguist is to explain how languages that seem so different can be products of this species-wide mental configuration.

2. Chomsky first inaugurated this idea in what was published in 1957 as *Syntactic Structures*. Within 10 years, this approach to syntax became the dominant one in linguistics, and it is taught universally today.

3. One of Chomsky's foundational concepts was that syntax is a module of the generation of a sentence that is distinct from its meaning (i.e., its semantics). Earlier, it was generally thought that expressing meaning and syntax were more or less the same process.

   a. Chomsky called attention to facts such as that *The dog bit the man* and *The man was bitten by the dog* have the same meaning but different syntax.

   b. Also, a sentence that is syntactically well-formed can be semantically meaningless, such as *Colorless green ideas sleep furiously*. This sentence is termed *grammatical* albeit nonsensical.

4. Chomsky proposed therefore that there is a mental level that generates grammatical sentences, with their meaning being a separate generative process.

**III.** Chomsky's basic idea was that this process is innate, and he called it *universal grammar*.

**A.** One of Chomsky's crucial insights was that children do not make all the mistakes that we would expect them to.

1. For example, to make a sentence into a question, in English we change the order of the subject and the auxiliary, such as: *The man is tall. Is the man tall?*

2. Thus we might think that the rule English speakers follow is simply "switch the order of the subject and the auxiliary."

3. But to make the sentence *The man who is tall is sad* into a question, we say *Is the man who is tall sad?*

4. *Is* appears twice in the sentence, but we do not put the first *is* up front and say *Is the man who tall is sad?*

5. This is because *who is tall* is nested within the sentence as a kind of subsentence. We are questioning the sentence, not the subsentence, and thus we extract the second *is*.

B. No one teaches children such a thing—and yet children do not start out trying sentences like *Is the man who tall is sad?* Chomsky argues that this is because we are born with an innate mental configuration to learn and produce language with this kind of nested structure.

1. That is, syntax is not a mere matter of learning the order of elements.

2. Syntax is a matter first of constituency and second of a nested, or *hierarchical*, structure that the elements are slotted into.

IV. Chomskyan syntax has worked out a formal representation of how sentences are represented in the brain in this structure-dependent fashion. The representation is in the form of "trees," in which words occur at the ends of the "branches."

A. The tree begins with a basic distinction between an *entity* and a *predication*, traditionally called *subject* and *predicate*: *Bill* (subject) *walked away* (predicate). The top *node* of the tree is rendered as S, for sentence. The subject is rendered as N for noun and the predicate as V for verb.

B. However, a subject can consist of more than just a noun. The noun can be modified by an adjective: *Black cats*. The noun can have an article: *The black cat*. For this reason, the subject node in our tree needs room for more than just a noun alone. The node is, instead, specified as for a *noun phrase*, abbreviated on the tree as NP. It has a hierarchical structure.

C. In the same way, a verb as often as not is followed by an object (*Bill saw Jim*) or modified by an adverb (*Bill walked slowly*).

**D.** The tree has a *verb phrase* node (abbreviated as VP) next to the noun phrase one as branches of the S node, and then the verb itself and the object noun are branches of the VP node.

**E.** NP structure can also occur under the VP node: *Bill saw the little man* would "tree" with the VP having two branches: one the verb *saw* and the other an NP, which would contain *the little man*.

**F.** Thus all nouns in a sentence, subject or object, are potentially NPs, with the same possible branching into definite article, adjective, and so on, in a hierarchical fashion.

**G.** The idea is that this is not simply a way to diagram a sentence but that we are born with an innate propensity to process and produce language as driven by this particular tree structure.

**V.** Motivation for the idea that we are born with a sensitivity to this kind of structure becomes clearer when we look further at how trees work.

    **A.** A verb can also take a complement that is, in effect, a separate sentence: In *Sue said that Bill lied*, the phrase *that Bill lied* is a sentence nested within the main one.

        **1.** On our tree, we indicate this with a node called the *complement phrase*, abbreviated CP, which comes under the VP.

        **2.** The CP branches into a complement node known as a *complementizer*, abbreviated as C, which takes the *that*, and then an S node for a whole new sentence: *Bill lied.*

    **B.** This brings us back to *The man who is tall is sad*. Here, *who is tall* is a sentence of its own, termed a *relative clause*.

        **1.** It fits into the tree as a CP as well, but *who* is the subject of this "sentence," and so the complement node itself hangs empty.

        **2.** That empty node is a hint that this is not just the parsing or diagramming that you may have learned in school. This is a different kind of formalism.

    **C.** Under the Chomskyan conception, a child would first hear a sentence and know, on a certain level—literally be genetically programmed to readily understand, although not able to put it in so many words—that there are possible sentences within sentences.

**D.** This happens even if the sentence heard is full of empty nodes, like that hanging complementizer in the last example. The child will hear the second auxiliary in *The man who is tall is sad* as higher, although the child has not been told this.

**VI.** The Chomskyan revolution was to study syntax as something autonomous from meaning and semantics and to propose that there is an innate capacity for learning, processing, and producing syntax of a particular kind that is universal to our species.

**Essential Reading:**

Pinker, *The Language Instinct*.

**Supplemental Reading:**

Radford, *Syntax*.

**Questions to Consider:**

1. I have necessarily given only a cursory portrait of the formalism that Chomskyan syntactic theory has entailed over the years. Some basic equipment was not necessary to present. How would you surmise, for example, that *The extremely fat man sat in a chair* would be represented in a tree like the ones above? Hint: Not only nouns and verbs but also adjectives and prepositions occur as part of "phrases" in the syntactic tree.

2. Were you taught to "parse" or "diagram" sentences in school? If so, parse or diagram a sentence from this lecture and consider the differences between that formalism and the Chomskyan one.

# Lecture Six—Transcript
## The Chomskyan Revolution

In this lecture, we're going to proceed to the next level of language structure, which is called *syntax*. We've seen sounds; we've seen how sounds make up morphemes, morphemes make up words, and words come together in sentences. In linguistics, syntax is the study of how that process works. For our purposes, the crucial insight is that syntax is not just a matter of learning to put words in the proper order. There is more going on from where sentences begin to how they actually come out than we might think. This is just like the other levels of language that we've seen in the course so far. There's the phonemic/phonetic distinction in terms of sounds. We've seen that words are actually a matter of conglomerations of morphemes in ways that you might not think about. In the same way, with syntax there's what underlies and then what is on the surface. We're going to take a look at how syntax works in linguistics over this and the next two lectures. In this one, the first thing I want to do is give a little bit of history of this way of looking at syntax, and then I want to introduce you to some of the basic tools in terms of how this kind of thing is studied in the academic linguistic field.

First, a little bit of history. What am I talking about—syntax—and why am I using that particular term? The fact of the matter is that phonology and morphology, in the ways that I've described to you so far in this course, were pretty well established and recognizable forms by the 1920s; these are relatively old things. But when it came to studying something like word order, this was something that was not done a whole lot. One of the oddest things about looking at a description of a language written in, say, 1910 is how little interest there often is in anything beyond phonology and morphology. It's as if there isn't anything else to be studied—or not studied very closely. There were two reasons for this: For one thing, if you were a linguist in, say, 1915, what you really were was a flavor of anthropologist. An anthropologist at this time, just like now—but this was a new paradigm for anthropology at this time—was committed to showing that there is no such thing as an inferior culture. To take a song from the aughts—the first decade of the 20th century—there is a very popular song that was supposed to be about a Zulu from Matabooloo and how he would sing a love song. It went: "If you like-a me like me like-a you and we like-a both the same." That was the idea of what a native was. Either you were a civilized, first-world person or you had a bone through your nose. You can even look at old Looney Tunes, and the native is somebody who yells "Bunga bunga

bunga." You get the feeling that the language is more primitive because it only seems to have one word and so on. That was the view that anthropologists were newly committed to fighting in, say, 1915.

For example, we saw how Edward Sapir noticed—in terms of languages—that Plato's language, his ancient Greek, was similar in structure to the language of a swineherd from Macedonia, and that the language of Confucius was similar in structure to the headhunter from Assam. This was the sort of idea one worked under. Another main promoter of that idea was Franz Boas. These were people who were linguists as well. If you were a linguist, you were committed to this idea that there were just cultures of equal value. Language was seen as something that comes from culture, and of course it does. The idea was how the words are put in order—just like everything else in language—is just something, chance, that happened at a particular time, in a particular place, maybe for cultural reasons, but that there's nothing systematic to be studied about it. Certainly there's nothing that we can say about which language has which words in what order and how these differences might mean something in the grander sense. It's just cultural.

In addition, this was a time when psychologists were under the influence of behaviorism. The general idea in behaviorism was that anything that human beings do is a learned kind of behavior. You start out as a blank slate—as a *tabula rasa*—and you watch people doing things; that's why you do them. This, supposedly, would include language. It's just a matter of what you've picked up. It would not be a matter of there being any kind of underlying system in the way that we've seen how phonemes work and how they come out as allophones, or how morphemes come together into words. The idea was that it was just a matter of culture. Linguists basically described the languages' phonemes and allophones, then you describe some morphemes, and then we wait for them to describe sentence structure—at least a linguist waits—and then it kind of just stops. They say a few things, and the next thing you know you're in the index and then you shut the book and it's gone. That is something that was changed by Noam Chomsky.

Noam Chomsky, of course, is best known to most people for his political views and his political writings. But he actually has led a kind of double life, because Noam Chomsky also founded the main perspectives of how traditional linguistics is done today. He's considered the grandfather of the field. For every political book that he puts out or political statement that he's known for, there's something he's done within the world of linguistics which is considered equally important.

Chomsky, starting when he was just an undergraduate at the University of Pennsylvania, hit upon a different way of looking at what syntax was. Instead of it being a matter of each language just happens to have a certain way of putting words in order for reasons that aren't particularly important and are probably tied up with local cultures, he thought, "It looks to me as if language's word-order patterns have certain things in common, which suggests that there is some kind of mental hardwiring that is innate to human beings—and that is all human beings—which allows us to 'generate' sentences," as he put it, "and which determines what the word order is in different languages." His idea is that it is not cultural, that there is something actually imprinted in our brains. There's actually something in our DNA that codes for the ability to use and process the syntax of language. His idea was that even if all of the 6,000 languages of the world's word order look very different, it must be that all of them are actually variant expressions of a single template that we are actually born with the ability to use.

That is not an idea that anyone had had before. I, myself, sometimes wonder how anybody—particularly as an undergraduate when I, at least, was busy doing all sorts of other things—would sit and look at all of the different syntaxes of the world and come to the conclusion that, wow, we must be born with syntax encoded in the neurons in our brain. That's what Chomsky did, however, and he has promulgated that idea very prominently for a very long time now. The official salvo was his book *Syntactic Structures*, and that was in 1957. There was a revolution of sorts in the study of linguistics. Suddenly, by only about 10 years later, *Syntactic Structures* was the way most people studying syntax were looking at things. The people who had done the old-fashioned kind of linguistics suddenly seemed like pipe-smoking people in tweed jackets with three names who were resentful that this Chomsky and people his age had come along and turned the whole field upside down. It was an acrimonious time. Those days are gone now, and the revolution has pretty much become accomplished.

The new idea was that syntax was something separate from phonology, morphology, and particularly semantics. It used to be thought that if you're putting a sentence together, then obviously meaning has something to do with it because we say things that we mean or we say things that we don't mean. The idea was that there is syntax and that's intimately tied up with meaning and that on some level the two must be the same thing. The way philosophy of language was done at the time, it was assumed that this was true. But Chomsky pointed out that we have to make more of a difference between the study of meaning—that is, *semantics*—and the study of syntax than has often been done. For example, you can say *The dog bit the man*. That's a simple, boring sentence. Then you can say *The man was bitten by the dog*. Those two things mean exactly the same thing. In both cases, you picture a dog kind of nipping at the gluteal region of some man or wherever the dog happens to bite the man. But the fact of the matter is that with *The dog bit the man* and *The man was bitten by the dog*, you've got different syntax, so obviously syntax is something different from meaning.

Or there is the famous sentence *Colorless green ideas sleep furiously*. That's a sentence: *Colorless green ideas sleep furiously*. I have not made any kind of grammatical mistake, but obviously that sentence makes not the slightest bit of sense. The problem is that the meaning is wrong, but it's not that the grammar itself is wrong. It's not that the syntax is wrong, so syntax seems to be separate. Suppose you heard somebody say, "Read you a book on modern music?" If I say that, you know what I meant, even though clearly there is something wrong. The meaning is there—"Read you a book on modern music?"—you all know exactly what I mean, but that's clearly not the way to say it. The semantics are fine; it's the syntax that's off. Or imagine saying something like, "Oh, look, that baby seems sleeping." You know exactly what I mean—"that baby seems sleeping"—you almost wish that you could say that, but you just don't. The meaning is clear. It looks like that very tiny human being is in a peculiarly inert state that we call sleep. But we don't say "seems sleeping"; the syntax is wrong.

Chomsky isolated that there is something, which he called syntax, which is worthy of study and which is going on in our brains on a different level than—or another way he often put it, *in a different module from*—where meaning (that is, semantics) is taking place. His idea was that if you look at something like *Colorless green ideas sleep furiously*, it's a morphological matter. The things from our earlier lectures—that *-ly* is being linked to *furious* and you have this new word *furiously*—so that's down here (on the morphological level). Then you've got meaning—the fact that *sleeping* and *furiously* would never be mapped together because *furiously* implies a deliberation and probably being awake that is incompatible with *sleeping*—that's on the semantic level. But as far as Chomsky was concerned, there's something in between—syntax—which could be called a kind of mezzanine. That's what he was interested in.

The basic idea was that this is innate; he called it *universal grammar*. The idea is that any human being has it. It's not that a Turk is born with some innate ability to understand Turkish but that all human beings are born with this ability, because, of course, children of any extraction learn the language that they're raised with, and they do it quickly. One of Chomsky's crucial insights was that children do not make all of the mistakes that you would expect them to make. This is another one of those things where I can't imagine why someone would have thought of this, but the fact of the matter is that he is right.

For example, let's take an ordinary sentence like *The man is tall*. We all know that to make it into a question, what we would do is say *Is the man tall?* We think, what's the rule? How do you make something into a question in English? In this case, it seems that you take the auxiliary and the subject—the *is* and the *man*—and you switch places. It's *Is the man tall?* That's easy, but if you take a slightly different sentence, *The man who is tall is sad*—that's a simple sentence—and if you make that into a question, we know instantly that you say *Is the man who is tall sad?* But the fact of the matter is that when we did that, we did not apply that rule that we came up with of the subject and auxiliary (AUX). At least, it's not clear exactly how we applied that rule, because there are two *is*'s in that sentence. We could take the correct *is*—the one that we know is the correct *is*—and we say *Is the man who is tall sad?* But that's the second *is*. Somehow, we just knew to do that. If we're going to go by our first rule—i.e., *Is the man sad?*—then you'd think that somebody might think, well, suppose we just take the first AUX and reverse it with the subject. What's interesting is that no child makes that mistake. You'd think that children, if it's just a matter of listening for the order that words come in, would think if you are going to make something into a question, then you take the subject and the AUX that follows it and you reverse the order. But in the case of *The man who is tall is sad* that would mean that you would get *Is the man who tall is sad?* That's not a sentence at all.

We know that children make mistakes. For example, it's very common for a child to go through a phase where they're saying *feets* instead of *feet*. When I was little, I remember going through a phase where instead of saying *have* I would say *gots*, and I insisted that was correct. My mother kept getting on me about it. I didn't grow up in a home where that was said. I just got it from somewhere: "I gots this book in my hand." My mother would say, "That is not the way you use the word 'gots.'" I had these vocabulary cards, and I remember the word *got* was on one of the cards. I said, "Yes, there is such a word: got." We would fight over it. Kids are very insistent about the mistakes they make. But no child says *Is the man who tall is sad?* That doesn't happen.

Why is it that a child never does anything like that? If the child is just listening for word order, then you'd think that that would happen. The question is answered—as far as Chomsky is concerned—by a simple statement that the child, in a sense, already knows when it's born that you can't do a sentence like that. This is why I'm saying this; this is the justification for what Chomsky meant.

There is a formalism that is used in the study of syntax. There's a way of doing what we call *treeing sentences*. I'm going to introduce you to a little bit of this formalism, because it can show you the answer to the question as to how children seem to automatically know how to make *The man who is tall is sad* into a question.

The way that this tree system works is we can start with a basic difference between an *entity* and a *predication*. Traditionally, this is called *subject* and *predicate*. For example, something like *Bill* can be the entity, and then *walked away* can be the predication. The way we do this is that the top *node* of the tree is rendered as an S, for *sentence*, and then let's render our subject as an N (*noun*) and our predicate as a V (*verb*) and put them under here like this.

A subject can consist of more than just a single noun. A noun can be modified by an adjective. Let's say our noun is *cats*, and then, with an adjective, we can say *black cats* because my cat is black. Or the noun can have an article, and so let's try *the black cat*. The noun can take all of these modifiers. For this reason, we need our tree to be able to handle more than just a single noun alone like *Bill*. The way we handle this is that we specify it for this whole kind of "noun-y" package. That, in syntax, is called a *noun phrase*. Typically, we abbreviate that as NP; we have this NP here. What's important is that you can take, for example, *the tall man* and that's one kind of entity. Then you can take *the man*. That's one kind of NP. Or, you can replace *the man* with something like *he*. For example, *the tall man walked away*, *the man walked away*, or *he walked away*. It can be *The tall man with the strange hat walked away*. All of those things seem to have a certain common status; you can substitute one for the other. That's why we think of this being a noun phrase, even if it was just *cats*. The idea is that in *cats* you've got other nodes within the noun phrase that happen to be unfilled. The noun phrase, because you have this kind of substitution and all these things have a certain status, that's called a *constituent*. We talk about more than just the fact that *black* is an adjective and *cat* is a noun. We talk about there being a noun phrase, which itself is a particular constituent.

In the same way, if you look at a verb typically in a sentence, then it will be followed by an object, for example, or it will be followed by an adverb. You'll have something like *Bill saw Jim* or *Bill walked slowly*. In *Bill saw Jim*, the way that we represent this in the tree is not simply to hang a verb underneath and then hang the other noun—which is in this case *Jim*—underneath, so that you've just got this kind of three-ball pawnshop-symbol-looking structure. We don't do it that way because actually there is a closer relationship between the verb and the object than, say, between the subject and the verb alone. The way that we know this is because if you look at something like *Bill saw Jim*, *saw Jim* is a constituent too. It is a unit, and that's because *saw Jim* can be substituted for by other things. *Bill saw Jim, and Jill did too*. The *did* is the substitution for *saw Jim*. There's no way that you can substitute for *Bill saw* alone, leaving *Jim* by itself. The idea is that with our verb—just like we have noun phrases—there's also a *verb phrase*, and that is typically abbreviated as a VP. Then, under the verb phrase, the verb alone is one branch. Then, for example in *Bill saw Jim*, you take *Jim* and hang that as a noun under our VP node.

The fact of the matter is that this object doesn't have to be just a single noun like *cats* or *Jim* either. This object can also be a full noun phrase itself. For example, you can have a tree of *Bill saw the little man*. In this case, you'd have an NP which was under our VP. You can see that in the diagram here. All the nouns in a sentence—not just the subject—are potentially filled-out VPs, all with the same potential branching into definite article, adjective, and so on. This is the crucial thing to see about the tree at this point, which is that the object NP—the one that is *Jim*—is lower in the tree than the subject NP. If we start with our S, then we have our first NP, and we have our first VP, you see that once we have our second NP—our object—underneath, it's lower in the tree. You can see that there's a hierarchal structure in this tree. Some nodes are higher up than others, and this ends up mattering for all sorts of things in terms of processing, in terms of how we produce sentences, and in terms of how children learn sentences, as we'll see in a bit. There's hierarchal structure. We have *constituency*, which is that we're not just dealing with separate words but that words come together in groups that actually have a coherence and a substitutability that is as noteworthy as the fact that we have a bunch of separate words. Then we have that the tree exists in a hierarchal structure.

The important thing is that this is not just a way of diagramming the sentence. The idea is that this kind of structure is something that we are innately programmed for. The idea is that we are born with a sensitivity to this kind of structure—with a propensity to express language with this particular kind of structure. The idea is that humans are born as parsers, so to speak, rather than just listening to people use words and using them the way they do. The motivation for that idea becomes clearer when we see one more thing about how trees work.

I mentioned that often a verb has an object or a verb has an adverb. A verb can also take a prepositional phrase. For example, we can say *Bill lived in San Francisco*, just as we can have an adverb, *Bill walked slowly*, or *Bill bought a cat*. In the same way, a verb can take something else. It can take a whole sentence. For example, you can say, *Sue said*, and then *that Bill lied*. In this case, if you think about it, *Bill lied* is a whole sentence in itself. *Bill* is a subject, and *lied* is a verb. In all of these cases, we say that a verb takes *complements*. There are different kinds of complements. There's an *object complement*. There's a *prepositional phrase complement*. You can have an *adverbial complement*, or you can have this kind of *sentential complement*. The way that you tree a sentence where there's a sentential complement is to append to the VP what is called a *complement phrase*. That's how you handle things like *Sue said that Bill lied*. This is how we handle a subordinate clause. If you think about it, there might be a question as to where you would put the *that* in *Sue said that Bill lied*, because *Bill* is our subject, our first NP, and *lied* is our verb, our first VP. The way we handle this is that the CP branches. You have first a C node, and that stands for *complementizer*. Don't worry why, but that is considered a complementizer; that's the terminology that's used. We hang our *that* there. Then *Bill lied* is a sentence, and so we have a whole new S node. The complement phrase— the CP—branches into a C, where you hang your complementizer. Then you've got a whole new sentence within a sentence. That's how the CP, the complement phrase, works.

This finally brings us back to *The man who is tall is sad* and how human beings seem to know so intuitively how to make it into a question, despite the fact that there are actually two auxiliaries. The idea is that in *The man who is tall is sad*, *who is tall*—as you might know—is what's termed a *relative clause*. That is handled as a sentence within a sentence, so to speak, just like *that Bill lied* in *Sue said that Bill lied*. We append it in the same way, here, only this time we do it on the subject NP. It's a matter of *the man*, and then *who is tall* is appended, and then *is sad* is our VP, and that's separate, and that's over here. In *who is tall*, *who* is actually the subject, if you think about it, and we have *is* as the auxiliary. That means that, in this case, the C node hangs empty. We're going to see more of that kind of thing in the way syntax works in a subsequent lecture, but that's just a hint that this is not just the parsing that you may have learned in school. This is a different kind of formalism. But the C is going to hang empty.

What we see here is that we don't have to make a clumsy stipulation that a child learns that in sentences with relative clauses you have to pick the second AUX when you're making it into a question. Obviously, that's not what goes on. Rather, this tree structure shows that the way that a human being might go at it is to think that what you do the inversion with is the highest auxiliary. The idea is that one of the auxiliaries is more prominent than the other and seems more central, even if there happen to be two or even three and even if it comes second in the sentence. It's not about counting; it's not about memorizing anything; it's about being sensitive to this structure. Under the Chomskyan conception, a child would hear first a sentence like *Is the man sad?* and know, on a certain level—literally be genetically programmed to readily understand, although not being able to put it in so many words—that there are possible sentences within sentences. This hierarchal structure is the way that language is actually built. This is even if, for example, in a simple sentence that they hear the embedded sentence, so to speak, is full of empty nodes, like that hanging complementizer that we saw. The child will hear that second auxiliary in *The man who is tall is sad* as higher, even though the child has not been told this—certainly, nobody would tell a child anything like this. But the idea is that we are programmed for syntax, which is organized according to the principles that we've seen in this lecture.

The Chomskyan revolution was to study syntax as something autonomous from, in particular, meaning and semantics and to propose that there is an innate capacity for learning, processing, and producing syntax of a particular kind that is universal to our species. His idea was that this is explained partly by the fact that there are mistakes that children do not make. They will say *feets* but not *Is the man who tall is sad?* Clearly, these are things that beg some kind of explanation. The important part is that this is not just a matter of the sentence parsing that some of you may have learned in school. This is the formalism, but the formalism differs from what you learned as parsing in many ways, as you've seen.

In the next two lectures, we're going to see that, with this formalism, Chomsky and the gang have taken the study of syntax far beyond anything that anybody would have been taught in elementary or middle school. In this lecture, what I wanted to present is just the basic tools as well as the history that we saw. Now we're going to play with those tools in the next two lectures. We're going to look at some of the insights on human language capacity that linguists have discovered in manipulating this basic syntactic tool kit that Chomsky created back in the 1950s.

# Lecture Seven
## Deep Structure and Surface Structure

**Scope:** Just as there is a difference between the phonemic and the phonetic and the morpheme and the word, under the Chomskyan paradigm it is argued that sentences that we utter often begin at "deep structure," with different constituent ordering than when they emerge at "surface structure." There are movement processes called "transformations" between the two levels. In this lecture, I demonstrate evidence for this claim.

## Outline

**I.** Under the Chomskyan conception of syntax, when we first generate a sentence mentally, the constituents are often in a different order from when we pronounce the sentence. That is, there is a *deep structure* and a *surface structure*.

    **A.** Sentences as they are formed at the level of deep structure are altered into their surface-structure form via changes in the order of constituents called *transformations*. For this reason, Chomsky's syntactic framework was, in earlier stages, called *transformational grammar*.

    **B.** We have already seen one transformation: the placement of auxiliaries first in questions. It is relatively intuitive that a sentence like *Is Bill walking?* is an inversion of a sentence *Bill is walking*. In "tree" terms, the auxiliary is moved to the front.

**II.** *Traces* are a less intuitive kind of transformation.

    **A.** An example is a sentence with *what*, like *What do you want to see?* Notice that you can use the *wanna* contraction in this sentence: *What do you wanna see?*

    **B.** Now, take the sentence *Who do you want to win the game?* Here, you would not use *wanna*: *Who do you wanna win the game?* sounds odd.

    **C.** Under the transformational grammar conception, the reason for this is that what begins at the end of the sentence is moved to the beginning between deep and surface structure. The original sentence, then, would be *You want to see what?*

**D.** There are three relevant facts:
1. In *What do you wanna see?* the *what* is the object of *see*, which gives some reason for thinking that on some level *what* actually came after its verb.
2. It is possible to phrase the question with *what* at the end: *You want to see what?*
3. There are many languages where words like *what* do not move to the front, such as Indonesian.

**E.** If *what* or *who* has been moved to the beginning of the sentence, then we can presume that it left behind an empty slot at the end of the sentence. This is called a *trace*.

**F.** Evidence that traces really exist reveals itself when we look at *Who do you want to win the game?* Here, *who* is the subject of the subordinate clause. This would mean that the original sentence at deep structure is *You want who to win the game?* Note that one could even say it that way.

**G.** If *who* left behind an empty slot, however, then this would explain why we do not say *Who do you wanna win the game?* There is a trace intervening between the *want* and the *to* in this case, such that a contraction cannot happen.

**III.** The trace conception is one of several phantom aspects of syntax, which under the Chomskyan conception are seen to be under the surface and not intuitive to ordinary speakers.

**A.** Quite typically there are traces or nodes imperceptible except via analysis like the *wanna* contraction case.

**B.** When *what* moves to the front in *What do you want to see?* for example, where in the syntactic tree does *what* fit? Where does *what* land, since there's no more tree leftward of the subject *you*?

**C.** Recall that subordinate clauses are appended with complement phrases, CP, which branch into a complement node that takes words like *that* in *Sue said that Bill lied* and then an S that a new "sentence" can fit onto.

**D.** Under Chomskyan theory, actually, the top S—the main clause—is a CP as well. The complement node is where the *what* goes.

**E.** Quite often, the C node above the top S stays unfilled; however, that C gives a certain uniformity that is scientifically elegant.

**IV.** Most sentences do not fulfill the entire potential of what the syntactic tree can be. There are phantom elements in most sentences.

    **A.** There's a degree of abstraction in the Chomskyan syntactic paradigm that is different from simply charting the sentences.

        **1.** We do not simply utter words in a sequential order.

        **2.** We package the words into constituent phrases, which are then often ordered at deep structure differently from how they end up being ordered on the surface.

    **B.** At that point, phonological processes are applied to the string of words, taking it from phonemic to phonetic representation. For example, *wanna* ([wanə]) is the phonetic expression of what phonemically is /want tu/.

    **C.** The phonetic distortion is the result of the fact that /n/ and /t/ are both alveolar sounds and thus naturally run together into a single sound during rapid speech. Then [u] becomes the schwa that is very common in unaccented syllables in English (*should have* becomes *should've*: [ʃʊdəv]).

    **D.** In *Who do want to win the game?* however, when phonology is applied to the string of words, there is a slot—a trace—between *want* and *to*, such that they are not run together because they are *not* together.

**V.** The formalism as Chomsky presented it decades ago is the way it is still conventionally presented in some textbooks. However, the formalism used by practicing linguists changes roughly every decade.

    **A.** The formalism I have presented is how syntax was done when Chomsky first presented his ideas. The current version of the formalism, known as *The Minimalist Paradigm*, is quite different. It is also so removed from laymen's conception of how language works that it is ill-suited to introducing the basic conception of how linguists look at syntax.

    **B.** However, the course wouldn't be complete without introducing what a modern Chomskyan syntactic tree looks like. Consider: *The boys are trying to help you*.

        **1.** Today, every node branches only twice. S is rendered as IP, for *inflection phrase*. Thus even sentences are a kind of phrase like a noun phrase, except where in a noun phrase the *head* is the noun, in an IP the *head* is a kind of "sub-I," called *I-bar*. The subject, here *The boys*, is a modifier of "are-ness."

**2.** *The boys* is rendered as a *determiner phrase* (DP). These days, the article—the determiner—is thought of as the *head* rather than the noun itself. In the same way, *you* at the end of the sentence is a determiner phrase.

**VI.** Funny things that happen on the surface do not make sense unless we posit that there are phantom elements underneath.

   **A.** The way constituents are ordered—the way constituents are arranged—and the way constituents move from one language to another seems to be more patterned than we might expect.

   **B.** Linguists have also found that there are underlying patterns in how constituents interact from one language to another.

   **C.** Our basic theme here is that what happens on the surface is less predictable, and yet in other ways more predictable, than just putting words in order.

**Essential Reading:**

Pinker, *Language Instinct*.

**Supplemental Reading:**

Radford, *Syntax*.

**Questions to Consider:**

**1.** Try to reconstruct the sentence *Who'd I see?* at the level of deep structure. Then reconstruct what the sentence was at phonemic level, when it first arrived at the surface but before phonological processes occurred such as the creation of contractions.

**2.** The typical person, even thoroughly intelligent or even learned, thinks of language as a collection of words and grammar as a collection of prohibitions such as "fewer, not less" and the like. After these seven lessons, what might you tell someone who sought enlightenment on what language actually is?

# Lecture Seven—Transcript
## Deep Structure and Surface Structure

In the last lecture, I hinted at the notion that the way we generate sentences underlyingly is different from the way they come out on the surface. However, in giving you the very basics of how syntacticians mapped out sentences into trees, I didn't really nail for you—the viewers—exactly how it is that the underlying is different from the surface in an explicit way. That's what I want to do in this lecture: I want to show that what's at the beginning is different from what's at the end.

This will help you answer a question that you may reasonably have had—especially if you have had a life that has had a certain amount of length—which is that there might be a question as to what's the difference between this business of constituent structure—the NP and the VP—and what you may have learned as parsing sentences or diagramming sentences. It may look like there's just this sort of replacement formalism for what you learned as subjects and predicates, etc. That's a very reasonable impression. There is one answer to that question that we can think of as a preliminary answer, which is that the question is how is it that children, in a sense, seem to know how to parse or diagram sentences mentally before they even know how to read or write? Why doesn't any kid make a mistake like "Is the man who tall is sad?" Children seem to have some sort of diagram, mental diagram, of the sentence long before they really are even particularly articulate. According to the Chomskyan analysis, that demands explanation. Furthermore, the issue is—when you are diagramming sentences and when you are parsing sentences—there was presumably not a particular focus on the fact that language is hierarchically structured. You could draw that conclusion from the parsing and the diagramming you were doing, but the issue being central that *Is the man who is tall is sad?* is a matter of understanding that there is a hierarchy in that sentence and that this is why you don't end up just taking the first *is* that comes along. Those aren't questions that are even asked under the diagramming and parsing paradigm.

More to the point, the reason that contemporary conceptions of how sentence structure—i.e., syntax—work are something different from the good old-fashioned diagramming or parsing sentences is that there's more that goes on. Once we've got these basic tools, in terms of the formalism, we see that that formalism ends up entailing various processes which were certainly not the kind of thing that was being taught when there was sentence diagramming and sentence parsing as a regular part of a curriculum. There's more going on than that. We're going to see some of that in this lecture.

We're going to look at what were once called *transformations*, and the basic concepts still exist in contemporary syntax. This is a basic insight of Chomsky's way of looking at language: That is that at the *deep structure*, a sentence may be in one form. You can think of it analogously as kind of a phonemic form, although that's not a technical use of the term. Then there's kind of a "phonetic form" of the sentence, which is how it comes out on top. The way that you get from the deep structure to the *surface structure* is through transformations of the order that constituents come in—not just words, because *cat, black cat*, and *the black cat* are all noun phrases. Order of constituents is something that is affected by a transformation. *Transformational grammar* was the way the Chomskyan paradigm was first referred to. We can look at this as one of the things that makes human's syntax interesting and unique.

We've already seen one transformation. One transformation is this business of inverting a subject and an auxiliary to form a question. That involves a transformation because we assume that, at first, the subject is where we think of a subject as being—at the underlying level—then, on a higher level, we imagine that the subject and the auxiliary have had their order switched. We have something like *Bill is walking* and then *Is Bill walking?* We know, on some level, that an inversion has taken place. We know that there's a sentence, *Bill is walking*, and we know that there is *Is Bill walking?* The idea in syntax is that *Is Bill walking?* begins, at first, as *Bill is walking* and then the intent to make a question. Then *Bill is walking* is transformed into *Is Bill walking?* as the result of a transformation. That's an easy transformation, but let's take a look at one that's less intuitive and see the kinds of effects that it has.

For example, how about this sentence: *What do you want to see?* That's an ordinary sentence in English: *What do you want to see?* If you know that that's an ordinary sentence in English, you also know that more colloquially you might say, "What do you wanna see?" And so: *Wanna see?* I think pretty much any English speaker has at least some relationship to *wanna*. Nobody walks around always saying, "What do you want to see?" or, if you did, you're alone. It's "What do you wanna see?" and so you have *wanna*. That's called *wanna* contraction. *What do you want to see?* becomes *What do you wanna see?*

Take another sentence: *Who do you want to win the game, the Steelers or the Rams?* I know nothing about sports. I really don't know what sports either one of those teams play, but I just hear people talking about them as I walk down the street. *Who do you want to win the game?* That's an ordinary sentence, but notice, "Who do you wanna win the game?" sounds kind of odd. It almost sounds like the *wanna win the game* refers to some entity that you haven't mentioned. *Who do you wanna win the game?* It's better to say, "Who do you want to win the game?" The *wanna* contraction doesn't happen easily there. It's very easy to say, "What do you wanna see?" But "Who do you wanna win the game?" is a little ambiguous; you get a little thrown around the *wanna*. There's a reason for this under the conception of transformational grammar; the reason for this begins with the fact that we think that something is starting at the end of a sentence or phrase and then moved to the beginning. And so, *What do you want to see?* The hypothesis is that it begins as *You want to see what?*—that's the initial—and then, on the surface, it comes out as *What do you want to see?*

There are three reasons for thinking that *What do you want to see?* starts out as *You want to see what?* with *what* at the end. For one thing, if you think about it, *What do you want to see?*—in that sentence, *what* is the object of *see*. We might think of *what* as just being a word that you use to ask a question, but there are a bunch of those. There's *what*, and *who*, and (if you insist) *whom*, and *where*, etc. This is a particular word that you use to ask a question, which also is the object. After all, *see* must have an object. We're not just talking about "I can't see"; I can't affect the process of seeing. We're talking about something having been seen. If you think about it, the see—or something that someone wants to see—and what we see is the *what*. You might give an answer, "I would like to see a baseball game," "I would like to see a hailstorm," or something like that. But in the question "What do you want to see?" it's *You want to see what?*; *what* is the object. There is some reason for thinking that on some level the *what* actually came after its verb, and therefore there was the verb-object order, just as in English, objects tend to come after their verbs. Then, notice that technically you can say, "You wanna see what?" It has a certain context, but you can say, "You wanna see what?" Or, you can even walk up to somebody and say, "So, you want to see what?" That's a comprehensible sentence. It's a little confrontational; it's not something you usually would say, but you could. Saying, "You want to see what?" is not as strange as wanting to tell somebody that they're a good boy and saying, "You're good a boy." That's just utterly wrong. "You want to see what?" is just not the usual case, but it is a possible sentence.

In line with this, there are many languages in the world where *what* does not move up to the front. For example, you can look at this Indonesian sentence (*Anda membaca apa?* "What are you reading?"), and you can see that the word for *what*—"apa"—is at the end. It doesn't have to be at the end—and it depends on which dialect of Indonesian you're talking about—but in thoroughly standard Indonesian, that is a place where *what* can very easily be without the confrontational indication of *You wanna see what?* or *You want to see what?* That's just their way of saying *What do you want to see?* You can put the *what* in that position.

It seems that there's some level at which *what* can be expected at some point to have come after *see*, because *what* is the object of *see*. In the general situation in a language, when you're making a statement, the object tends to come after the verb. Let's say that we assume that *what* starts out at the end of the sentence, and then it gets moved to the beginning of the sentence. We can presume that it left a kind of a slot at the end of the sentence; we can presume that it left a trace. That's what it's called: a *trace*. It's presumed that you say, "What do you want to see?" Then, although we don't utter it, there is a slot where the *what* used to be. It's "What do you want to see _____? That _____ is the trace. In itself, that can seem rather perfunctory or rather forced, or it might seem like linguists just enjoy positing all of these sorts of things because it makes things look more complicated than they are, but there are various reasons that lead linguists to believe that there actually is such a thing as a trace mentally inside of our brains when we're generating language.

The reason for this you can see, in part, because of looking at our other sentence *Who do you want to win the game? Who* can be assumed under the same way of looking at things as having not started where it is. This is because, if you think about it, we've got a subordinate clause here—and that is the *to win the game*—and *who* is the subject of that. Winning is something that someone is going to do, and that someone is not Bill, it's not John, it's not Andrew; it's *who*. We can assume that the original structure of this sentence—even though on the surface it comes out as "Who do you want to win the game?"—is *You want who to win the game?* where *who*, as the subject, is in the place you would expect before the verb. *You want who to win the game?* Notice again that you can actually say that sentence. You might very well say something like that: "You want who to win the game?" This means that *who* can be seen as having left a trace, just like *what* did when it left the end of *You want to see what?* In this particular case, we would have this trace but in a different place. The place would be *Who do you want*—and then _____ —*to win the game?* There's this empty slot before the verb. The subject started there, but it moved out. The subject is *who*, and so it's *Who do you want* _____ *to win the game?* There's a trace there.

Go back to the difference between *What do you want to see?* and *Who do you want to win the game?* We've seen that *wanna* is easy with "What do you wanna see?" *What do you want to see?* becomes "What do you wanna see?" But "Who do you wanna win the game?" is not as likely. Why don't we say that that's because there is a trace between *want* and *to* in *Who do you want to win the game?* Where there is no trace between *want* and *to*— because in *What do you want to see?* the trace is at the end of the sentence—then *want* and *to* can be smudged together into *wanna*. But when they're separated by this trace that's underlying—that still is represented in the brain even though it isn't given an utterance—it means that "Who do you wanna win the game?" doesn't end up happening because there's something in between *want* and *to*. That gives an explanation for something that otherwise seems rather difficult to explain: the fact that the *wanna* contraction will apply in one kind of sentence but then not in another.

The trace conception is one of several aspects of syntax, which under the Chomskyan conception is seen to be under the surface, not intuitive to ordinary speakers'—or even extraordinary speakers'—eyes or ears or thoughts but which can be shown to be there via various tests such as looking at the issue of the *wanna* contraction. Here's another example: Take *What do you want to see?* again. Based on our syntactic trees, where at the top there's always S branching into a noun phrase and a verb phrase, where exactly would *what* go? Where does *what* land? *You* is already the subject, and it kind of stops there; there is no more tree above that. Where would *what* go? It can't just float; it's not like this UFO. We're supposed to actually put it in the tree. Remember that we have this thing, the CP; the complement phrase. *Sue said that Bill lied*: The *that Bill lied* is a complement phrase where the *that* goes under the C of the complement phrase; then the complement phrase has another whole S, and that takes care of *Bill lied*. That's the way we handle that kind of complement phrase.

Under Chomskyan theory, actually even the first S that we've seen—the main S—is actually under a CP node itself with a C hanging. That C is often unfilled; however, that C gives a landing place for the *what* in something like *What do you wanna see?* The idea is for there to be a certain uniformity; there's supposed to be something that is scientifically elegant. One way we would handle where *what* goes is to come up with some way of having some sort of super S, and then hanging a W and calling it the *what* phrase or something like that. But that's not the way science is done. It's more elegant—it's more scientifically graceful—to suppose that actually any S is actually an S under a potential CP and that that CP then will have a naked C, a complement node, hanging, and that that's where things like *what* can go when they wind up in the front of the sentence. It seems intuitive when you think of something like the title of a play by Sidney Howard in 1924 about a woman who marries an old vintner in Napa Valley. It became a musical called *Most Happy Fella*, which is one of the most beautiful two CDs, these days, ever recorded. But in any case, the original play—it's kind of like *My Fair Lady* and *Pygmalion*—*Most Happy Fella* and *They Knew What They Wanted*. *They*, and so you have here the noun phrase. Then you have *Knew What They Wanted*; that's your verb phrase. *Knew* would be a nice V right there, and then *What They Wanted*, well, what's that? That has to be a CP, because *They Wanted* is already a noun and a verb, so you have your CP, and what's in the C is *What*. And so: *What They Wanted*. You can have *what* hanging in C. In the same way, *What do you wanna see?* is in a C. There's a phantom C.

There's a basic tree, and that basic tree is actually not one that begins with S. That basic tree is one that actually begins with CP. Not all the nodes are always filled, but that CP is there. There are these phantom elements that are there. Most sentences do not fulfill the entire potential of what the syntactic tree can be. These phantom elements—such as the trace and the fact that sentences are all actually underlyingly CP rather than just S, good old vanilla sentences—those are the sorts of things that diagramming and parsing were not concerned with. There's a degree of abstraction in the Chomskyan syntactic paradigm that is different from simply charting the sentences. The basic insight is that we don't just utter these words in sequential order. We package the words as constituent phrases, which are then ordered at deep structure differently than they end up being at the surface; that's part of the process. They wind up on the surface, at which point phonological processes are applied to the string of words taken from phonemic to phonetic representation.

For example, [wanə] is the phonetic expression of what phonemically is /want tu/. This is based on very ordinary processes of sound change that we saw. The phonetic distortion [wanə] is based on, to review, the fact that *n* and *t* are not just two letters of the alphabet but that those two phonemes are alveolar sounds; [n] is an alveolar nasal, and [t]—*t*—is an alveolar stop. As a result, they naturally run together into a single sound during rapid speech because they are both alveolar sounds. Thus the *n* wins out, and so: [wanə]. Then the *wanna*—it's encoded as an *a* on the page, but it's not [wana] or [wanæ] or anything like that; it's [wanə]; that is the schwa sound. Phonemically, we may have had a vigorous /tu/, but then, phonetically, it ends up being just [ə]. The schwa is a very common sound in English because it is the vowel of unaccented syllables, syllables that don't have stress. In the same way, we don't say "should have" as much as we say "should've." We mean *should have* (/ʃʊd hæv/), but in rapid speech it's "should've" ([ʃʊdəv]). An [ə] is again our schwa sound; that's something that happens on the phonetic level, whatever we're generating on the phonemic level.

It's interesting about schwa and how shy we can be about public acknowledgement of that sound. You're always hearing people on TV shows—even TV shows where people think that they're speaking casually—and they'll say, "Well, tell them to send it here." Whereas, in real life—if you listen to the way people talk in real life—it's "Tell th'm to send it here." There is "them" ([ðɛm]), which is your explicit pronoun, and then there's this other pronoun, "th'm" ([ðəm]), which is used in rapid speech in particular circumstances. There is a word: "th'm." It's just like "Tell him later": It's much more likely to say, "Tell 'im later," and there's no *h* there at all. If a Martian came down and transcribed the English language, the Martian would say there are strong pronouns used for emphasis, like [hɪm] and [ðɛm], then there's this other group, like [əm] for the third-person singular masculine and [ðəm] for the third-person plural and [jə] for the second-person single. Actors are always taught that somehow we won't understand them if they say, "Tell 'im," or maybe it's supposed to be low class when all of us say it. "Tell them to get their butts down here" doesn't really make any sense. But in any case, we do have schwa.

But in *Who do you want to win the game?* we have the phonemic level, and it presents you with the kind of uptight, very clean "Who do you want to win the game?" But it doesn't, at the phonetic level, become "Who do you wanna win the game?" because there is this trace. The phonetic processes happen, but then they hit that trace and it's like _____. They have to kind of jump over the trace—_____—and then keep going. Definitely, it's "Who do you want to win the game?" It'll be "who do," not "whoo doo"—all the sorts of things that make something from phonemic to phonetic happen, but not making *want to* into *wanna*, because something is in the middle. Those are some slices of how syntax is thought of.

At this point, I need to broach a certain issue, which is that the formalism that I have presented to you is more or less the formalism as Chomsky presented it at first, very early on, many decades ago. This is the way it's still conventionally presented in some textbooks. However, the formalism changes roughly every decade, which is fine—that just means that it's a vigorous science. But the current version of the formalism, which is called the *Minimalist Paradigm*, is quite different from what I have given you. It's so removed from how any layman would think of how language works that I figured it wouldn't be wise to present that, because, really, you'd need half of a course to make any of that make sense, much less be at all engaging, unless you'd had all sorts of other preparation. With the Minimalist Paradigm, it helps to have been doing syntax before it existed, I highly suspect. I opted not to give you these basic concepts there because frankly, as ingenious as the Minimalist Paradigm is, it's terribly ill-suited to introducing people to the basic conception of how linguists look at syntax.

However, the course wouldn't be complete if I didn't show you what a syntactic tree looks like in a modern academic linguistics journal. Today, every node branches only twice. There is binary branching, and so no more three-ball, pawnshop, subject-AUX-verb little tridents. What used to be called S is now rendered as IP; that means *inflection phrase*. Inflection here refers to what you can think of in shorthand as tense. There are tensed sentences like *She slept*, and then there's the infinitive *to sleep*; something like "Room to Let" could be considered related to it. That doesn't have tense, so that's kind of dead. Inflection is the issue of how the sentence alights. For the inflection phrase, the *head* of it is inflection, which is rendered as a kind of a sub-I called *I-bar*. Then the subject (in *The boys are trying to help you*)—which here is *the boys*—is in a relationship to the head, which is today called a *specifier*. There's what's called a *spec-head relationship* here. If you look at what should be the noun phrase, it is a DP. That D stands for *determiner*, which we can think of as definite articles. For various reasons, today the determiner is considered to be the head of what we think of as the noun phrase rather than the noun, and so it's called a DP. The organizing principles within DP are very different and yet the same from what they were in the old days, but that's why that says D; it's not that it's a down phrase instead of a noun phrase or something like that. There are very interesting differences. The IP is in some paradigms nowadays exploded, so to speak, into a *tense phrase* and an *agreement phrase* as well, the idea being that tense is something that should have a branch of its own and then agreement—as in whether something is third person or second person or first person—is something that should have a branch and therefore have things hanging off of it, although in the case of those two things, often it would be just endings that the verb then comes and gets. This is the way minimalism trees work.

As you can see, this is a highly abstract conception of the way language works. There is a great deal of heterogeneity in how different practitioners do their work under this paradigm. There are many different conceptions of what a proper tree is. That is just a sample of the way a syntactic tree looks in this era. If you're interested in learning more about how minimalism works, then I recommend to you the sources that I've given in the written materials, where you'll find in particular a very useful introduction to minimalism—at least the most useful one that I know. But in the meantime, what I'm trying to show is that there is more going on in how we put sentences together than just the simple matter of word order. It's beyond just parsing the sentence. What we've seen in this lecture is that it's beyond just parsing the sentence because we have these phantom elements, which we can tease out by noticing funny things that happen on the surface that can be seen to not make sense unless we posit that there were these phantom elements underneath.

Then we'll find in the next lecture that another reason that we must go beyond the simple fact of diagramming sentences or parsing sentences is because the way constituents are ordered—the way constituents are arranged—and the way constituents move from one language to another seems to be more patterned than it would be if all we needed to know about sentence structure was a matter of diagramming the sentence in a static way. Linguists have found that there are underlying patterns in how these constituents interact from one language to another. Certain things seem to almost never happen, while certain things seem to almost always happen in particular patterns. All of these things seem to confirm that there is indeed a tree representation of the kind that we've seen, as well as various other factors in language that can be switched on or off in fascinating ways. That's what we're going to hit upon in the next lecture. But our basic theme here is that syntax, or sentence structure, is more than just putting words in order. There seems to be something going on in our brains that determines what happens on the surface in a less predictable, and yet in other ways more predictable, way than that.

# Lecture Eight
## The On-Off Switches of Grammar

**Scope:** One school of syntactic thought proposes that languages' syntaxes differ according to whether certain features are set "on" or "off," such as whether objects come after or before verbs and whether or not subject pronouns can be dropped (Spanish *hablo*, "I speak"). Children learning a language, then, would engage in a task of learning how the switches, or parameters, are set in the language they are exposed to.

## Outline

I. We begin with the Japanese for *Pam bought the book in Tokyo*.

  *Pam   wa  Tokyo   ni   hon   o  katta.*
  Pam         Tokyo   in   book      bought.

  **A.** It looks as if Japanese's word order is simply randomly different from English's. In fact, we will see that it is different in only one way.

  **B.** This is the perspective of many scholars of Chomskyan syntax, who propose that the differences between languages' syntactic patterns is due to different settings of a number of "on-off" options called *parameters*.

  **C.** This conception of parameters in syntax has the possibility of explaining in relatively few strokes what appears so chaotic at first glance: the immense variety among the world's languages.

II. The *Head-First Parameter* is especially noteworthy.

  **A.** Recall from Lecture Six that on the syntactic tree, the noun is the head of a noun phrase, a verb is the head of a verb phrase, and so on. In English, the verb comes first, or close to it, in a verb phrase: *kissed the woman*, *drank the potion yesterday*.

  **B.** Prepositions are considered the heads of what are called prepositional phrases, such as *in the car*, *behind the sofa*.

  **C.** Prepositions come first in their phrases. In general, English is a head-first language.

**D.** Japanese, however, is head-final. One says, "*hon o katta*" (*the book bought*) for *bought the book*, not "*katta hon o,*" because in its verb phrases the verb comes last while the object is before it. For the same reason, "*Tokyo ni*" (*in Tokyo*) comes before the verb as well. Then the preposition *ni*, the head, comes last in *Tokyo ni*. The Japanese verb phrase is the mirror image of the English one.

**E.** Syntacticians have formed a theory called *Principles and Parameters*.

    **1.** The *principles* are the same in all languages. For example, the tree structure we met in Lecture Six is considered innate to our species: *universal grammar*.

    **2.** What differs from language to language is how parameters are set. In English, the Head-First Parameter is set on; in Japanese, off. This explains what to English speakers looks like "crazy" word order in Japanese.

**III.** Some proposed parameters have less noticeable effects.

**A.** To say in French *Jean often kisses Marie*, one must reverse the positions of the verb and the adverb, *kisses* and *often*: *Jean embrasse souvent Marie*. It is incorrect in French to say *Jean souvent embrasse Marie*.

**B.** This word-order fact is true in many languages, and what they tend to have in common is that they are languages, like the Romance languages, with a considerable number of suffixes used to conjugate verbs. English has far fewer of these conjugational suffixes.

**C.** In modern conceptions of the syntactic tree, there is a node high in the tree where verbs are thought to go to join with suffixes like the conjugational ones.

**D.** There is something called the *Verb Attraction Parameter*.

    **1.** Under the parameter conception, the difference between French and English is that in French, verbs must move upward in the tree—i.e., to the left in terms of how a sentence looks on paper—in order to meet their suffixes.

    **2.** However, in English, there are relatively few suffixes of this kind, and so the verb stays in place and its suffixes go down the tree to meet it.

**E.** One piece of evidence that there is such a parameter is that if a language loses its conjugational suffixes over time, the order of the verb and an adverb in sentences like *John often kisses Marie* changes from the "French" way to the "English" way.

    **1.** This happened in English.

    **2.** In earlier forms of modern English, one would say: "In doleful wise they ended both their days" [Christopher Marlowe, *The Jew of Malta*, III, iii, 21 (1589)], whereas we would say "they both ended."

**IV.** Parameters seem to not exist in isolation from one another; instead, it seems that there is a kind of parametrical flow chart.

    **A.** Some parameters seem to only be set on if another one is on, and these relationships appear to be hierarchical.

        **1.** *The Pro-Drop Parameter*, when on, means that it is possible to drop the subject pronoun when using a verb: In Spanish, *hablo* alone means *I speak*, even though there is a word for *I*: *yo*.

        **2.** A Pro-Drop language is always one with the Verb Attraction Parameter set on.

            **a.** Spanish and French are both Verb Attraction; Spanish is Pro-Drop and French is not. English is not Verb Attraction; therefore, we could predict that it isn't Pro-Drop.

            **b.** Pro-Drop seems to depend on the Verb Attraction, as if it were a subsequent step in a process of setting the language's switches.

        **3.** All languages with Verb Attraction are ones with the Head-First Parameter on. If a language doesn't have Verb Attraction, then the Head-First Parameter might be on, as in English, or it could be off, as in Japanese.

        **4.** The relative popularity of *All About Eve* and other Bette Davis movies offers a possible analogy: If you've seen her obscure films, you've almost certainly seen the famous ones. If you have the "lower" parameters on, you definitely have the "higher" ones on.

    **B.** This does not mean, however, that languages like Japanese with the Head-First Parameter set off are not situated within a nested hierarchy of parameters. Rather, there are other parameters that start applying for head-final languages.

**V.** Linguist Mark Baker hypothesizes that learning to speak involves learning how the parameters are set in the language one is born to and that the task is made easier by the nested relationship of the parameters.

    **A.** A child would learn that the language has the Head-First Parameter set to on, which would then eliminate the need to search for various parameter settings that are only possible in a language with that parameter set off. Instead, the child would now set the Verb Attraction Parameter, and if the setting is on, then eventually he will set the Pro-Drop Parameter on or off.

    **B.** For example, Baker proposes that there is a *Polysynthesis Parameter* at the top of the hierarchy. Polysynthesis describes the kind of language in which a sentence is often a single word.

        **1.** For example, in Mohawk one cannot say *He likes babies* as separate words.

        **2.** Instead you have to either have *babies* as part of a compound word with the verb: *He baby-likes.*

        **3.** Or you can have the verb include affixes that express the subject and object, with the word *babies* tacked on as an option: *He likes them, babies.*

        **4.** Children, then, would decide first whether their language was one like this, and, if so, other parameters fall under the Polysynthesis Parameter set to on.

    **C.** Children appear to learn parameter settings in their order down the tree.

        **1.** Even at the age of one, children have learned what the head order of their language is. For example, an English-speaking toddler might say *Give cookie*, while a Japanese one might say *Cookie give.*

        **2.** By about a year and nine months, French children are moving their verbs, with the Verb Attraction Parameter set on: For example, English-speaking kids will say *Not have coffee*, French-speaking ones, *Veux pas* ("Want not").

        **3.** Only by about two years and three months do English-speaking children stop saying things like *Not making muffins* and French ones *Est pas mort* ("Is not dead") and add their pronouns.

    **D.** Parameters' relationships of this kind can be represented as a grid of possibilities that may show us how children acquire language as well as why and how languages differ as they do.

**Essential Reading:**

Baker, *Atoms of Language*.

**Supplemental Reading:**

Lightfoot, *How to Set Parameters*.

**Questions to Consider:**

1. Modern developments in the study of genetics and biology are uncovering how significant differences between organisms are determined by genetic "switches" set on or off, such that a switch set the wrong way in a *Drosophila* fruit fly can create, say, an extra set of legs. The parameter concept in linguistics is analogous to this mechanism. As counterintuitive as it may seem that we have such switches in our brains relevant to how we speak, does the parallel with biology make the concept less peculiar or implausible?

2. One problem with the parameter concept is that it is hard to conceive of it being selected for according the Darwinian principle of natural selection. How would a parameter mechanism make a human more likely to sire offspring? In his work on parameters, Mark Baker even ventures the possibility that only God might know what the benefit of parameters was to early humans. Can you think of a more mundane reason a parameter mechanism may have evolved in *Homo sapiens*?

# Lecture Eight—Transcript
## The On-Off Switches of Grammar

There is a language spoken in Japan, and it has the name Japanese. Here is a sentence in that language: This is *Pam bought the book in Tokyo*. I love the name Pam; I don't know why. I like Laura, I like Jocelyn, and I like Pamela; it tastes good somehow. If Pamela had a flavor, it would be apricot. Let's use Pam: *Pam bought the book in Tokyo*. In Japanese, that is "*Pam wa Tokyo ni hon o katta*." I can barely speak Japanese without using a higher voice, and I'm sorry about that, but I tried. "*Pam wa Tokyo ni hon o katta*"—then you sound like you're in a Kurosawa film. What that sentence means is that Pam bought the book in Tokyo. But the way it pans out, word for word, is *Pam Tokyo in the book bought*.

That seems really weird from the perspective of English. The fact is, however, that in terms of Chomskyan syntax, the Japanese sentence's pattern is different from the English sentence's pattern in only one way. This is how many Chomskyan syntacticians work, and the idea is that the differences between languages' syntactic patterns is a matter of different settings of a number of what we can call *switches*. It's whether these switches are *on* or *off*, and these on-off options are called *parameters*. The idea behind parameter theory is that you can explain the differences between the syntaxes of the world's 6,000 languages in a relatively economical way. The idea is to be able to do it in relatively few strokes. Instead of there being this multifarious and completely systemless variety between the syntaxes of the world's languages the way earlier linguists thought, the idea here is that all of it can be reduced to some systematic options that human beings choose from in learning their languages and operate from in producing their languages.

For example, if we look at the Japanese sentence, what we're seeing is a simple alternation in where we place what are called *heads*. In a syntactic tree—remember, we saw noun phrases—the noun is what's called the head of the noun phrase. It's what has the juice, so to speak; it's what is being modified. In the same way, in a verb phrase, the verb is the head. In English, heads come first, or close to it, in the verb phrase. For example, you'll say something like *kiss the woman*, *drank the potion yesterday*. The head comes first, whereas in Japanese we have something different: We have the head coming last. If you look at "*Pam wa Tokyo ni hon o katta*," you see that it's "*hon o katta*"—*book bought*—rather than *bought the book*.

You would never say "*katta hon o*"; that would make no sense in Japanese. The object comes before the verb because the head, in this case, is last. We say that English is *head-first* in its verb phrase; we say that Japanese is *head-final*.

In the same way, you can look at prepositions. Prepositions are considered heads within what's called a *prepositional phrase*, so *in the car* or *behind the sofa*. In the Japanese sentence, what we have is "*Tokyo ni*." It's obvious that if this means *in Tokyo* that *Tokyo* probably means *Tokyo* and not *in*; and so the "*ni*" is the *in*. But this isn't a preposition at all, because it's not pre-post, it's post-post; and so we call this a *postposition*. Prepositions are heads just like nouns and verbs. What we see here is that the head in "*Tokyo ni*" comes finally. There's something systematic going on. In a VP—in a verb phrase—the verb comes at the end in Japanese. In a—now get ready to giggle—in a PP, a prepositional phrase, it is the preposition, i.e., in this case postposition, that comes at the end and is therefore post. The neutral way to refer to this object of reference here is *adposition*. That respects the fact that in some languages an adposition comes before and in other languages it comes after. Prepositions and postpositions are adpositions; that was a side bar.

What we're seeing is that there is a systematic issue here. Also, in the Japanese sentence, instead of saying *Pam bought the book in Tokyo*, you say *In Tokyo the book bought*. You have the reverse order of the way the verb phrase pans out in English. The difference between English and Japanese, in terms of word order, on the surface looks like it's just frankly weird, or it's crazy, or—as it's often put by a layman—just so different, when in fact what it is, is it's based on a simple parametrical difference between English and Japanese. English has what's called the *Head-First Parameter* set for on; Japanese has the *Head-First Parameter* set for off. That takes care of that difference. If you wrap your head around that—and if you think about Japanese as having syntactic trees just like English, which of course it does because all languages do—then the whole crazy word order in Japanese actually looks very predictable. It's very easy to handle, even if you were learning Japanese, to understand that it's not "just crazy," but it's just based on the head being final rather than first; then you have a valuable insight about how Japanese works. It's important to realize that—even though I'm saying the Head-First Parameter is set on, implying that if the Head-First Parameter is set off that it's somehow inferior—the fact is that there are a great many languages in the world where, for example, the verb comes at the end of the sentence. In fact, there are more languages in the world with the order subject, object, verb than there are languages like English with subject, verb, object. If anything is exotic between those two, it would be the SVO languages. It's a little ethnocentric of me to say that the Head-First Parameter is set on. If Japanese linguists developed this formalism, then certainly their idea would have been "Head-Final" is set on or off.

In any case, what syntacticians call this tradition is the *Principles and Parameters* perspective. The principles in question are the same for all languages. For example, the tree structure that we met in Lecture Six: That is a *principle*. That's set; that's in our DNA. The *parameters* are what are different from language to language, because each language sets its parameters in different combinations. You've got these universal principles and then these parametric variations upon them. The Head-First Parameter is one of a bunch. It varies from tradition to tradition, but I think that there is a vague consensus that perhaps there'll be about 15 parameters, and that might take care of human language. I suppose it's possible that there were about 100, but that would be not a very economical theory. In any case, in this lecture, we'll just see a few and look at the ways that they interact.

There are other parameters that have less immediately noticeable effect, but they definitely seem to be active on some level. For example, we'll say in English, "He often kisses Mary." But to say that in French, you'd have to reverse the position of the verb and the adverb. You'd say, "*Jean embrasse souvent Marie*"; and so "John kisses often Marie." You can't say, "*Jean souvent embrasse Marie.*" You could; just like in English a French person might say "He kisses often Marie" and you understand what he meant, but it's charmingly foreign because it has to be "He often kisses Marie." That order is part of the grammar of French. What's interesting is that that's true in a lot of languages that you have to say, "He kisses often Marie," rather than "He often kisses Marie." What those languages have in common is that they have a lot of suffixes used to conjugate verbs, such as in the Romance languages. English has many fewer of those. You can see how in the classic Spanish present tense you've got these six different endings for first-person singular, second-person singular, third-person singular, first-person plural, second-person plural, and third-person plural; you have to master all of that. In English, we've just got our scanty little third-person singular *-es*: *I kiss*, *you kiss*, *he/she/it kisses*, and then *we kiss*, *you all kiss*, *they kiss*, and that's just all you've got. We are poor in that kind of conjugational suffix, we Anglophones. But that is not true in, for example, the Romance languages.

Under the modern conception of the syntactic tree, there's a node high in the tree where verbs are thought to move to go get their suffixes. The idea is that on the preliminary level—the deep level—the verb is in one place and that then on the surface it has come to get its suffixes. The idea is that if the language is relatively suffix poor, then the verb does not have to go up and get it; the verb stays in place and the suffix goes down to meet it. This is the idea as to why you have this different kind of placement. When you say, "*Jean embrasse souvent Marie*," the important thing to realize is that *embrasse* comes before the adverb. The idea is that underlyingly, it was "*Jean souvent embrasse Marie*" but that the verb had to come get its tense marker. As a result, you have that order. In English, "He often kisses Mary" is the order because *kisses* doesn't have to move up before *often* since English just has its skimpy little -*es* and the language doesn't bother to have your sort of suffix store high up in the tree; the suffixes are further down. That seems to be a matter of a parametrical alternation, and that is called the *Verb Attraction Parameter*, because the verb is attracted to this pre-adverbial slot—this slot higher in the tree or to the left of the tree.

One piece of evidence that that really is a parameter is that if a language loses conjugational suffixes over time, then often the order of the verb and the adverb in sentences like "John often kisses Mary" changes from the French way to the English way. For example, think about "Olde Englishe." It wasn't really called "Olde" English; they did not call it Old English, by the way. Somebody walking around in 800 was not saying, "Boy, the language I speak is Old English." We call it Old English. In Old English, you had a lot more to deal with in terms of suffixes than we do. Anybody who suffers through learning Old English—actually, it can be a lot of fun—finds that it is a language very much akin to German in terms of conjugational suffixes and all different conjugational classes, and "the nouns are conjugated," i.e., there are case endings and different declensions. That's what it was like. In earlier English, you had a similar situation where the verb had to move up. From Christopher Marlowe's play, *The Jew of Malta*, there is one sentence: "In doleful wise they ended both their days." I don't know why it's in that accent, but it just looks like it. What's important is that it's *they ended both*; the verb has moved up ahead. Whereas today we would say, "In doleful wise they both ended their days." The point being that *ended* stays where we kind of feel like it should be. The reason for that could be that Old English—Anglo-Saxon—was jangling with suffixes for the verb to go up and get, whereas our English is a language that likes to take it all off. It seems that the parameter shifted, and so the Verb Attraction

Parameter went away because there was no longer a suffix store, so to speak.

In any case, parameters seem to not exist in isolation from one another, but it seems that there's a kind of parametrical flow chart. It seems that some parameters are set on only if another one is on; there seems to be a hierarchical kind of relationship. For example, there is a parameter called the *Pro-Drop Parameter*, and "pro" we hear is short for pronoun. What this refers to is that in a language where the Pro-Drop Parameter is on, you can drop the subject pronoun when using a verb. For most of us, that is most familiar from Spanish. To say *I speak*, you can say, "*Yo hablo*"—that's perfectly proper—but you can also just say "*Hablo*," and the *-o* suffix takes care of indicating that it's first-person singular present; you don't need to have the pronoun. French has the Pro-Drop Parameter set to off. If you want to say *I speak*, you say, "*Je parle*." You cannot just say "*Parle*" because you have to have the pronoun, for one thing, because French's suffixes for indicating present tense are not as rich as Spanish's, and so there would be more of an informational loss.

What's interesting about Pro-Drop languages is that if a language is Pro-Drop, then the Verb Attraction Parameter is always set on. If a language isn't Pro-Drop, then it could go either way. You can have a language which isn't Pro-Drop, where the Verb Attraction is set on. You can have a language that isn't Pro-Drop where it isn't. For example, you can look at Spanish, French, and English. In Spanish, if we talk about this business of kissing Mary or Marie—very common in linguistic example sentences; for some reason it is very often John and Mary who are involved, and there's an awful lot of hitting and there's awful lot of kissing in these example sentences. It's a tradition. I'm not sure why that it is; I'm not quite old enough to know. But that's partly why I'm using these; there's a lot of kissing in linguistics. But in Spanish, if you want to say *I usually kiss Maria*, then you say, "*Beso normalmente Maria*." In this case, you see that the verb has moved up because "*normalmente*" comes afterward. You could say, "*Yo beso*"—*I kiss*—but "*Beso*" is fine. *I usually kiss Maria*: It's got the Verb Attraction Parameter, and it's a Pro-Drop Parameter on language. Then, French and English are both languages where Pro-Drop is set off; you can't drop the pronoun. French, as we've already seen, nevertheless is a language where there is the verb attraction, whereas in English there is not. We have this situation where it seems as if the Pro-Drop Parameter being set on has something to do with the Verb Attraction Parameter being set on.

It's as if the Verb Attraction Parameter being set on is a first step in the Pro-Drop Parameter being set on, and you can see that in this diagram.

If a language is Pro-Drop, as we say, and has the Pro-Drop Parameter set on, then the Verb Attraction Parameter is definitely set on, too. Wait, there's more: If the Verb Attraction Parameter is set on, then the Head-First Parameter is set on as well. If a language doesn't have verb attraction, then maybe the Head-First Parameter is set on. English ain't got no verb attraction, and it is a nice Head-First language. But then Japanese does not have verb attraction, and it has its Head-First Parameter set off. Remember that the head is final. You can see in this diagram that there's that same kind of relationship. If a language has Pro-Drop set on, then it has Verb Attraction set on; if it has Verb Attraction set on, then it has Head-First set on.

It's like Bette Davis—and believe me, this analogy is actually going to work. Long, long ago, Madonna had a song called "Vogue" that was very popular. You were supposed to get out and dance to it in certain ways, as I recall. There's this one lyric that went, "Katherine, Lauren, Lana too; Bette Davis, we love you." I don't know why it always bothered me a little bit, but I always thought, given the segment of life and the ethos that that song "Vogue" was supposed to be about, I always wondered, "How many Bette Davis movies have those people in a sense actually seen?" When these people are saying, "Bette Davis, we love you," haven't they really only just seen *All About Eve*? How much love have they really given her? I don't know, but I was always thinking what they really mean is we've all seen *All About Eve*, because that is Bette Davis's most popular movie.

If you've seen *All About Eve*, you might have seen some of her second-rung movies, in terms of their memorability today. There's *Dark Victory* where she goes blind, and *Now, Voyager* where she doesn't, and *The Letter* where she shoots somebody. These are the middle-level types. There's *Jezebel* where she wears a red dress—even though the movie's in black and white—and she's in the South. These are sort of the Bette Davis DVD box set classics. If you've seen *All About Eve*, that doesn't mean that you've actually bothered to see *Jezebel* and *Dark Victory*. That's what I always worried about with these people out on the dance floor pretending to be old movie fans or really caring about Bette Davis. But you do know this: If you have watched Bette Davis go blind in *Dark Victory*, if you have seen how somehow the dress does look red even though the movie is in black and white in *Jezebel*, you've seen *All About Eve*. There's no such thing as "Oh, *Dark Victory* is one of my favorite movies; *All About Eve*, I've never gotten around to that." One kind of implies the other. If you have seen *Dark Victory*, you've seen *All About Eve*.

Then—talk about giving Ms. Davis love—there are movies like *Three on a Match* from 1932, where she and two other women are so poor that they have to light their cigarette with one match. In 1934, she did one called *Fog Over Frisco*, and in 1961 *Pocket Full of Miracles*, where she plays a kind of bad woman who sells apples; it's a long story. These are the ones where you have to really dig. This is like Turner Classic Movies, mild fanaticism, and things like that. If you've seen *Dark Victory* and *Jezebel* and *The Letter* and those sort of solid classics, you might have seen *Three on a Match*; but maybe you don't go that far. Maybe you've got a life. But if you've seen *Three on a Match* or *Fog Over Frisco* or *Pocket Full of Miracles*, then we know you have seen *Dark Victory* and *Jezebel* and *The Letter* and *Now, Voyager*, and you've also seen *All About Eve*. There's no such thing as, "I sat through *Fog Over Frisco* from 1934, then *All About* ... what? No, I gotta go see that one." That's how the parameters work. If you've seen *Three on a Match*, then your Head-First Parameter is set on, so to speak.

In any case, this does not mean that if, say, Japanese has its Head-First Parameter set off, that this means nothing else happens in Japanese. There are other parameters that have these same sorts of implicational relationships that we can't fit into this lecture. You can see here that it's not that Japanese is dead; it's just that Japanese is kind of another world; it's over on the other side of the planet or something like that.

In any case, Mark Baker, the linguist, hypothesizes that learning how to speak is a matter of learning how these parameters are set in the language that you're born to. His idea is that this nested relationship of the parameters makes learning a language's syntax easier. The idea is that these things are inborn. A child would learn that the Head-First Parameter is set on, and that would eliminate the need to search for other parameter settings that would only apply to a language where the Head-First Parameter was set off. The next thing you know, you've got your Verb Attraction Parameter set, and next you're trying to figure out whether your language's Pro-Drop Parameter is set on or off.

There are other kinds of parameters. There are decisions that, under this analysis, children make that we would never think of. For example, remember how we saw that in a language like Chinook—the Native American language—what we think of as a sentence is often just one word. That kind of syntax is under, for example, Mark Baker's conception based on a parameter. That kind of language is polysynthetic, as we saw, and there could be a *Polysynthesis Parameter*. The way it would work is something like in Mohawk. In Mohawk, if you want to say *He likes babies*, the way to say is it not "He likes" and then the word for *babies*. Believe it or not, that doesn't work in Mohawk. That sounds as funny in Mohawk as "He kisses often Marie" does to us, if not funnier. It's really quite incorrect. That's because in Mohawk, you have two choices. "He likes babies" is wrong. You can say it in two ways: You can either say, *He baby-likes*, where you take the noun and do what's called *incorporate* it into the verb—we have a little of it in English, "I babysit," etc.—or we can even say something like, "I bear-hunt," or something like that. But if you're tooling around with your new plasma screen, you will not tell somebody, "I'm TV-fixing"; that's quite bizarre. In Mohawk, that's one way you have to say it, and so, *He baby-likes*. Or you can say, *He likes them, babies*, with *babies* kind of set off with a "comma." Of course, comma is a matter of writing, but: *He likes them, babies*. You get it all expressed with pronouns, which are actually affixes on the verb: *He likes them, babies*. That's what you have to do. That could be determined by a parameter. According to Mark Baker's hypothesis, children first decide whether or not their language is polysynthetic or not, and then there's a whole nest of parameters that go underneath being not polysynthetic and some that happen if your language is polysynthetic.

Baker's hypothesis is that parameters would be set, and that this would be in order, and that you supposedly would see this in how children acquire language. Perhaps we do. For example, at the age of one, children seem to have already set their Head-First Parameter. We can imagine a kid in English saying something like, "Give cookie," because they do. They've got their verb first: Head-First language. They don't say, "Cookie give." I think you can't imagine your child starting to babble that. It sounds even more wrong than a child would make it. But in Japan—as you might expect if you think about it—kids do babble "Cookie give." It is very rare in Japan that they babble "Cookie give" in English while everybody around them is speaking Japanese, but in Japanese, they say, "Cookie give," and that's because very early children perceive in the language swirling around them that their language is Head-Final. Of course, they can't put it that way, but that seems to indicate that their parameter is already set.

Then it's by about a year and nine months that it seems that the Verb Attraction Parameter is set. For example, English-speaking kids will say, "Not have coffee," talking about some sort of negative experience with the possession of a wonderful beverage. "Not have coffee" is a situation where *have* is after the *not*; it hasn't moved up. Whereas a French kid will, around this age, start saying, "*Veux pas*"—"I don't want something"—"want not," "*veux pas*," instead of "*Pas veux*." The verb is already moving up, so to speak. Then it seems that the Pro-Drop Parameter is only set much later. It's only when kids are maybe two years old and change that French kids and English-speaking kids, whose languages that they're learning are not Pro-Drop, stop dropping pronouns. An English-speaking kid will say, "Not making muffins," instead of "I'm not making muffins." Or, a French-speaking kid saying that something isn't dead—I never thought until right now how sad that actually is, but maybe some little bird is lying half-dead—will say "*Est pas mort*," and so "Is not dead," instead of "*Elle n'est pas mort*," whatever is being referred to. These are languages—French and English—which are not Pro-Drop, but kids don't seem to learn that until they're two years old and change. It seems that the acquisition of the parameters goes in the order that they've been proposed to fit in our little flow chart; it's an interesting idea.

It's a little bit challenging in that what these people are proposing is that something is configured in our brains to allow us to be sensitive to whether or not our language has things like Verb Attraction, Polysynthesis, and Pro-Drop. It's difficult to figure out how it would work anatomically, I think. There's also a challenge in figuring out how something like this would have evolved in our species along the lines of natural selection, which presumably it did. In other words, it's very hard to see how having a Verb Attraction Parameter would get a creature more sex or ensure that a creature would survive longer. Boy, your verbs move up and so you don't get a cold in the rain and women like you! It's difficult to imagine how that would work. Mark Baker himself has even said, after having developed this theory—and he's not the only one—but after having developed this theory in two books (and I highly recommend the one he wrote for the general public, *The Atoms of Language*), he actually says at the end of one of them that, as far as he's concerned, it is so challenging to imagine how this could have evolved that maybe it was something that God created, and that's just going to be the answer. I personally would like something a little more concrete and systematic in an explanation. Research continues, but it's an interesting idea in any case.

What we have seen is that syntax, under the conception that is held by linguists, is a matter of a possibly innate configuration, which is characterized by constituency, rather than words just coming in order individually; which consists of hierarchical structure in our tree; in which all of this is the breeding ground for transformations that take a language from deep structure to surface structure. There are traces that are underlying in our sentences, although we don't perceive them or pause for them when we speak. It would seem that there are parametrical settings that determine how a language's syntax works and how it will differ from the syntax of another language. There are all sorts of variations upon this.

According to standard practice, I have given you Chomsky 101. There are other schools of syntax with now-massive literatures and fierce adherence. As I've noted, the actual practice of syntax has changed considerably from the kind of Tinkertoy kit that I necessarily gave you in introducing you to the very basic concepts. Nevertheless, the basic ideas that I've given you about what syntax is to a linguist apply to pretty much all of the schools of syntax. You now know what all the excitement is about in one of my little worlds.

# Lecture Nine
## Shades of Meaning and Semantic Roles

**Scope:** Languages differ in how they express basic concepts of meaning such as person, space, and tense. What is evident to all humans is conveyed in speech in a different fashion from one language to another. More generally, basic syntactic concepts such as subject are more multifarious on the level of semantics, where the subject in *Tom kicked the ball* is treated as quite a different thing from the subject of *Tom likes nectarines*. This lecture introduces the concepts of deixis and semantic roles.

## Outline

I.  All human beings process the world according to the basic cognitive endowment of *Homo sapiens*. The area of linguistics known as *semantics* studies how to convey meaning in all of its shades. There is a semantic level of how we use language in addition to phonology, morphology, and syntax.

   **A.** Languages differ in terms of what aspects of reality make it into the surface form, i.e., the sentences that are normal in that language.

   **B.** Languages also differ in what grammatical constructions they use to express the basic concepts that all human beings experience and wish to express. Concepts from syntax such as subject and object do not suffice: There are different kinds of subjects, and there are different kinds of objects.

II. How a language splits up, or points at, reality is called the *deictic* aspect of semantics.

   **A.** The word *deixis* comes from the Greek word for pointing. Strategies of deixis in a language orient and position events in time and space.

   **B.** *Personal deixis* (the deixis of personhood) varies from language to language.

   **1.** All languages have a way of distinguishing first, second, and third person. Often, the third person has no marker because it doesn't require indication in a conversation between two people, such as in Hungarian.

2. Personhood can be divided into finer categories than in English. For example, the Ghaimuta language of the Solomon Islands indicates all possible permutations of what is indicated in English as simply 'we"; exactly how many people are involved is encoded in their grammar.

C. *Spatial deixis* involves pointing out how close or how far things are from us.

1. Many languages distinguish things close to the speaker, things somewhat removed from the speaker, and things more distantly removed.

2. In Tukang Besi of Sulawesi, spatial deixis is indicated in three grades like this, then with a different set of words if the referent has already been spoken of, and yet another set if the referent is being explicitly pointed out.

D. *Modal deixis* is not something we might necessarily think of as pointing, but it is.

1. Languages differ in how they indicate a speaker's attitude toward the truth of a proposition, permission, or suggestion. All languages express this kind of thing, but they differ in just how. In English, this is done with auxiliary verbs like *may* and *must*.

2. In Spanish, however, the meaning conveyed by *must* in terms of probability (*He must be at the door*) is expressed with the future marker: *Será él a la puerta* ("It will be him at the door").

III. *Semantic roles* show how syntactic concepts of subject and object can only take us so far.

A. *The dog bit the man* and *The man was bitten by the dog* express the same concept. Both have a subject. However, the subject in the two sentences is a different entity.

B. There is a separate level of grammar distinct from grammatical roles like subject and object. Linguists say that in both of these sentences, *dog* is the *agent* while *man* is the *patient*. These are termed *semantic roles*.

C. Not all subjects in active sentences are agents. In *Jocelyn likes sunshine*, the subject is not an agent but has the semantic role termed *experiencer*.

**D.** The noun within the prepositional phrase of a passive sentence is not necessarily an agent. In *Harold got hit by a rock*, rock is a *cause*. In *Harold got hit with a rock*, the rock is an *instrument*.

**E.** In the same way, in *The rock knocked him out*, rock is a *cause*, while in *The key will open that door*, key is an *instrument*.

**F.** Here is a full array of the semantic roles that a subject can have:

> *The janitor opened it.* (agent)
> *The door was opened.* (patient)
> *The job expanded his possibilities.* (instrument)
> *Snow hid the barn.* (cause)
> *The cat was feeling good.* (experiencer)
> *Jocelyn got a Lego set.* (recipient)
> *Cincinnati harbored the future wife of William Howard Taft.* (location)
> *Tomorrow is another day.* (temporal)

**IV.** Different languages have different expressions of semantic roles.

**A.** Languages differ in how semantic roles are expressed on the surface, as opposed to the fundamental meaning of the sentence apart from its particular arrangement in the language. For example, in Spanish, *I like the house* is expressed with the patient as subject rather than as object: *La casa me gusta*.

**B.** In Hindi, the *I* in *I broke your mirror* is expressed as an instrumental if it was an accident but as an agent if I did it on purpose:

| (by accident) | *Apka šiša mʊjh-se ʈuʈ gəya.* |
| | Your mirror by-me broke. |
| (on purpose) | *Apka šiša mɛ̃-ne ʈor ḍala.* |
| | Your mirror I broke. |

**C.** Understanding semantic roles allows you to understand *ergativity*.

   **1.** In a language that did not mark case or grammatical relations at all, there would be one form of, say, a pronoun whether subject or object and whether in a transitive or an intransitive sentence, e.g., *She went* as well as *She saw she*.

   **2.** In English, the "wrinkle" is that pronouns differ when used as object: *She saw her*.

3. In a great many languages, however, the pronoun is marked when it is the subject of a transitive sentence, not when it is an object, as if in English we had a different form of *she*, "sheb," used in this way:

> [intransitive] She went.
> [transitive] Sheb saw she.

4. This is called *ergativity*, where languages mark subjects differently according to whether they are agents (thus engaged in a "transitive" activity like kicking, painting, or hugging something) or experiencers or other semantic roles (thus engaged in something "intransitive" like going, sleeping, or liking). Here is the Yidin language of Australia, which adds an ergative marker when the subject is in a transitive sentence:

> [intransitive] *Wagudya gundal.*
> The man is cutting.
>
> [transitive] *Wagudya-ŋgu dyugi gundal.*
> The man is cutting the tree.

5. Note that the object in the transitive sentence and the subject in the intransitive one are marked the same; in many ergative languages, there is also a marker for not being ergative called an *absolutive* marker, such as in Yupik Eskimo:

> [intransitive] *Doris-aq ayallruuq.*
> Doris travelled.
>
> [transitive] *Tom-am Doris-aq cingallrua.*
> Tom greeted Doris.

The insight here is that intransitive activities "happen to" a person on some level, and thus the person is a kind of patient.

6. Ergativity can be thought of as a parameter of the type we saw in the previous lecture. It is, in fact, possibly a parameter that would fit in the slot we left empty in that lecture regarding Japanese. Ergative languages are usually head-final (i.e., with the verb coming last). Thus an *Ergative Parameter* would be nested under the off setting of the Head-First Parameter.

**Essential Reading:**

Note: There are no books written for the general public, at this writing, treating the subject matter of this lecture in any substantial way. Thus I refer those interested to books not explicitly devoted to the goals of this lecture but useful in any case.

Payne, *Describing Morphosyntax*. This book, although intended as a guidebook for describing an unknown language, is also a great way to get acquainted with the basic semantic concepts of language and how they are expressed differently from one language to another.

**Supplemental Reading:**

Comrie, *Language Universals*. This book, in addition to being a standard introduction to issues of universals and typology covered in Lecture Thirteen, also contains a bracingly clear introduction to ergativity, a concept that is uniquely well-suited to get across the difference between syntax and underlying semantics.

**Questions to Consider:**

1. In the sentence *Sausage tastes good*, the subject is *sausage*. However, of the semantic roles we have seen in this lecture, which would you attribute to *sausage*? Note that, for example, *sausage* is too inanimate and inert to qualify as an agent as *Billy* is in *Billy threw the paper airplane*.

2. In Japanese, "I like Masako" is "*Masako ga suki*." *Suki* means, roughly, "like" (more like "likeable"). Then, *ga* is a particle that marks *Masako* as a subject. So *Masako ga suki* means, literally, *Masako is likeable*. Both "I like Masako" and "*Masako ga suki*" contain words with the *grammatical role* of subject. But what *semantic role* is expressed in the English sentence but not in the Japanese one?

# Lecture Nine—Transcript
## Shades of Meaning and Semantic Roles

So far, we have looked at the way sounds come together in a language and the way they interact. We have looked at what a word actually is, and we've seen the fact that there's a difference between a word and a unit of meaning, which is a morpheme. Then we've pulled the camera back, and we've looked at how sentences are put together. In this lecture, we're going to take a look at another kind of linguistic analysis and that is a look at how languages convey meaning. Obviously, that's what a sentence is for; but there is the issue of structure. We've seen our parameters, for example, and how word order and whether or not a language has bound morphology interact. These are the sorts of things that have to do with traffic rules, in terms of how the pieces of the language are arranged. Beyond that, there is an issue of how you convey meaning in all of its shades, how you use these building blocks that we've seen in order to communicate about and receive messages about the full range of reality that we know. That is what, in linguistics, is called *semantics*.

There is a phonological aspect of linguistics; there's the morphological aspect of linguistics; there's the syntactic aspect; and then there is a separate semantic aspect. There are two parts of this that I want talk about during this half hour. One of them is the fact that languages can differ greatly in terms of what aspects of reality they find it necessary to express in an ordinary sentence. It's pretty clear that all people speaking all languages can call attention to anything that they want. But languages are different in terms of which aspects of reality have to be put forward in ordinary sentences as one speaks every day. Then there's another aspect of semantics, which is a matter of the fact that subject and object alone— we've talked about those things, and those things are very relevant in syntax—subject and object alone will not suffice in looking at the way some things happen in language. There is a different level of things. There are different kinds of subjects; there are different kinds of objects. That's where semantics also comes in, because this is a different level of language than just the traffic rules and the traffic-type interactions that we've seen in how constituents move around and for what reasons.

We're going to look at those two aspects of things. First, how we split up reality: There is what is called the *deictic* aspect of semantics. *Deixis* is from a Greek word for pointing. Strategies of deixis in a language orient and position events in time and space. All languages have deictic strategies, but they're just variations in how those things are done. For example, there is *personal deixis*: deixis of personhood. All languages distinguish first person, second person, and third person. Very often, however, there is a general rule that the third person does not need to be marked at all, that the third person is default. For example, in Hungarian, to say, "I am an engineer," you have a word for *am*, which is the final word in our sentence for "I am an engineer" in this Hungarian example (*én mérnök vagyok*). If you say, "You are an engineer," then the final word for *are* is marked for second-person singular (*te mérnök vagy*), but it's there. But if you say, "He or she is an engineer," then you just say the equivalent of "she engineer" or "he engineer" (*ö mérnök*), and there is no word for *to be* that has to be used. The idea is that the third person doesn't need to be marked because, if you think about it, when you're speaking, the third person is usually what you're referring to. If you're talking about something, that is by definition third person. Then we all talk about ourselves to a large extent, too, but third person is default; often it's not even marked.

There are even languages in the world where you don't have to mark number at all. We might assume that one would have to mark *I*, *you*, *he*, and *she* and then also *we*, *you* in the plural, and *they*, but there are some languages where it's just a matter of first person, second person, or third person. If you say *I* or you say *we*, you use the same kind of morphology and there's the same word, which can mean either *I* or *we*. It depends.

In addition, personhood can be subdivided much more finely than anything that we're familiar with. The grid of six that I talked about—the *I*, *you*, *he*, *she*, *we*, "you all," *they* grid—is actually only one of many choices that a language might make. Many languages actually cut things up much more finely and would find our system rather denuded and almost rude in not acknowledging that there are so many variations and how many people can be around and how they are related. For example, in the Solomon Islands on Guadalcanal—this particular island is famous for historical reasons, but there are also fascinating languages spoken on it—one of them is called Ghaimuta. In Ghaimuta, you have a different pronoun to express, as we see here, *you and me* (*kogita*), *me and him* (*kogami*), *me and you, too* (*lugita*), *me and them, too* (*lugami*), *me and all of you* (*gita*), and *me and all of them* (*gami*). All of those are different words. To them, that is as natural as it is to us that we distinguish between *I* and *we*. For them, the issue of exactly how many people are involved is actually encoded in their grammar. This is just something that would be normal to them, exotic to us. There's personal deixis, and that's very important in communicating.

In the same way, there's also *spatial deixis*. Spatial deixis involves pointing out how close or how far things are from us. Many languages are, again, more—you might say—anal about this than we are. In English, we say, "There is this podium" and then "There is that podium over there" (presuming that there's a podium over there). There's "this podium" and then let's say "that chair," and that'll do. Whereas actually, in earlier English—if you think about how you imitate "Olde" English—you could also say "yon chair," and that meant a chair that was further removed. That happens to have dropped out of English. We can, if necessary, say "that chair over there," but in terms of there being a single word that you have to use, we say "this chair," "that chair."

It's very different in a language like Tukang Besi in Sulawesi. Sulawesi is an island in Indonesia; it's shaped kind of like a starfish, except I think you'd say that it only has four arms. On old maps, it used to be called Celebese; now it's called Sulawesi, which is that in Indonesian. One of the many languages spoken on Sulawesi is Tukang Besi. Not only do they distinguish between *this*, *that*, and *yon* as a matter of course with three separate words—it's not a matter of there being an option of "over there," or "way over there," or "that there," but a separate word for something that is actually significantly removed rather than slightly removed—but, if you've already referred to this item in conversation, then there's a set of three separate words that you use for *this*, *that*, and *yon* to indicate that it's something that you've already talked about; there's a different set. For them, something that is just mentioned for the first time can be subdivided into whether it's close, far, or really far. Then, for them, whether or not that thing was actually mentioned before is different enough that there's a different set of words. If you're actually pointing out in a very explicit way—like if you're going to say something about "that woman," as someone once did—then, depending on whether she's "this woman" or "that woman" or "yon woman," a whole other set—notice I didn't say "a whole 'nother"—a whole other set of words completely separate from the other two sets meaning *this*, *that*, and *yonder*. That's how Tukang Besi works, and that's something you find in a few of its relatives. There are languages in the world that subdivide even more finely.

That is one of many examples of a lesson that I often mention, which is that, actually, the smaller a population that a language has of speakers, the more likely there is to be something like that. It's not true that if people are living in villages relatively distant from technology—and are not what you would call "first world"—that their language is somehow simple. Actually, the further you get from "civilization," the more you can expect the language is going to be fascinatingly complicated. That's one of those examples. Tukang Besi, again and again, leaves you almost wondering how anyone could speak it, whereas we don't have that feeling when we encounter French. Of course, part of the reason for that is that French is related to our language, but part of it really is a quantitative difference in how many things a language sees it necessary to actually point out. That tends to increase the more "uncivilized" the language is. That's just an observation.

But in any case, these things are not parameters; this is something different from that. For one thing, as we saw, parameters are a matter of on and off. You can imagine, actually, a light switch: It's either clicked on or off. It's supposed to be binary, whereas these things are rather clinal. There are some languages that have personal deixis that's very fine; some have it rather fine, some have it very coarse, but there's no binary alternation. Or, in terms of deciding whether something is here or there or yonder, there are languages that handle that in all sorts of different ways. There's no switch that can be switched on and off; it would be more like a dimmer switch, and that's not how parameters are supposed to work. In addition, parameters are about syntax; they're about traffic. We saw that it's about things like the Pro-Drop Parameter, whether or not you need to express a pronoun depending on whether or not there are certain suffixes around. There is the Head-First Parameter, in terms of what order constituents come in based on issues of head order. These are syntactic things. These things are about chopping up the world into units of meaning, and whether or not these things are expressed. It's about semantics rather than syntax. Languages differ in these ways, but these are not things that are called parameters, because parameters are supposed to be a syntactic issue.

In any case, there is also *modal deixis*, and this is not something we necessarily think of as pointing, but it is. Languages differ in how they indicate a speaker's attitude toward the proposition that they are putting forth, or some kind of permission, or some kind of suggestion. All languages express this kind of attitude—there's no language where you can't—but languages differ very much in the extent to which they do it and also in just how. For example, in English, we talk about "He must be over there." That use of *must* means that we think that he probably is over there; we're expressing probability. Or we can say something like "He may cross the street"—you know, little Justin has gotten old enough that, okay, yes,

Justin, you may cross the street—and so we're giving permission; our attitude is one of permission. That differs from language to language, though, how that kind of thing is done.

For example, in Spanish, where we would say, "He must be at the door," they would use the future tense to indicate that. To use the word for must-ness—and there is one—would be rather peculiar, and it would mean that he is absolutely required to be at the door. Instead, you have to say, "*Será él a la puerta*"—"It must be him at the door"—and what you're saying in the literal sense is that *It will be him at the door*. But that's how modal deixis is done in Spanish versus the way it's done in English in one particular case. Languages vary there.

The amount of variation can be rather spectacular, again, especially with the lesser-known languages. There is a language spoken in New Guinea, and this is an island that is home to as many as 800 languages. There are only about 6,000 languages in the world; about 800 of them are spoken just in New Guinea. Many of the groups are very separate and, until very recently, did not have much interaction with the outside world or often even with one another. As a result, the linguistic diversity is fascinating. The languages themselves can be truly flabbergasting—and I mean in a positive way—in terms of showing how different human expression can be in societies that have had quite different experiences than ours. For example, there is one of them called Berik, and in Berik, you have to specify when you are using a verb, things such as if the verb is about wielding an object, you have to specify how large it was on the verb with an affix. That has to be on it. You have to specify the sex of the person who you are affecting. Even if you mention that person elsewhere in the sentence, you have to have an affix on the verb to express it. Of all things, you have to express, when you're talking about something, whether or not it happened when the sun was up or not. It's the oddest thing. For example, "*Kitobana*," in Berik, sounds like a very innocent kind of word. It's just four little syllables. "*Kitobana*" means *Gives three large objects to a male person in the sunlight*. It would be a completely different word with only the *give* left if you gave it to a woman at night and if the object were like a KitKat bar instead of a coconut, in which case it would be a small object. That affix would be something different. Things vary, which is to say that what we do in English is actually just an arbitrary choice among all sorts that a language might actually make. That's the issue of deixis and how we express the reality of the world around us. That is one aspect of semantics.

There's another aspect of semantics—somewhat more abstract, but I think it's quite interesting—and this is what is called *semantic roles*. This is what I meant about how subject and object can only take us so far. Let's try this: "The dog bit the man." There is an exquisitely boring sentence, so I'll say it again: "The dog bit the man." There's another sentence: "The man was bitten by the dog." Those two sentences mean the same thing; they refer to the same event. You imagine a man, and a dog is kind of chomping in—like Pablo the German shepherd did on my leg one day in 1973; I bled and bled, he only just pierced the skin—"The dog bit the man"; "The man was bitten by the dog." Both of those sentences have a subject. In "The dog bit the man," the *dog* is the subject. In "The man was bitten by the dog," *man* is the subject. But the subject in these two sentences is a different entity. Nevertheless, the sentences mean the same thing. We need some sort of mechanism that can capture that the *man* is the same person in "The dog bit the man" and "The man was bitten by the dog" and that the *dog* plays the same role in both of those sentences, whether or not the dog is the subject. That is something that we do in linguistics by positing what are called semantic roles. In both "The dog bit the man" and "The man was bitten by the dog"—although the *dog* is only the subject in one of those sentences, in both of them the *dog* is what's called the *agent*. The dog did something; the dog is the doer. In both of those sentences, although *man* is only a subject in "The man was bitten by the dog," the man in both of them is the *patient*; it happened to him—it's not the patient because he got bitten and he's hurt; that's just an accident—it's the patient because of something that he underwent. In both of those sentences, we have the same agent and patient. Those are called semantic roles, and that is the semantic level of analysis.

What's important is that not all subjects in active sentences are agents; it's not as simple as that. Jocelyn—that is my favorite female name after Laura; I really like Laura (that's why I named my cat Laura), and then Jocelyn. No one likes that name except people named it, their parents, and me. I don't know why that is. "Jocelyn likes sunshine": The subject is not an agent because, if you think about it, liking is not that active. It's not like "I'm going to go like me some sun"; it's just that Jocelyn is pleased when the sunshine happens to hit her. Jocelyn, in that case, is not an agent. She's a subject, but she's not an agent; she is an *experiencer*. That's what it's called. "Jocelyn likes sunshine"; that's an experiencer. You had an experience. Your semantic role is an experiencer, even if you are a subject. Here's a little bit of terminology: Your *grammatical relation* is subject— that's what we say—but your semantic role is experiencer. Subject and object are grammatical relations. I know, rather arbitrary; that's life. She is an experiencer.

You can keep going. Let's say that "Poor Harold got hit by a rock." In that case, *rock* is not an agent. The man was bitten by a dog, and that dog is barking and trying to bite the man; he's an agent. But if Harold got hit by a rock, the rock doesn't have legs; the rock didn't chase him. Harold got hit by the rock. The rock is what we call a *cause*; it was the rock that created the result. We presume that the rock was either thrown at him or it fell on him or something like that, but it did not run barking after him and bite him on purpose, and so it is a cause. "Harold got hit with a rock": In that case, again, the rock didn't come chasing him; it's not an agent. He got hit with it; it's the *instrument*. That's a semantic role, when things are instruments.

You can have many semantic roles, all of which are subjects on our one level. On our syntactic level, these are subjects. Their grammatical relation is subject, but they're different. "The janitor opened it": That's an agent because the janitor went up and he opened the door. Or with "The door was opened": You know somebody did it; presumably it was that janitor. In that case, the door is the subject. But in terms of the semantic role, it's a patient. Something happened to that door, and so it's a patient. Or "The job expanded his possibilities." In that case, the job is an instrument because he expanded his possibilities with said job. "The cat was feeling good." The cat's the subject, but the cat didn't go feel something. Even when we feel good, it's usually not something that we go accomplish in some deliberate way; it's something that happens to us. If the cat was feeling good, the cat was having an experience; she was an experiencer.

"Jocelyn got a Lego set"—we're going to use Jocelyn again—"Jocelyn got a Lego set": If Jocelyn went and obtained a Lego set from Target, then Jocelyn is an agent. But if what you mean by "Jocelyn got a Lego set" is, "Oh, look, it's Christmas and little Jocelyn got a Lego set," Jocelyn did not run and go get it—Jocelyn, if she's getting a Lego set, probably doesn't have any money to buy herself a Lego set yet. She is, for one thing, having an experience, but more specifically, she's what we call a *recipient*. She's the subject, but then there's another aspect of being a subject: She is a recipient.

"Cincinnati harbored the future wife of William Howard Taft"—which it did; Nellie Taft happened to grow up in Cincinnati. Nellie Taft smoked and drank, both a little bit too much; that was considered vaguely scandalous in her time. William Howard Taft died, and she lived on. She started wearing her dresses a little bit short, right around the knees, which was considered interesting for a woman of her particular time. That's Nellie Taft. I hate to admit it, but I read a book about Nellie Taft and I can't really tell you why. But "Cincinnati harbored the future wife of William Howard Taft"—that would be a *location*, and so on.

It's not just subject and object that can help us; there is more to it than that, because in "The dog bit the man" and "The man was bitten by the dog," we certainly have subjects. Basically, the dog is an agent in both of those cases. Semantic roles allow us to describe that.

For example, in Hindi, what semantic role you express something in is crucial to conveying a certain nuance. You can say, "I broke your mirror." You can see here that you can say that in two ways. Ordinarily, if you say, "I broke your mirror," the *I* is a subject—that's fine—but you express it in the instrumental. You kind of say, *Your mirror broke by my agency*. That is the way to indicate something about the breaking of the mirror, which is that you probably didn't do it on purpose. It's going to be, "Whoops, I slipped and I broke your mirror," "Whoops, I dropped your mirror," and that took care of that. If you want to say, "You know what, Rajiv? I broke your mirror and what are you going to do about it?" To say that, then, you have it in the ordinary case where it's an agent. If *I broke your mirror* is a matter of you taking it and banging it down, then, yeah, you broke the mirror. If you say, "I broke your mirror" usually—which is the usual case in terms of how mirrors get broken—you make yourself an instrument. That's how semantic roles are real; that's something going on beyond the level of just whether or not something is a subject.

If you understand semantic roles, it allows you to understand something that happens in a lot of languages which otherwise seems quite arbitrary and counterintuitive. That is something called *ergativity*. Here's how ergativity works. Imagine a sort of ideal language where you didn't have to deal with case marking or that kind of thing. You have an intransitive sentence and a transitive sentence. Intransitive, remember, are the ones without objects, and transitive sentences have objects. Let's say that you had a language where, for intransitive, you said, "she went"—that's an intransitive verb— and then for transitive, if you wanted to say that a female person saw another one and you're using pronouns, you would say, "She saw she." That makes a kind of a sense; we don't have to have a *her*, like in English. Let's say that *she* was always just *she*. So "She went" and "She saw she." That's not an impossible language; there are some that are like that. Ours isn't. We say, "She went"—intransitive—and then "She saw her." We have this marking; when the pronoun is an object, it changes. We have *her* instead of *she*; we have *him* instead of *he*.

Here's the wrinkle: There are many languages—not just one weird one spoken somewhere where there are giraffes or, you know, vines or something like that—but lots of languages where instead of it being "She went" and "She saw her," it's "She went," and then what's different is the subject pronoun in the transitive version. We just have to make something up because I don't want to make it *her*. Imagine if there were a pronoun *sheb*; and so, "She went" and "Sheb saw she." There's no *her* at all. It's not a matter of marking it as the object; what they mark is the subject of the transitive sentence. It is very peculiar if you don't think about semantic roles. This is called ergativity, and this is how that works.

The reason that you say "Sheb saw she" in these languages is because, in languages like this, they're distinguishing whether the subject was an agent or whether the subject was, for example, an experiencer. If "Sheb saw she," the reason that it's *sheb* is because there was a she that a sheb saw. This indicates that something happened: "Sheb saw she"; there was something done. That's an agent, whereas if you just say, "She went," that's not an agent; that's not something that you actually went and accomplished. That is a language, therefore, that is sensitive to semantic role in terms of the expression of subject.

We can look at how this actually works in Yidin; this is a language of Australia. You see that "the man is cutting." Just saying "the man is cutting" in an intransitive way is "*Wagudya gundal*," and so "the man is cutting"—then, in the transitive, this is an SOV (subject, object, verb) language, and so you have *gundal* at the end. *Dyugi* means tree. You don't say, "*Wagudya dyugi gundal*"—"The man tree cut." You have to put this marker in the case of the transitive, and so it's "*Wagudya-ŋgu dyugi gundal*." For any Yidin speakers out there, I'm sorry if I'm mispronouncing your language, but you have "*Wagudya-ŋgu*." That is your ergative marker, and that ergative marker shows that this is an agent and not, for example, an experiencer or instrument, etc. Of course, speakers of ergative languages can't tell you that's why this is, but the reason that those markers exist is because these semantic roles are real. They affect how a language develops.

In many languages, there isn't only a marker of the ergative, but then the other elements are also marked as well. You can see that in Yupik Eskimo. You can see the transitive sentence, "Tom greeted Doris." Tom has this marker, *-am*, on it to indicate that he's doing something; it's an agent marker, in a sense. But then, on the other hand, Doris has a marker, -*aq*, and then Doris also has that same marker in the intransitive. There's this marker of not being ergative. That is the other element; that's called an *absolutive* marker. There are many languages with both an ergative and an absolutive marker. The intuition behind it is that an intransitive action is something that kind of happens to the person who's experiencing it, and so you're going to mark that in the same way as you will mark a person having undergone the experience of being affected by an agent. If Tom greets Doris, something happened to Doris. If Doris travels, then in a sense, traveling happened to Doris. If she sleeps—which is intransitive— something slept her, so to speak. That's ergativity. It's a matter of how you mark your subject, and it's based on these semantic roles. That explains it, whereas if we don't think about semantic roles, then it just looks like something deeply peculiar about how these people see the world, when really they see the world just like we do. We just don't happen to mark subjects in that way; we leave it to context.

As it happens, ergativity can be thought of as a parameter, and some have parameters, as we saw in the last lecture. In fact, it's possibly a parameter that would fit in the slot that we left empty under head-final languages in the last lecture, because ergative languages, for various reasons, are usually head-final. An ergative parameter, we can see in this picture, could be nested under the offsetting of the Head-First Parameter.

Anyway, that is the world of semantic roles. In the next lecture, we're going to talk about meaning from a completely different perspective.

# Lecture Ten
# From Sentence to Storytelling

**Scope:** This lecture treats the investigation of pragmatics: how we move beyond the literal meaning of the sentences that we produce and link them to real-world matters such as our attitude, general presuppositions assumed within the context, and what is known versus what is new. Pragmatics is what makes strings of words express the full range of humanity and consciousness.

## Outline

**I.** We begin with a passage that has no grammatical errors and yet clearly sounds very odd, especially compared to a normal-sounding equivalent.

    **A.** What is so peculiar about the first passage is that its *pragmatics* are wrong.

    **B.** Pragmatic factors in how we use and interpret language bridge the literal meaning of sentences with real-world factors such as context, personal orientation, and background assumptions.

**II.** When we talk, we are always negotiating what is given versus what is new information.

    **A.** Sentences typically do not simply impart a brand-new conception alone. Rather, they contain both information that has already been established and information that is new.

        **1.** "Who took my pen?" "Some guy took it."—*some guy* is the new information.

        **2.** Given information is often shortened or omitted.

    **B.** Given information can also be conveyed by *fronting*: "The show about makeovers I only like so much." (Implying that the new show is a known quantity.)

    **C.** *Passivizing* marks the agent as new information: "This message was brought to you by the makers of Tide."

    **D.** In languages with a lot of suffixes to distinguish subjects from objects, etc., given and new information can be linked to positions within the sentence. In Russian, generally new information comes at the end of a phrase, whether it is a subject or object.

*Što    presleduet    sobaku?*
what    chases        dog
"What is chasing the dog?"

*Sobaku    presleduet    koška.*
dog        chases        cat
"The cat is chasing the dog."

Here, in the first sentence the new information is the dog; to answer that the cat is chasing the dog, it is not impossible to do what an English speaker would intuit and have dog still be at the end of the sentence. But in more authentic Russian, the dog, although still an object, is old news and the cat is new information.

**E.** Some languages express this distinction with markers.
   **1.** In Saramaccan Creole, the word *nóo* marks new information.
   **2.** One of my informants for Saramaccan once said *nóo* to me when saying, in effect, "I'll be waiting for your call." Later in the conversation, he said the same thing but without the *nóo*, because the fact that he was going to be waiting for my call was no longer new information.

**III.** From the perspective of pragmatics, a sentence has a *topic* and a *comment*.

**A.** How would you "parse" a sentence like "Me, I was so tired I could barely make change"? *I* is already the subject.

**B.** *Me* is what linguists call the *topic*. The topic is the center of attention in a sentence. The rest of the sentence is called the *comment*.

**C.** There is a similarity in function between a topic and given information.
   **1.** "Norman Lear sitcoms, they were what made TV start to grow up." The presumption is that all people over roughly 30 saw some of these sitcoms.
   **2.** However, in "Books with no covers, that's a business I want to get into," the topic is new information (i.e., the utterance could be made when *books without covers* had never come up).

**D.** In many languages, most expression is in topic-comment sentences rather than the subject-predicate ones that are normal in English. Chinese is such a language.

**E.** Many languages more familiar to most of us are more *topic prominent* than English. Spoken French is an example.

    **1.** To say, "The clam is down there, too," an Anglophone is tempted to say, "*La palourde est là-bas aussi.*" However, a French person would almost always actually say, "*La palourde, c'est là-bas aussi.*"

    **2.** This is because spoken French is a rather topic-prominent language (*L'état, c'est moi*).

**F.** Topic prominence can be seen as a parameter à la Lecture Eight.

    **1.** Japanese is a topic-prominent language to the point that it is a standard and conventionalized aspect of even basic utterances (rather than being one strategy in the toolkit, as in French). The way "Mike is an American" comes out in Japanese is "As to Mr. Mike, he's an American."

    **2.** Mark Baker nests topic prominence under ergativity, the idea being that topic prominence is something especially likely to happen when a language is head-final.

**IV.** A final aspect of pragmatics is the issue of conveying nuances of attitude.

    **A.** Notice that it is difficult to imagine a newspaper headline reading "Assemblyman Just Fails to Attend Meeting." The *just* conveys a personal judgment, which seems out of place in writing (other than in *The Onion*, where it would be funny). Notice also, however, that these words used in this way are crucial to communicating in the spoken language.

    **B.** Some languages have more *modal particles* of this kind than others. German has quite a few, conveying meanings such as:

        **1.** Uncertainty: *Auch*, which has the core meaning of *also*, is also used to convey uncertainty that something happened that should have.

            *Hast du auch deine Socken eingepackt?*
            "Are you sure you put your socks in?"

        **2.** Surprise: *Denn*, with the core meaning of then, is also used to convey surprise.

            *Was machst du denn da?*
            "What are you doing?!?"

3. Urgency: *Schon*, with a core meaning *already*, is also used to convey urgency or impatience.

> *Nun, gib es schon her.*
> "Well, give it to me!"

This is the likely source of the English expression "Do it already!" when Yiddish speakers translated their very similar usage of their "already" word into English.

V. Pragmatic markers are an indication that there is another level of language beyond sounds, morphemes, syntax, and even the simple semantics.

   A. Pragmatics are part of what it is to learn to speak a language with true fluency, either as a child or as an adult.

   B. *The New York Times* had a headline that uses a pragmatic construction: "They Kind of Knew It Wouldn't Work." Notice that the effect is rather humorous.

### Essential Reading:

Finegan, *Language: Structure and Use*. The chapter in this textbook on "Information Structure and Pragmatics" is my favorite summary of this area—more thorough than in most linguistics textbooks and with much insight.

### Supplemental Reading:

Horn and Ward, *Handbook of Pragmatics*.

### Questions to Consider:

1. What does *even* mean? Literally, *flat* or *temperate* or *fair*. But how about in *Could you even consider giving me a refund?* It can be deliciously elusive to explain, say, to a foreigner what such words "mean."

2. A sign reads:

> "IT IS FORBIDDEN TO
> BRING DOGS INTO STORE!"

Why is this common but nonstandard use of quotation marks funny to those aware of what "air quotes" are technically taken to convey? What pragmatic meaning *do* air quotes convey, and why is this infelicitous on signs such as this one?

# Lecture Ten—Transcript
## From Sentence to Storytelling

Listen to this—let's pretend I'm a newscaster:

> As for the Santa Clara Fire Department, it evacuated two apartment buildings at the corner of Country Club Drive and 5<sup>th</sup> Avenue at 3:00 am last Sunday. There was someone who had discovered a furnace in the basement in one of the buildings from which oil was leaking. What was sprayed by firemen over the oil for several hours was chemical foam.

All of those were perfectly well-formed sentences, but do you notice that there's something kind of wrong with that? It sounds vaguely off. There's something a little Martian-like about it, especially compared to this version: "At 3:00 am last Sunday, the Santa Clara Fire Department evacuated two apartment buildings at the corner of Country Club Drive and 5<sup>th</sup> Avenue. Oil had been discovered leaking from a furnace in the basement of one of the buildings. Firemen sprayed chemical foam over the oil for several hours." Now, that's normal.

What's the difference? The difference is that the first one calls attention to elements in a way that is not felicitous in terms of the way a newscast is couched or in terms of the way we would narrate the event. For example, the first sentence of the first version was: "As for the Santa Clara Fire Department, it evacuated two apartment buildings at the corner of Country Club Drive and 5<sup>th</sup> Avenue at 3:00 am last Sunday." That brings the Santa Clara Fire Department to the fore, as if that were what you wanted to talk about, as opposed to the evacuation of the apartment buildings. The felicitous version is: "At 3:00 am last Sunday, the Santa Clara Fire Department evacuated two apartment buildings at the corner of Country Club."

What's going on here is that there is a part of language that is about what you highlight and what you leave in the background. What's peculiar about that first passage I read is that its *pragmatics* are wrong; that's how we put it in linguistics. Pragmatic, of course, means in general English somebody who is practical, etc., but we're using a different meaning of the word pragmatics. Pragmatics is this issue of how we bring one element into the foreground and leave others into the background. That is something which languages differ in terms of how they do, but all languages do it because you have to do that to actually be a human being and use the language in the world as we know it. It also bleeds over into how we convey our attitude about what we're talking about, how we give shades of human nuance to what we're saying. That's pragmatics. Semantics is one thing; pragmatics, this business of backgrounding and indicating attitude—in other words, making our statements into human engagements with reality—is something different. In this lecture, I want to talk about a few aspects of what linguists call pragmatics.

This is the first aspect that's important, and this is what was amiss in the first paragraph. When we speak, we don't just string out observations in a neutral fashion. When we talk, we're always negotiating what is given information versus what is new information; what is information that we already knew—that's already set—versus this new thing that we want to communicate; why we opened our mouth, probably, at all. A typical sentence does not impart a brand new conception alone. Generally, there is information that's already been established and information that is new. For example, someone says, "Who took my pen?" Then somebody else says, "Some guy took it." *Some guy*; that's the new information, because this person didn't know who took the pen. But then, notice that the person says, "it," not "Some guy took your pen." That's a little bit Martian to mention the pen again; you say, "Some guy took it." What a pronoun is for is to indicate that something is given information. It's already been established that there's a pen, and then you say just "it," because that's already within the orbit of the conversation. You could even say, "Some guy did." You know that "did" stands for "took the pen." The reason you can shorten like that is because the information is already given.

Then there is another way of conveying given information—it might seem kind of random—and that is *fronting*. You could say, "I only like that show about makeovers so much." You know these shows nowadays, where somebody gets made over in terms of their wardrobe or their house; really, I don't get it. "I only like the show about makeovers so much." I might also say, in ordinary speech—if you think about it, this is very common—"The show about makeovers, I only like so much." That's not a random choice. If you say, "The show about makeovers, I only like so much," then when you front it, what you're indicating is that this is given information. When you say that, it's assumed that everybody knows what the show about makeovers is and probably has certain opinions about it, and these are opinions, such that you saying that you don't like it is of interest. You're conveying that it is given information by doing the fronting.

Another way that you indicate given information is by *passivizing*. For example, to go back into the announcer tone, "This message was brought to you by the makers of Tide." Putting it that way is making it passive, and it highlights the Tide. You could say, "Tide brought this message to you," and it's kind of inert. "This message was brought to you by the makers of Tide": The purpose of that is to indicate that the Tide is what you're supposed to be thinking about. "The man was bitten by the dog" is actually a similar kind of case. There are all sorts of ways to indicate given information. These are things that a person is not usually conscious of, but they're very real nevertheless.

The fact of the matter is, there are languages in which this sort of thing can be done in ways that are not done in our language. For example, word order. In Russian, for example, conveying whether something is given or new information is based on word order. For example, let's take the word for dog. Dog is *sobaka*. If *dog* is an object in Russian, it's *sobaku*. Because the ending makes this difference between subject and object, you don't have to have the rigid subject, verb, object order that we tend to have in English. You can ask the question in Russian: *What is chasing the dog?* "*Što presleduet sobaku?*" *Sobaku* is marked as an object. Then there's the issue of what the answer to that sentence would be. You could say, *Cat is chasing the dog.* You could say, "*Koška presleduet sobaku,*" and that would be fine. But, rather more authentically, what you would do is you would say, "*Sobaku presleduet koška.*" What that is, is *The dog chases cat.* It still means that the cat is chasing the dog. *The dog* is an object, but you can put it first because in Russian, when you put it first, it's one way of conveying that it is given information. It's been asked: *What's chasing the dog?* We all know about the dog; the dog is "in the room," so to speak. Then when you want to say, *Well, the cat is chasing the dog*, what they say is, in effect, *As for the dog, the cat is chasing it.* So, it's "*Sobaku presleduet koška.*" But in their language, it means that you have what looks to us like a reverse and counterintuitive word order. All of that is based on the fact that there's this difference between given and new information.

I've just discussed ways of marking information as given. As you can imagine, there are also ways of marking information as new. For example, Saramaccan is one of the roughly 6,000 languages of the world. Saramaccan did not exist before the late 1600s. It was developed by African slaves in

Suriname in South America who were lucky enough to escape from plantations on the coast. They settled in the rainforest, and their descendents still live there today. They have a language of their own, where the words are a combination of English and Portuguese and Dutch. The grammar of the language is a combination of English's grammar, of one African language's grammar called Fongbe, and then also things that have just happened in the language by itself as it's developed in relative isolation over 300-and-change years. As it happens, I have been writing a grammatical description of Saramaccan, and it's interesting the things that you find out are going on in a language's grammar when you're trying to describe it as completely as you can.

For example, Saramaccan has a little word which at first seems kind of random. You can see in this sentence: "*Té mujée sí Kobí, nóɔ de tá kulé.*" This sentence means *When women see Kobi, they run.* The way this comes out in Saramaccan is "*Té mujée sí Kobí, nóɔ de tá kulé.*" What you see in this is that there are words for *when, woman, see, Kobi,* and then there's *they be running,* so to speak. "*de tá kulé.*" Then there's this world *nóɔ. Nóɔ* does not mean *now*; there's a whole different word in Saramaccan for *now.* It would be a little strange for them to say, "When women see Kobi, now they run." It just kind of looks a little bit like *now.* What *nóɔ* actually is in Saramaccan is a marker—an explicit marker—that something is new information. We don't do that in English in any regular way, but Saramaccan happens to have conventionalized something to mark this, which shows that these pragmatic considerations are real and languages are attending to them, just like they're attending to whether something is an agent or an experiencer or a subject or an object, etc.

Here's one way of seeing that it's a matter of new information: One day, one of my informants—we call native speakers who we're consulting for doing grammatical work informants; it's not that he was telling on somebody or something like that—but I asked one of my informants, "Can we have a session tomorrow?" It's gotten to the point where I can speak Saramaccan fluently and badly, but more badly. I can talk fast, but making lots of mistakes. But you have to be able to fake speak it if you're really going to get things on the fly. So we were talking, and I said, "So, when can we do our next session?" We figured it out, and then my informant said in Saramaccan, "Good, so I'll be listening for you": "*A búnu. Nóɔ mi ó tá háika i.*" What he meant was *I'll be waiting for your answer.* We had to nail down one last aspect about the time, so he said "*A búnu*"—*good*—"*Nóɔ mi ó tá háika i*." So there's this *nóɔ* thing, "I'll be listening for you," "I'll be waiting for your call." That's what he said then.

Then we kept on talking, and later—because so much of casual conversation is about repetition—he said, "*A búnu. Mi ó tá háika dí kái fíi tidé néti*." He was saying the same thing. *Good*: "*A búnu*"; "*Mi ó tá háika*": *I will be listening*; "*dí kái fíi*": *your call*; "*tidé néti*": *tonight*. He said it again; this time, he didn't use the *nóɔ*. That wasn't just random; it was because then it wasn't new information. We had already discussed this issue, and so it doesn't get introduced with a *nóɔ*. If you look at how Saramaccan is used in running speech, and if you look at folk tales and things like that, you can see that *nóɔ* is used to indicate "Here is something new." This is not given information; here's a new thing. Saramaccan has actually conventionalized that marker; that's new information versus given information. Even though we're not usually conscious of it—when we're taught about grammar, we're not taught that this is what's going on—that pragmatic consideration is central to actually expressing yourself in a way that sounds like you are a human being.

There is another aspect in that way: There is what is called *topics*. What I mean by that is something like this: I remember one time I was in a supermarket, and a woman who was working there was, literally, she must have been seven feet tall. It was quite spectacular; I mean she was what would have been called a giantess. That's why I was frankly kind of looking at her and listening to her. She was having a casual conversation with the normally sized other cashiers, and she just said, "Me, yesterday, I was so tired I could barely make change." I just said, "Okay, that's a sentence." For some reason it stuck in my head, partly because she was so tall. Around the next day, I was thinking—people who are parsing or diagramming sentences, I wonder how they would classify what *me* is in that? For example, I just used a sentence: *People who are parsing or diagramming sentences, I wonder how they ...* what is *People who are parsing and diagramming sentences* in terms of how you parse and diagram? The fact is that *me* in that sentence that the giantess uttered is called the topic, and then the rest of it—the "real sentence"—is called the *comment*. In *Me, I was so tired I could barely make change*, there's already a subject; it's the *I*. What are we going to call the *me*? We don't just call it, well, some other subject; it's the topic, and then the rest of it is the comment, and the comment contains a subject and a predicate.

There's a similarity in function between a topic and given information often: *Norman Lear's sitcoms, they were what made TV start to grow up*. Remember, like Maude: she had a facelift; and Archie Bunker was a bigot; and *Good Times* was in the slums. All of that was considered very advanced at the time. *Norman Lear's sitcoms, they were what made TV start to grow up*. The presumption is that all people over roughly 30 saw at least some of these sitcoms. *Norman Lear's sitcoms* is given information in that case, but it's not always that a topic is given information. If you say, "Books with no covers, that's a business I want to get into," *Books with no covers* is not given information; that's not an established topic, especially if you're talking about someone saying that in about 1940, when paperbacks weren't so common. If you said, "Books without covers, that's probably something new," what you're doing when you're using a topic is highlighting in a more general fashion.

However, that's only in English, because there are many languages where actually topic-comment sentences—topic-comment constructions—are the default way of expressing yourself. To only speak in tidy subject-predicate sentences would sound either bookish or a little bit autistic. For example, in Mandarin Chinese—I can't even pretend to pronounce Mandarin Chinese. I will probably learn one day, but I'm not going to insult the speakers by coming up with something silly sounding, so just look at it here on the screen (*Zhèi běn shū, pízi hěn hǎo kàn*)—this sentence means that *This book's cover is very pretty*. The way you say that in good Mandarin Chinese is "This book's cover, very good looking." That's the way you say it. So whereas I listened to the giantess saying, "Me, yesterday ..." and I was thinking that is a good, solid, but very colloquial sentence, in Mandarin Chinese, that's the way one talks; that's how it goes.

That is something that is called *topic prominence*. Some languages are topic prominent; some languages are *subject prominent*. English is subject prominent; Chinese is topic prominent. Actually, spoken languages that are more familiar to us than Chinese is to most of us are often more topic prominent than we're used to and more topic prominent than they are taught to us as. For example, in French, if you wanted to say—let's take a perfectly ordinary, vibrant, real-life sentence, like *The clam is down there, too*—let's say you wanted to say that: *The clam is down there, too*. You would be taught to say "*La palourde est là-bas aussi*"; and so, *The clam is down there, too*. You would be taught to say in French, *The clam is down there, too*, but actually, in terms of how French people actually speak, it would be more likely that they would say, "*La palourde, c'est là-bas aussi*." *The clam, it's down there, too*. If you learn to actually speak the language, you learn that really speaking French involves using an awful lot of topic-comment constructions. This is not something that is necessarily street or mouthful or anything like that because think of "*L'état, c'est moi*." It wasn't "*L'état est moi*": *The state is me*. "*L'état, c'est moi*." That was something said by somebody who was decidedly not street. This is that French is a more topic-prominent language than English is.

In fact, topic prominence can be seen as possibly another parameter, as we discussed in the previous lecture. Japanese, for example, is topic prominent to the point that it is a matter of basic utterances. You get this in 101, first day, in textbooks if you're taking Japanese, for example. It's not a matter of a certain choice you might make as in French; it's part of the language. If you want to say, "Mike is an American," then "*Maiku san wa, Amerikajin desu*." There is that high voice again! All right, "*Maiku san wa, Amerikajin desu*." That is Japanese. The way it pans out is, "As to Mr. Mike, he's an American." That's the way you say it. You could hammer out a way of rendering it as "Mike is an American," and that would sound like an American student of Japanese butchering the language. It's right, but it isn't quite right. And so, "*Maiku san wa, Amerikajin desu*." That is the way you say it in Japanese. Mark Baker actually puts topic prominence under ergativity on his tree, as we see here. His idea is that languages that are topic prominent are particularly likely to be head final, i.e., to have the Head-First Parameter set off. Some people would argue with that, but if that is true, we can see how Japanese would fit in here. Japanese is not ergative, but it is highly topic prominent.

There is a final aspect of pragmatics, and that is the issue of conveying the nuances of attitude. You don't usually just say things; you're also encoding how you feel about the thing that you're talking about. Just as pragmatics is about highlighting one thing rather than another, that is intimately tied up in how you're relating to what you're talking about it, i.e., why you are speaking at all. To get a sense of what the machinery is in one's own language for that is to show that these sorts of things are not used where the idea is to convey as little attitude as possible and to be as objective as possible.

For example, here is a fake newspaper headline: The newspaper headline on the story is "Assemblyman Just Fails to Attend Meeting." Notice how you probably would not read a headline like that, except maybe in *The Onion* where it would be funny. What's funny? It's not the word *assemblyman*, and it's not the word *attend*; it's the word *just*. That *just* conveys a personal judgment; it conveys that the assemblyman promised that he was going to come and then, look at that, he's supposed to be an assemblyman and he just doesn't show up at a meeting. That's the way you talk, and that's a perfectly grammatical, perfectly well-formed way to talk, but that is not something that you have in a newspaper because there is this attempt in a newspaper to not convey attitude, to be objective. Here's this story about this meeting, and you have this assemblyman that just fails to attend the meeting. That *just* is what is called a *modal particle* or a *pragmatic particle* because, of course, *just* can mean *just around the corner*, in the sense of right around the corner. *Just*, of course, can also mean *fair*; but then, in this *just*, try to explain what that *just* means. Or if you say that it means *simply*, well, what's simple about it? Why would you talk about simplicity in this case? It's a very subtle issue; it conveys a faint disapproval after having expected that the opposite was going to happen. We have that modal particle: *just*.

There are some languages where you use modal particles like this more in spoken language. Using the modal particles is part of actually being a speaker of the language, rather than somebody who's just kind of faking it or who only has competence in the official, written variety. For example, German: One of the hardest things about learning to speak German—and I don't speak German at remotely this level, but I have watched other people doing it and I have struggled with this myself—is learning how to use their modal particles. This is because you can be darn good at the declensions, and you can know the irregular plurals, and you can know how to use your *dars* and *deses* and *doses* and *eins* and things like that, but in terms of how the language is actually used, there are all these little bitty words that have these very subtle meanings that a dictionary really can't help you with. What those are is *pragmatic markers*; they're how you express your actual humanity when you're speaking German. For example, there's the word *auch*. *Auch* technically means *also*, *too*. That's very easy to learn; that's German 101. But there are uses of *auch* that don't translate as *also*. You gradually have to learn that this *auch* conveys attitude. You can ask somebody, "Did you pack your socks?" What you would say is "*Hast du auch deine Socken eingepackt?*" It's very simple: *Have you packed your socks?* But in real life, you're probably asking that question for a reason; you don't just ask that out of nowhere. It's probably that the person didn't pack their socks last time, and that there was a big to-do because you had to go the store and get other socks, and they weren't really good or something like that. The idea is, "Did you pack your socks? You better, because you didn't do it last time and I don't want you to say that you did this time and then it turns out that you don't have any socks and we have to go to Woolworth's and find you some socks." That is when a German will say, "*Hast du auch deine Socken eingepackt?*" That *auch* means, "Come on, make sure that you have packed your socks; don't mess us up this time."

Or if you ask somebody, "What are you doing?!" the way you could say it in German is "*Was machst du da?*" *What are you doing there?* That's not really what you would say; that's what an American student would say. What you really are supposed to say is "*Was machst du denn da?*" *Was machst du denn.* *Denn*, in terms of its cognate in English, is *then*, but we certainly wouldn't say, "What are you doing then?" That doesn't work. This *denn* means something different; this *denn* means surprise. You are looking at somebody who's digging in the closet and you don't know why—"*Was machst du denn da?*"—you know, with your butt up in the air, digging around; that's what the *denn* means. To really speak German, you have to put the *denn* in. We would say, "What are you doing?" We do it with melody: "*What* are you *doing*?" Germans have the melody too, but then there's also this bit of stuff: "*Was machst du denn da?*"

Then there is *schon*, which to me is the most elusive of the German particles; i.e., it has eluded me. I'm not pretending that I've ever gotten it; I can talk about it, but using it is tough. It is used in something like, "Well, give it to me." Now you could say, "*Nun, gib es her*"—*give it* and then *to here*: "*Nun, gib es her.*" That could be said. But really, what a person would say is "*Nun, gib es schon her.*" *Schon*, in this case, technically it translates as *already*, but it seems like a strange thing to say because, really, you can't talk about *already* when nothing has happened yet. What it really conveys is urgency or impatience; that's what the books say. You can see that, or you can hear it when you listen to people using it, but it's a particular grade of urgency and impatience.

As it happens, when we say in English something like "Do it already!"—if you think about it, that is an odd use of the word *already*. It is highly likely that the reason that we say, "Do it already!" is because of Yiddish speakers. Yiddish is very close to German. People don't like it when one says this, but although Yiddish is culturally a language spoken by people who are not of Germany, the fact of the matter is that in a bird's-eye view, Yiddish is a dialect of German with a lot of loaned words from Hebrew and Slavic in it. Its grammar works out very similarly to other German dialects because it basically is one of them; that includes these uses of modal particles. In Yiddish, when you want to convey urgency or impatience, you would use this *already* word. Yiddish speakers, of course, came to the United States in massive numbers starting in the late 1800s and continuing into the 1900s. There were many second-language English speakers whose first language was Yiddish, a great many people who might have said, "Give it to me already," because they were translating from Yiddish into English. For whatever reason, that happened to catch on, and so that's why we say, "Do it already," in English, most likely.

We have, in this case, these pragmatic markers. They're small; they feel kind of random in that they're small and that their uses are rather elusive, but actually there's nothing unusual about them. They are an indication that there is another level of language beyond the sounds and the morphemes and the syntax and even the simple semantics, and that is the pragmatic. That is part of what it is to learn to speak a language with true fluency, either as a child or as an adult. That's because these things are as crucial to expressing yourself in a language as the things on the other levels.

I want to close by mentioning that I wrote this lecture, and then a month later I found a *New York Times* headline that actually said, "They Kind of Knew it Wouldn't Work." This was way back in the days when the candidacy of Rudolph Giuliani for the Republican nomination fell apart. *The New York Times* had a very nice headline right after I had said that you would never find a headline like this in real life, saying, "They Kind of Knew it Wouldn't Work." But, as you notice, that is intended ironically, and it partly channels into a sense that New Yorkers have a certain vibrant, streety way of speaking. Nevertheless, it shows that there is pragmatics as well as there are the other things that we have discussed, and they're an integral part of what a language is.

# Lecture Eleven
## Language on Its Way to Becoming a New One

**Scope:** In the early 19th century, linguists began to understand that the world's languages are the product of sound changes that took place gradually over vast periods of time. The discovery of Grimm's Law in Germanic languages spurred the development of a scientific way of charting sound changes, which was the foundation of the modern field of linguistics. This lecture will present the origin of *historical linguistics*—the study of how language changes over time and how the world's languages are related in a "family tree" sense.

## Outline

I. Today there are 6,000 languages, and those 6,000 are all the product of branching from the first language, or a first few languages, in the past.

    **A.** Languages are subdivided into families, though the number of families is very controversial.

        **1.** *Indo-European* is a language family that covers most of the languages that are spoken in Europe, as well as those of Iran and a great many of those of India.

        **2.** The Indo-European language family traces back to one hypothetical language, which is called *Proto-Indo-European*.

        **3.** Other language families include *Sino-Tibetan* and *Austronesian*.

    **B.** We know so much about language change thanks to recent technological developments—namely, world travel, as well as widespread printing and literacy.

II. The ancients, even in literate societies, had only a limited conception of language change.

    **A.** The ancients understood that words came and went and that spoken language in their own era was somewhat different from the language of older written documents. However, they were aware of relatively few languages, and thus the idea of language families did not beckon.

**B.** Even after the Renaissance, educated Europeans typically believed in the Biblical account of the origin of the world's languages, in which there was once a single language but God punished humankind by creating thousands to impede communication between groups.

**C.** As a result, the idea that languages had changed over enough time so as to form a vast branching tree of related tongues was only dimly perceived.

**III.** However, developments in biology spurred a new way of looking at languages.

    **A.** The first glimmers were by the pioneering linguist Rasmus Rask (1787–1832), who took a page from the taxonomic system for classifying the animal kingdom developed by Carl Linnaeus (1707–1778).

    **B.** Rask noted that just as animals could be classified according to a hierarchy of species, genus, order, family, etc., a language like English could be classified in the same way, as a member of a group of languages that was itself a member of a group.

    **C.** Rask also noticed a pattern in how sounds were different between *Germanic* languages and other languages. This, studied more carefully later by Jacob Grimm, became known as *Grimm's Law.*

    **D.** Most of the languages of Europe belong to the large Indo-European family. This family is comprised of several subfamilies, of which one is called Germanic. It includes German, English, Swedish, Icelandic, Dutch, and others.

    **E.** Rask, and then Grimm, noted that where most of the other Indo-European languages' word for a concept began with a certain consonant, in Germanic languages it very often began with another one.

        **1.** This could be represented as a table of sound correspondences:

| Typical Indo-European | [p] | [t] | [k] | [b] | [d] | [g] |
|---|---|---|---|---|---|---|
| Germanic | [f] | [θ] | [x], [h] | [p] | [t] | [k] |

2. There were many exceptions to Grimm's Law, but those have been systematized by adding corollary laws.

3. This pattern suggested that there had been some kind of process of change, which led to the basic idea that the Germanic languages had emerged chronologically later than, for example, Sanskrit.

IV. The *Neogrammarians*, who used the word "grammar" in a broader sense that linguists still use today, saw *analogy* as an important principle for explaining irregularities in how language changes.

A. Influenced by Charles Darwin's theory of natural selection, this school laid the groundwork for a conception of language changing gradually through time in a regular, rather than random, fashion. They concentrated on sound changes.

B. The Neogrammarians proposed that all sound change is regular, except that in certain cases, sounds are detoured from changing regularly because of a countervailing process, in which speakers tidied up the grammar in some area to create a pattern (rather like colloquial English *mine, yourn, his'n*).

C. For example, in the ancestor of what would become Old English, in which nouns still had case as in Latin, the way to decline *foot* was like this:

|  | *singular* | *plural* |
|---|---|---|
| nominative/accusative | fōt | **fōti** |
| genitive | fōtes | fota |
| dative | **fōti** | fotum |

1. Now, regular sound change over time changed *fōti* to *fēt*. This left a new situation with *foot*, in which in certain places (the dative singular and the nominative and accusative plural), the vowel was *ō* instead of *ē*:

|  | *singular* | *plural* |
|---|---|---|
| nominative/accusative | fōt | **fēt** |
| genitive | fōtes | fota |
| dative | **fēt** | fotum |

2. There is a natural human tendency to iron out things like this, and what happened in English is that the *ē* was reinterpreted as indicating the plural. Therefore, in Middle English (whose orthography, unlike Old English, does not have vowels with

macrons such as *ō* because vowel length no longer meant the difference between one word and another), things were tidy again:

|            | *singular* | *plural* |
|------------|-----------|----------|
| nominative | fot       | fet      |
| genitive   | fotes     | fete     |
| dative     | fote      | feten    |
| accusative | fot       | fet      |

3. The genitive and the dative plural took on the vowel from the nominative and accusative. This is the process of analogy.

**V.** Regular sound change is a hallmark of all human language.

**A.** The result of the Neogrammarians' discovery was not limited to European languages. They revealed a general principle of how human language changes worldwide and always has.

**B.** For example, comparing languages of the Semitic family, which today includes Arabic, Hebrew, and the Amharic language of Ethiopia, we can see that where Hebrew has [š], Arabic and Amharic regularly have [s].

**C.** This insight traces back to Sir William Jones, who, in a presentation to the Bengal Asiatic Society in 1786, made what is considered to be the first coherent and official statement that language changes systematically over time and develops family relationships.

**Essential Reading:**

Sapir, *Language.*

**Supplemental Reading:**

Hock, *Principles of Historical Linguistics.*

**Questions to Consider:**

1. English was once an unwritten Germanic tongue, which itself descended from an Indo-European language, which itself was descended from a language spoken by hunter-gatherers in Africa. Most laymen, of course, are not aware of this. What has your own conception been of where English came from?

2. As late as the 17<sup>th</sup> century, learned folk writing on language assumed that the first language was Hebrew, since the Old Testament was written in Hebrew. Meanwhile, physician and linguist Johannes Becanus (1519–1572) assumed that the first language was his native Dutch. In your mind, do Adam and Eve speak English? Have you ever had an impression as to what the "first" language would have been?

# Lecture Eleven—Transcript
## Language on Its Way to Becoming a New One

In the first 10 lectures of this course, what we have looked at is how linguists study language, specifically language's grammar on all of its levels, as it is now. There is another module, so to speak, of linguistic analysis which studies how language changes over time. This is a whole subfield of linguistics which is called *historical linguistics*. In this and the next few lectures, we're going to take a survey of how historical linguists ply their trade and what has been found out about how language changes through time. It's important to realize that this is not the realm of *etymology*. Words certainly do change through time, and they do so in many ways. To an extent, those ways are idiosyncratic to each word, although there are patterns. Here we want to look at how languages change through time in terms of the things that we've learned about already—in terms of a linguist's conception of what grammar is. There's a present-tense aspect, and we've seen that, and now we're going to look at the past tense, or better, the imperfect—as you may have learned from a Romance language—because we're talking about something that's ongoing. Languages change in an ongoing way.

Basically, we have to start with the fact that there was probably one original language—maybe a few; I'm inclined to think one—and now there are 6,000. Those 6,000 are all the product of branching from languages in the past, and those languages were the product of branching from languages into the past, until you get to the first language or few languages. That's how languages work in this world.

The languages are subdivided into a bunch of families. It's very controversial how many families there are, but there are certainly more than a few. For example, *Indo-European* is a language family that covers most of the languages that are spoken in Europe, as well as those of Iran and a great many of those of India. The Indo-European language family traces back to one language, which is hypothetically called *Proto-Indo-European*. That language is now represented by several subfamilies within the Indo-European family.

*Sino-Tibetan* is another family. Sino-Tibetan includes Chinese—or, more properly, the Chinese languages, given that Mandarin and Cantonese are not mutually intelligible, nor are any of the other major what are called Chinese "dialects." Then there is also Tibetan, and there are various languages of Southeast Asia, most of which are not familiar to laymen. But Sino-Tibetan is a family. Austronesian is a family: So this is Tagalog and other languages of the Philippines, Indonesian, or Malay, and languages akin to that. Then Austronesian stretches all the way to Taiwan—where there are some languages that are thought to be the first Austronesian languages—and then way off into the Australia region, and so the languages of Melanesia, Micronesia, and Polynesia. All of those are Austronesian languages. Families: That's how languages are distributed across the world.

That is something that we know really because of relatively recent technological developments. By that I mean the possibility to travel around the world, and also widespread printing and literacy. The ancients knew, as any of us know, that words come and go. It's hard not to notice that there are things older people say that you might say less. The ancients knew, to an extent, that if they were in a literate society such as Ancient Greece that the language that they saw on the page sometimes indicated that language had changed in certain ways since that was written. Everybody knew that that was something that went on. But, in this time, there was no way of understanding that actually the world is coated with languages that have family relationships and that language change is the source of all of them. There was no way for anyone to know that, because, for example, even if you were a highly sophisticated person living in Ancient Greece—even if you were a thinking person and a scholar, even if you were wealthy—you really were not capable of traveling but so far. For you, the world was basically the Mediterranean, and you knew of some distant other places. How much, really, were you going to know about language? Wherever you went, writing in the world that this person lived in was a relatively marginal activity. Literacy was not widespread; there were only so many written sources produced. The vast majority of languages that you encountered would not have been written anyway, so you're only hearing them falling out of people's mouths.

The idea that there are families and that there is a historical process of language development was something that you could not grasp in that era. What people tended to believe—and this is educated people, this is people of all temperaments—was that, for example, if the Judeo-Christian tradition was relevant, that the Tower of Babel story was actually the way that the world's languages had come about. There were variations on the notion that everybody had once spoken one language but then as a punishment there were several languages in the world created. Many people were only in the position to know that there were several, rather than 6,000, so only dimly perceived was what we know of historical linguistics today.

But new developments in biology started changing people's ways of thinking about this kind of thing. The first glimmers of the fact that there might be a science of how languages change that is applicable to all languages was glimpsed by a man named Rasmus Rask. His life straddled the 1700s and the 1800s. He was a Dane, and he is best known for the factoid that he spoke 25 different languages—which I doubt, for the record. I mean, you have to be careful with claims like that, because with languages either you use it or lose it. What would the conditions be that would allow you to speak 25 languages all the time, especially when you're living in, say, the year 1800, and it's so hard to actually go anywhere? Rasmus Rask was quite the genius, but I wonder what this "speaking" was. Nevertheless, he is always recalled as this marvel for having this command of 25 languages. He was the first person to describe the language of Iceland. As late as his life—when the United States of America exists, and the steam engine is about to be invented—no one had actually described how the Icelandic language worked, which was interesting because that language was ancestral to the languages of mainland Scandinavia: Swedish, Danish, and Norwegian. This was something which was perceived—it was perceived that there was a similarity between these languages—but Rask was the first person to really start working that out, and that included doing that description.

Rask's work was a lot of what formulated the idea that there was an Indo-European language family. Even if you were a literate person in 1800, there just weren't enough sources written describing languages yet for you to have a sense that there is a group of languages, that there are identifiable sub-groups of languages, and you're going to identify what these relationships are with several different grammatical descriptions. You didn't have it; you had to travel. Rask did quite a bit of traveling and helped to describe quite a few languages—acquired a competence in them. He was quite diligent in doing this kind of thing. As he looked at various languages—for example, as he noticed the similarities between Icelandic and his native Danish—he started realizing that languages seemed to work, in terms of their relationship to each other, the way that flora and fauna did according to the new work of Carl Linnaeus, who was the person who came up with the taxonomy of animals and plants into species, genus, order, family, etc., classified with the Latin names. His idea was that actually English could probably be classified in the same way: English could be classified as belonging to some higher-order group; in this case, it would be the *Germanic family*. Then Germanic, as a family, seemed to have a whole lot in common with a whole bunch of other languages. He was getting towards the idea that there was this kind of taxonomy. Actually charting it was something that other people did, but Rask was the person who kind of set the tone.

But Rask did notice something that really did give birth to the study of *historical phonology*: how sounds change. Rask noticed a certain pattern in the Germanic languages. Then Jacob Grimm picked up on this and made the most prominent statement of it, although Rask really had lit the flame. The result was something called *Grimm's Law*. Jacob Grimm was a man most of whose life took place in the 1800s. He was an interesting character. I think if we could meet him today, we would find him to be a bit of what I'll call for the purposes of this medium a jack … anapes. However, he collected folk tales. So yes, this is the Grimm who, with his brother Wilhelm, collected the Grimm's Folk Tales, which are very grim if you actually read them, which Disney made into cotton candy. This was something he was doing not just because he liked a good story, but because he was a devoted German nationalist and he was interested in charting the noble history of the German nation, as it would be. As part of that, he wrote a grammar of German; it's where he started noticing these patterns. The reason that he noticed the pattern that he noticed was because writing a grammar in his time—writing a grammatical description in his time—was something different from what it is now. Now somebody listens to somebody speaking the language and figures out what the phonemes are, what the morphemes are, of course what the words mean, and then figures out how the syntax works. This is something that linguists now do on a regular basis. If you wrote a grammar in, say, 1822, then what you did was you wrote a historical description of how the language has changed from its earliest written sources to today; that was considered to be the thing to do. Because, remember, at this point there's no such thing as a modern conception of syntax, and in this era where even before anybody knows what a phoneme is or a morpheme is. So, if you're going to describe, to them, it meant being a historical linguist—very different kind of glasses.

It's just like if you went back to 1905 and if a woman was about to give birth. Our first impulse would be, "Let's get her to the hospital." That would sound very strange to a woman then. Why are we going to go to the hospital? If a woman was about to give birth, she went upstairs and she was taken care of, and the baby was born at home. This was among people of all classes. Here's a factoid—now I'm going to sip for suspense—here is a factoid: Who was the first president of the United States to be born in a hospital? It's a fascinating factoid, and I'm not going to answer it until the end. But the fact is, just like in 1905, you would be kind of surprised by the fact that birth was something that took place at home with people getting towels and hot water. Back in 1822, if you wrote a grammar, you were describing the history of the language. That's what Grimm did. What he noticed, and what Rask noticed, was that there was a kink in the Germanic languages compared to the languages that were related to it in the larger Indo-European family.

Germanic is a group which consists of officially 11 languages; you might want to call it 12, 13, or 14, depending on what you call a language. In the Germanic language, of course, there is German, and there's also Dutch and Yiddish; English is in there, Swedish, Norwegian and Danish and Icelandic, one language called Frisian, Afrikaans down in South Africa, and I'm probably leaving one out. Did I leave out Dutch? I don't know. Anyway: the Germanic languages. What Rask and Grimm noted was that where most of the words in this Indo-European family began with one consonant, in the Germanic cognates the word would begin with some other consonant. This seemed to be a systematic kind of relationship. For example: If in Latin there is a *p*—like in *pater* for father, which comes down to English as *paternal*—then in English, we have *father*; and so *paternal*, but *father*. Or if a case is *tenuous*, then that comes from the Latin *tenare* for *to hold*. "It's a tenuous case"; that root comes down into English as *thin*, instead of with the *t*. "Cardiac arrest": The *cardiac* part comes from the Greek root for heart. They said *card*; we have the same root as *heart*. Or for example *labial* in Latin: The *b* in this case is important. In English, we have *lip*; and so instead of the [b] we have the [p]. *Gynecologist*: and so the "g" in that case, that root comes down into English as *queen*. You see that there are always these differences—and this is in all words beginning with those particular sounds; notice I don't say letters, but sounds—it ends up being kind of a correspondence chart. You can see the correspondence chart here (in the outline, III.E.1).

It's interesting: Let's kind of get a sense of what Lectures Two and Three were for. What this is, superficially, is just a bunch of letters in a couple of rows. But then take a look at what these letters actually are. Remember [p], [t], [k]? That is not unrelated; it's not the author Chaim Potok. Those are our unvoiced stops. Remember those? Those were important. Then look how next is [b], [d], [g]. Is that something like "bad dog," or something like that? No, those were what we met as our nice voiced stops. There's some system here. Then look how under [b], [d], [g] what you have in terms of where the letters went is, again, [p], [t], and [k]. See, I don't have to memorize any of this, because actually these are regular sorts of correspondences. Something happened to [b], [d], and [g] in becoming [p], [t], and [k]; what happens is that they *devoiced*. You can see that this is a regular issue. A linguist doesn't say, "Well, [b], [d], and [g] turned into [p], [t], and [k]." Who wants to remember that? Who cares? What happened is that the class of voiced stops devoiced. You might say, "Who cares about that?" But it's more systematic. Then, as far as what happened to the unvoiced stops from, for example, Latin and Greek, you see that what happened was [f], [θ] and then [x] or [h]. All of those are fricative sounds, so what happened was that there was a *fricativization*.

This is what was known as Grimm's Law. It's known as a law because this is what happened to pretty much all of the words beginning with those sounds. These are correspondences that you find between the body of cognates between, say, Sanskrit, Latin, and Greek and Germanic. There's something kinky about what happened to these sounds in Germanic. What's interesting is that, to the extent that there are exceptions to Grimm's Law, it has been found that you can systematize them, too, by adding corollary laws. This was the first encounter that scholars had with the notion that you could see, in languages that were written a very long time ago, an original state which languages that are more recent preserve a development of. This was the realization that what we see in the Germanic languages seems to represent a state *after* the one represented by Sanskrit, Latin, and Greek. There's a time relationship between these languages, which suggests that there is a process of sound change that happens. It isn't something that happens willy-nilly, idiosyncratically to each word, but that it's something that happens to the sounds themselves throughout the sound system, throughout the vocabulary, throughout the grammar, as we put it, in a systematic way.

By the time this was well established among linguists—people who were doing what we would now consider linguistics—Darwin's theory of natural selection had become influential, and basically we had a new school of thinkers. They called themselves the *Neogrammarians*. They called themselves that because grammar to them was not just a matter of the difference between nouns and verbs, etc., but also the sound system of a language—the entire system. Modern linguists still use grammar in that way, as I actually did myself a few beats ago. But the idea was that just as animals and plants can be seen as the products of evolution, so can be languages. The idea was that languages change in a regular fashion throughout time and that these sorts of things can be charted. Their basic idea was that the way language changes—and what they were interested in was the way language changes on the phonological level—they thought that when language changes, there are two things that happen: One is the ordinary processes of sound change that are regular, such as the ones that turned the original Proto-Indo-European root stock into the Germanic one on the basis of those regular sound changes. On the other hand, they did notice that there were differences between languages' earlier and newer states that could not be explained in terms of these regular sound changes. Really, there seemed to be a countervailing process where speakers were tidying up the grammar in order to create a pattern that they could dimly perceive. For example, standard English *mine, yours,* and *his.* In certain nonstandard English varieties, you can have *mine, yourn,* and *his'n.* That is not something that's only found in Lil' Abner; there actually are dialects where that is said: *yourn, his'n.*

It's not that *yours* changed to *yourn* in a regular way with [s] changing to [n]; there'd be no real reason to expect [s] to change to [n] just out of nowhere. Certainly, for an [n] to just pop up after *his* would be rather unnatural and unmotivated. Really, what happened was that *mine* is the form that's uttered the most because we are a self-centered creature. As a result, *yourn* and *his'n* were created to make something that seemed to pattern with *mine* because human minds seek patterns. That's called *analogy,* because *yourn* and *his'n* were created on analogy with *mine.* This is something that creates a lot of new material in how language changes. For example, in the ancestor of what would have become Old English where nouns still had case—as in Latin—the way that you would add cases to the word for *foot* was like this (in the outline, item IV.C.): What you can see is you had a form for the nominative and the accusative. Then you had a genitive form and you had a dative form—all very Latin-like. This is what you would have had in pre-Old English. This is something that we can reconstruct based on deducing from English and other Germanic languages; that would have been the original situation. So we have nice endings.

But then regular sound change would create something that would interfere with the system. What would happen is that where you have the form *fōti* in Old English—and so you see that for example in the nominative, accusative plural—where you had *fōti,* then regular sound change would change it to *fēt.* Here's how this would happen—and, once again, we realize now why we had to learn the classes of sounds—why would *fōti* go to *fēt*? It's actually very systematic; you would almost expect it. Notice that there's a relationship between the *ē* sound in *fēt* and the *ō* sound in *fōti*; those are both mid sounds, as you can see when we put up our old vowel chart from Lecture Three. They're both mid sounds. We notice that -*i* is this high front sound ([i]). What happened was that in anticipating pronouncing this high front vowel, the *ō* was pulled forward; it was pulled forward into *ē*. There was an intermediate step, which was that at first the *ō* was pulled forward; but remember how we talked about how roundedness is not something that only applies to the back, you can be rounded in the front. The cute French vowel *u* ([y]) for *lune* in *moon* is a nice high front rounded vowel. There's no reason why you would only have to have them high and front. You can also have a mid and rounded vowel, and that is the one that you produce when you shape your mouth for *boat* and say "bait" and so "beut" ([bøt]) and so *la peur* in French for *fear*. Here, the sound being pulled forward would be *ō*. Then pulled forward it would become a front mid but rounded sound, and so "fuh-tee" ([føti]) is what it would have been. Then it would lose its roundedness, as often happens, and then you have *fēt* ([fet]). It would have been a gradual process, very understandable if you think about how the vowels are actually arranged inside of our mouths. It just looks like something random, if you think of vowels as being *a, e, i, o, u*.

This left a whole new situation with *foot*, in which in certain places—namely, the dative singular and the nominative and accusative plural—you had a new kind of vowel. The vowel wasn't [o] anymore; it was [e]. This was messy. It was also the case that the [e] was present, for example, in the nominative and the accusative plural. You use the nominative and the accusative a lot; those are some pretty basic, Ozzie-and-Harriet, Wonder-Bread, beef-stew cases. Those are the ones that come up again and again and again. People don't always like it when you've got this wrinkle that's scattered randomly. So, in the nominative and the accusative plural, and then in the dative singular, the vowel is [e] instead of [o]. Over time, people are going to start pulling the *mine*, *yourn*, *his'n* thing on something like that. People saw that it was in the nominative and accusative plural. They heard it like that so often that there came a sense that the [e] itself was a plural marker—that that's how you make *foot* into plural. As a result, by the time you get to Middle English, you've got the situation that we're familiar with now, which is that the plural of *foot* was *feet*—back then still pronounced [fet]; the great vowel shift hadn't happened yet. But in all of the singular forms now, you had [o], no more the dative singular being the kind of odd lady out—notice that I didn't say man—and then in the plural, all of the plural are [e]. The analogy process ended up creating a new situation. This wasn't regular sound change; this was a matter of pattern making, and that plays as much of a part in how sounds, and also how affixes, end up changing as the regular process does.

This is something that happens everywhere. The Neogrammarians, of course, studied European languages the most, because that's what was available to them. But this is something that is just a hallmark of all human language. For example, the Semitic family—actually it's a sub-family within the Afro-Asiatic family, but that need not concern us—the Semitic family includes Arabic and Hebrew, and also Amharic of Ethiopia. You can see how in Hebrew where the word for *seven* is [ševa]; in Arabic, it's [sabʕa]—I'm trying to pronounce the *pharyngeal*; I don't really do it well. The pharyngeal is another place of articulation on our chart of where consonants go—but it's [sabʕa]; something like that. So [š] in Hebrew is [s] in Arabic. It's not just an accident, but that's what you find systematically in the differences. *Rastafari* from Amharic is actually two words; it's *ras* and *täfäri*, which means *feared*. *Ras* means chief. *Ras* is the same root as *rosh*, as in *Rosh Hashanah*; Rosh Hashanah in Hebrew. So *Rosh*, systematically, the cognate will have a [s] in Amharic. These sorts of correspondences are quite regular.

All of this traces back to a day in the late 18th century when a certain *Sir William Jones* gave a presentation to the Bengal Asiatic Society. He made what is considered to be the first coherent and official statement that languages change systematically over time and develop family relationships like creatures. He said:

> The Sanskrit language, whatever be its antiquity, is of wonderful structure; more perfect than the Greek, more copious than the Latin, and more exquisitely refined than either, yet bearing to both of them a stronger affinity, both in the roots of verbs and in the forms of grammar, than could possibly have been produced by accident; so strong, indeed, that no philologer could examine them all three, without believing them to have sprung from some common source, which, perhaps, no longer exists.

No one understood that as clearly as he did until then, and it created a revolution in thought about how language changes. It seems so natural to us now, but this is something that could only come about when certain technological changes such as travel and widespread print allowed people to perceive the multifariousness of human language and the fact that there were certain correspondences between them, which seemed to have a relationship to the passage of time.

I know you're worried, and so I'll just say it: Jimmy Carter.

# Lecture Twelve
# Recovering Languages of the Past

**Scope:** Referring to tendencies in how sounds change as first examined by the Neogrammarians, linguists can reconstruct what earlier languages were like by comparing their modern descendants. In this lecture, we see the methods of comparative reconstruction as applied to the recovery of the ancestor of the Romance languages, the ancestor of the Polynesian languages, and the ancestor of the main Chinese languages.

# Outline

I.  Historical linguists are able to reconstruct what older stages of language were like by using the fact that sounds change in regular ways; this allows linguists both to trace back what earlier languages must have been like and to explain changes that are happening in them now.

II. We can reconstruct languages because we know what typical sound changes are.

   A. *Assimilation*, one of the most important changes, is when a sound becomes more similar to one it is adjacent to.
      1. Assimilation in place of articulation is when one sound takes on the place of articulation (bilabial, alveolar, etc.) of the nearest sound. For example, in Latin, *inpossibilis* changed to *impossibilis* because both [m] and [p] are bilabial sounds.
      2. Assimilation in voicing is when a sound takes on the voicedness of the other sound.
         a. An unvoiced consonant between two vowels will often become voiced.
         b. If we see a voiced sound between two vowels, we can almost assume that at some point it was voiceless.
      3. Assimilation in *nasalization* is when a vowel becomes nasal (indicated with a tilde) if adjacent to a nasal consonant, e.g., Latin *bonum* became French *bon* ([bɔ̃]).

   B. A scale of *consonant weakening*, moving down the phonetic chart from Lecture Two, shows how consonants tend to morph into different ones.

**C.** Final sounds tend to erode, e.g., old French [maðyr] became *mûr* ([myr]).

**III.** Knowing these tendencies, we can trace modern groups back to ancestor languages. This is called *comparative reconstruction*.

**A.** For example, the Romance languages (such as French, Spanish, Italian, Portuguese, and Romanian) all trace back ultimately to Latin, but between Latin and the modern languages was an intermediate stage called *Proto-Romance*.

**B.** Here are the cognates for four words in modern Romance languages:

|  | Spanish | Sardinian | Romanian |
|---|---|---|---|
| "river" | [rio] | [riu] | [riu] |
| "laugh" | [riso] | [rizu] | [ris] |
| "shore" | [rißa] | [ripa] | [rɨpə] |

**1.** With the first example, based on a principle in comparative reconstruction that, usually, "majority rules," we assume that the Proto-Romance form was [*riu]. (An asterisk is used to note a reconstructed form.)

**2.** In the second example, we assume that the Proto-Romance form had a final vowel, because final sounds often drop off but rarely just grow from nowhere. We can assume that the vowel was a [u] that changed into an [o] in Spanish, because that is what seems to have happened in [riu]. We can assume that the original second consonant was [s] rather than [z], because the typical process is that voiceless consonants change to voiced ones; thus [*risu].

**3.** In the third example, Spanish has a consonant not in English, a voiced bilabial fricative [ß]. Since it is voiced, it cannot be the original sound, which was thus [p]. The central vowels in Romanian then lose out by "majority rules"; thus [*ripa].

**IV.** There are also cases where we can reconstruct a language that is truly lost, as with Proto-Polynesian.

**A.** In the Proto-Romance case, we can check on the validity of the reconstruction with Latin. However, the ancestor to the Polynesian languages was not written.

**B.** We know only that people settled the Polynesian islands starting in about 1500 B.C.E. and that the language would have been spoken then.

|           | Maori | Hawaiian | Samoan | Fijian |
|-----------|-------|----------|--------|--------|
| post      | pou   | pou      | pou    | bou    |
| forbidden | tapu  | kapu     | tapu   | tabu   |
| cry       | taŋi  | kani     | taŋi   | taŋi   |
| stay      | hono  | hono     | fono   | vono   |

1. For *post*, "majority rules": [*pou].
2. For *forbidden*, "majority rules" is applied to both consonants: [*tapu].
3. For *cry*, we must resist a sense that [ŋ] is a "strange" sound that could not have been first; "majority rules" again: [*taŋi].
4. For *stay*, we apply the fact that [h] is a "weak" sound that various consonants have a way of turning into. Thus it was not the original sound. [f] wins over [v] because it's voiceless: [*fono].

**V.** We see this same general principle when going back to old Chinese.

**A.** We can deduce words in old Chinese that gave birth to the seven main Chinese "dialects," which are actually languages as different as French, Spanish, and Italian.

**B.** The word for first-person singular *I* is massively variant:

| Mandarin (Beijing)     | uo   |
|------------------------|------|
| Mandarin (Xian)        | ŋə   |
| Cantonese (Guangzhou)  | ŋo   |
| Cantonese (Taishan)    | ŋoi  |
| Min (Fujian)           | gua  |
| Min (Taiwanese)        | goa  |
| Min (Shaowu)           | haŋ  |
| Wu (Shanghai)          | ŋu   |
| Wu (Suzhou)            | ŋəu  |
| Hakka                  | ŋai  |
| Gan (Nanchang)         | ŋo   |
| Gan (Jixi)             | a    |
| Xiang (Chengbu)        | ŋo   |
| Xiang (Shuangfeng)     | aŋ   |

**C.** Based on this, we can reconstruct that the word for *I* in the language that morphed into all of these languages was [*ŋag].

## Essential Reading:

Arlotto, *Introduction to Historical Linguistics*.

## Supplemental Reading:

Watkins, ed., *American Heritage Dictionary of Indo-European Roots*.

## Questions to Consider:

1. Have you noticed that the most common processes of sound change are also typical of how colloquial pronunciation differs from formal? For example, another common process is the simplification of consonant clusters. Therefore, one would expect a tendency to separate the consonants in the cluster [kl] with a vowel. How, then, would the word *nuclear* come out?

2. Some languages are more "conservative" than others in sound change. For example, the Latin word *augustus* has become in Italian [agosto] and in French the word spelled *août*, in deference to its history, but actually pronounced [u]! In your view, is French "broken down" or "innovative"?

# Lecture Twelve—Transcript
## Recovering Languages of the Past

One of the things that historical linguists do is that historical linguists reconstruct what languages were like, deep in the past, that we will never hear spoken again and that we barely—if ever—will see written. Not only do historical linguists chart the regularity of sound changes over time, but they have also used this knowledge of the regularity in order to get a sense of what languages were like which are otherwise unrecoverable to us. It's sobering to think that our species has been around for in between 150,000 and 200,000 years and that we can presume that most likely—science is gradually zeroing in on being able to figure out whether this is true, but most likely—in terms of genetic evidence, we probably were able to speak from the beginning (that means 150,000 years of language), yet writing was only something that was done starting about 6,000 years ago. That means that if language had existed for 24 hours, then writing only came along after 11:00 pm. That is an awful lot of unrecorded language.

Historical linguists are able to reconstruct what older stages of language were like using the fact that we know that sounds change in regular ways and therefore tracing backwards. This is something that you can understand if you understand how sounds relate to each other, as opposed to what order letters come in the alphabet. Now that we have been through the lectures about sounds, we're in a position to understand, for example, how it would be that linguists have traced what Proto-Indo-European—the father language to most of the languages of Europe and a great many of Iran and India—would have been. We'll never hear Proto-Indo-European; the people who spoke that language had no writing, so we'll never see it scratched on the back of a bone or anything like that. But we can reconstruct what it was like based on looking at all the Indo-European languages now and tracing backwards, because we know how it is that sounds change typically.

To do a kind of basic grab bag of what typical sound changes are, one of the most important is called *assimilation*. Assimilation is what happens when a sound becomes similar to the sound that it's adjacent to. This is something that happens, for example, with Latin, where the word for *eight* was *octo* and the word in Italian is *otto*. This is a *geminate t* or a double *t*, and this is a situation where what was originally the [k] sound has become identical to the [t] sound that followed it. As a result, now: instead of *octo* we have *otto*. That happens in language change all the time; it has a lot to do with what makes one language different from another one, in terms of classifications. If enough of that kind of thing goes on, then there is no mutual comprehension between languages.

You can have assimilation in what we've learned is place of articulation. For example, in early Latin, the word for *impossible* was *inpossibilis*—*inpossibilis* with an [n]. In later Latin—and this is a word passed down to us (listen, like John Kerry: "possed" down to us; "passed" down to us)—it is *impossibilis*; and so [n] has become [m]. That's not just a random process; the reason that the [n] became an [m] before [p] is because both [m] and [p] are bilabial sounds. You remember that from our sound grid: [m] is a bilabial nasal; [p] is a bilabial stop. Naturally, if an [n] comes before a [p], it's almost inevitable that over time that [n] is going to change into an [m]. It'll probably be processed as a mistake by some people, but you can't stop the beat; that has to go on. That's assimilation in place of articulation.

You can have assimilation in voicing. For example, *freed* was *liberatus* in Latin. In Spanish, it's *liberado*. What was a [t] between vowels in Latin is a [d] between vowels in Spanish. We know that [t] and [d] have a relationship: [t] is an unvoiced stop, and [d] is a voiced stop. Vowels have voices; vowels are very voicy sounds. If you have an unvoiced consonant—an unvoiced stop in between two vowels—chances are that it's going to voice because it's assimilating to the voicedness of the two segments that it's sitting between. That's another kind of assimilation that happens all the time; we can expect it. If we see a voiced sound between two vowels, we can almost assume that at some point it was voiceless, because this is the process that we can see happening the other way in languages around the world.

There's also assimilation in *nasalization*. A vowel will become nasal because it is adjacent to a nasal consonant; that is what makes French out of Latin. If the word in Latin for *good* is *bonum*, then over time we can assume—it's kind of like if you make some peas, unless you really strain them carefully, when you put them on the plate there's going to be this kind of light green puddle of fluid that kind of comes out. Then when you smack down that pork chop, the pork chop is going to get colored a little bit by that peas' juice; that's what's going to happen. In the same way, if the nasal consonant is next to a vowel, then the vowel is going to take on a nasal flavoring. For example, in French, the way the word for *good* is written is *bon*. That makes it look like the word is [ban], which it's not. It's not [ban] jour; actually, that is an approximation of what is actually pronounced as [bɔ̃]. If you think about it, there is no [n]; if you put your tongue up near your teeth, you don't say [ban]; it's not really there at all. In the IPA, *bon* is written as b, and then we have our nice open o—the o with the bite out of it that is the sign for "aw"—and then we indicate the nasality with a tilde over it, like from Spanish, and so it's just [bɔ̃]. The reason that it has that nasal quality is because that is a footprint that the [n] that used to follow it left behind. That is assimilation in nasalization. This business in French—"aw, aw, hee, hee, hee, haw, haw, haw" in *The Little Mermaid*—that "aw" is from what in Latin would have been just boring *on*'s; and so: onum, bonum, [bɔ̃]. That's assimilation in nasalization.

In general, you can see something that happens to consonants all the time. There is a scale of consonant weakening that you can see in family after family after family; it becomes almost predictable. What it basically is, is that a voiceless stop—for example, our famous [p], [t], [k]—will develop into a voiced stop; very often voiceless goes to voiced. In this case, it would be the [b], [d], [g] series. Then the voiced stops will become voiced fricatives—very commonly—and then the voiced fricatives will become nasals, then those will become liquids, those will become glides, and then the glides will become nothing. If we go back to our consonant chart, we can see that that is really that the consonants will go down our chart in terms of manner of articulation: Voiceless becomes voiced and stops become fricatives, and then we slide on down and you have nasal, liquid, glide, and then nothing.

If something was *mature* in Latin, then it was *maturus*, and we had a nice [t]. Latin became the Romance languages. One of them was Spanish; one phase of Spanish was what is called Old Spanish, and the word *maturus* in Old Spanish had become [maduro]. Now, [t] became [d] because we so often see the voiceless going to the voiced. Then, in Castilian, the word [maduro] came out as [maðuro], and what you saw here is that a voiced stop became a fricative and a voiced one. The voiceless one would be [θ]: [maθuro]; but it's not that, it's [maðuro]. Then, in Old French, the word was [maðyr]; and we have a change in the vowel. In New French, the word is just *mûr*; that consonant is gone completely. In the IPA, *mûr* would be spelled [myr]; and so it's our high front rounded sound: [myr]. That's what happened to the consonants. That is perfectly normal; that's what consonants do.

You can even recapitulate the process yourself involuntarily. I made a bet with someone in early 1997. For the life of me, I can't remember what the bet was, as if I'm 75 and my memories are fading; I was somewhere in my 30s. We made this bet. I lost the bet, and the conditions were that if I lost the bet, I had to go buy a cat. It was a serious bet; it must have been, because I actually did go buy a cat. That cat's name is Laura. She is now a healthy 11, and she likes me better than anything in the world. She's very cute. She has very large eyes, and she kind of thinks she can talk, and so she makes all these little sounds and things. When I greet her, one of my nicknames for her has always been "Precious," but I think this would happen to anybody. As I pick her up and hold her—and when no one's looking—I might say something like, "My widdle Bwezhuz! My Bwezhuz!"

Why do I say "bwezhuz"? Just because I'm silly? Maybe partly, but there are all sorts of things I could do for *precious*. There are all sorts of sounds I could make. Why does it come out as "bwezhuz"? I'm not thinking about sound classes when I do it, but notice first that to go from *precious* to *bwezhuz* means that I am voicing that initial consonant; I'm sending "precious" along its historical way; and so [p]. Then, instead of saying [r], I use the [w]. That could also be put as I'm making the liquid into a glide. For example, Elmer Fudd, that little trick he has where he says "west and wewaxation" for "rest and relaxation"; to a linguist, he's gliding. It's not because of anything physical he's doing but because his liquids are becoming glides. Interesting.

Let's see, I say "bwezhuz"; so "bwezhuz" comes from "precious." What I had at first was this nice alveolar palatal sound—this [ʃ]—and that was a voiceless sound. When I make it a [ʒ], all I'm doing is taking it a notch down on our chart and making it into a voiced sound. I just feel this intuitively—we all do—and what we're doing is taking the word along in its developmental process. Instead of "precious," I say, "bwezhuz." Remember, there's that relationship between [s] and [z]; a [z] is an [s] with a voice. When I'm grabbing Laura, I am kind of pushing all these processes ahead. It is perfectly imaginable that if language in a written form, where there was widespread literacy, changed as quickly as unwritten languages do—the reason that they don't is actually something that's discussed in another Teaching Company set on language—I forget who the professor was who did that one—but there is this other one that talks about language change, the rate of it, and things like that. I wish I could remember his name. But, anyway, if English was one of those, then certainly in some future development of English, the word for *precious* ([prɛʃʌs]) would be something like [bwɛʒʌz] or something like that; that's what happens.

These are the sorts of things that we know are processes of sound change. They're things that you just know. When on *The Sopranos* once—I hope you watched that; every episode is worth it. And you should have watched *The Wire*. It has a boring name (nobody wants to watch a show about a wire), but that's something very metaphorical. It's the best show that's ever been on TV since *The Sopranos*. Once, Tony was running around in the kitchen and he said, "Carm, give me some gabbagool." Now I'm not Italian—as you've probably guessed—and so we didn't have "gabbagool" in my home. But I thought, since these people are Sicilians and Sicilian Italian is further advanced in terms of its phonetic evolution than standard Italian, I thought, let's trace back what "gabbagool" would refer to. I thought, well, [g], that's a voiced sound, so probably originally it was unvoiced; so [k]. Then "gabbagool"—[b]—that must have begun as its voiceless alternate; so [p]; [k]-[p]. Then, okay, he says "gabbagool"; well there's another [g]. Let's say that he was saying "cuppacool"; and I thought, oh, all right, because then there's this business of [o] changing into [u] under certain circumstances. I thought, he's saying "Capicola"; he wants Capicola ham. If you have this sound chart in your head, that's instant. I remember hearing him say "gabbagool" and thinking, "What? 'Capicola'; okay." That's how sound change works.

Speaking of Tony and Carm, we can look at this kind of thing in, for example, the Romance languages. The Romance languages trace back to Latin; Latin is their father or their mother, whatever you want to call it. There are a whole bunch of Romance languages today. The big five are French, Spanish, Italian, Portuguese, and Romanian. Then there are a bunch of other ones. For example, Occitan are the varieties that are spoken in the South of France, and that included the Provençal variety that the troubadours sang in. Catalan is a fascinating language. Italian is really a whole bunch of different languages; Sicilian might as well be a different language from Italian. There are bunch of Romance languages spoken by very small groups in the Swiss mountains and the Italian mountains, which aren't really that closely related. There was one called Dalmatian spoken on the Adriatic coast. They found it when it was only spoken by one dying old man, and because he didn't have any teeth, they were never quite sure what the consonants were in it; but it was there. So there are a lot of Romance languages.

We can look at them and, of course, we already know what Latin was like, sort of. Except the classical Latin that's written on the page is very codified—it's very much a written language—and it's highly suspected that no one actually spoke the way, for example, Cicero wrote, or any of those people; those people were putting something on paper where you could chew on it slowly. There was a Latin that was actually spoken. It's often called Vulgar Latin—not because people who spoke it were fond of picking their noses, but because vulgar in that sense means just people, the common folk—and we have often wondered, what was the spoken language actually like? Or even what was the intermediate stage between today's Romance languages and that highly antique classical Latin that we see written on the page that probably nobody was really speaking in that way when it was written? We have reason to believe that there was something that we call Proto-Romance. There was a language that was spoken before the Romance languages existed that was not the Latin that we see on the page. You can see bits and pieces of Proto-Romance in the way "lowly people" are portrayed as speaking in some of the plays, which is very different from classical Latin. In graffiti on the walls in Pompeii, for example, you see a Latin that is definitely not-in-Kansas-anymore Latin—and not just in the cursing and the references to sex, but the sounds seemed to have changed.

What's Proto-Romance like? The only way that we can really figure it out beyond those shreds is comparing Romance languages spoken today. You can take, for example, Spanish and Romanian and Sardinian. Sardinian is spoken on the island of Sardinia. It's kind of like Italian, but it isn't. That's a Romance language we don't encounter much. (I once met an old Sardinian couple. If they were standing on this podium, they were both like that high; they were very tiny people. Good food in Sardinia.) Anyway, Spanish, Sardinian, and Romanian. We can look, for example, at the word for *river*. In Spanish we have [rio], in Sardinian [riu], in Romanian [riu]. That [u] looks a little odd to a lot of us. If you're Romanian, it'll look familiar, but for most of us, we think that the [o] must be original because we're used to it from Spanish in particular. But actually there's a basic principle, which is that "majority rules." Therefore, we can assume that if we have two of them that say [riu], and then in Spanish we have [rio], then [o] was secondary. So the original form—the Proto-Romance form—will be [riu]; so we can figure that out. Now in notation, because we don't know what the Proto-Romance form was and we cannot exhume and reanimate a Proto-Romance speaker to ask this person how to say *river*, we have to just assume. It's reconstructed form, and so we put an asterisk on it, and so that's what the star is on [*riu]; that's a reconstructed form.

Then, what about laughing? How would you talk about laughing in Proto-Romance? Spanish has [risa], Sardinian has [rizu], and Romanian has just

[ris]. Looking at these, the first thing that we know is that there was probably a vowel at the end, because it's much more common for vowels to drop off than for a vowel to just appear out of nowhere. For example, if you go back to our Latin *liberatus* example, not only in Spanish is it *liberado*, but that [s] is gone. That's because final sounds do tend to erode in that way. We can assume that a vowel fell off, not that the original word was something like [ris], and then all of a sudden people said, "Well let's just say [riso]!" There's no reason for that; much more likely is [riso], [riso], [ris], [ris], [ris]. That's how sound change happens. Now, what vowel was it? To my eyes, especially looking at this chart—and with my natural American sense that Spanish is somehow more real than little Sardinian and weird Romanian—you want to think, "Well, the vowel must have been [o], and then this [u] is just something that tiny people do." But no, because we're talking about systematic changes. Remember how we talked about how Grimm's Law taught us that these things happen in a regular way? If the word for *river* was [\*riu], where this [u] won out, and so it looks like in Spanish [u] became [o], we have to assume that that's the case with *laugh* too. The word for *laugh* is going to end in a [u] and not an [o].

What about the consonant? We have [riso] in Spanish and we have a [ris] in Romanian, and we have a [rizu] in Sardinian. For one thing, majority rules, and that's our first clue that there's an [s]. But then, there's also something else we can think about, which is that [s] is voiceless and [z] is an [s] with a voice. How do consonants tend to change? It tends to be that just as I call my precious cat "bwezhuz"—[prɛʃʌs]; [bwɛʒʌz]—they called their precious laughing [\*riso], and then it became [rizu]. We can assume based on those principles that what we have is majority rules plus the fact that the original sound is voiceless, and then in Sardinian a natural change happened where it became voiced. But that didn't happen to everything; the original sound would have been a voiceless one.

Then, with our other word, we have the word for *shore*. Sardinian has something very, very nice, which is [ripa]. Then there are some odd things elsewhere. Spanish has this sound that we don't have in English, and what this is, is what you learn in classes often is kind of like a [b] and kind of like a [v]; it's the [ß] sound. But we don't talk about "kind of like a [b] and kind of like a [v]" in linguistics; that doesn't really make any sense. What it is, is it's a different sound completely than anything that we have a classification for: It's a bilabial fricative, because it's fricative—it's hissy: sssssss—and what do you make it with? Not your larynx; you're making it with your bilabes, so, [ß]: bilabial fricative. We already saw the voiceless bilabial fricative back when we talked about how Japanese don't say [f] right. You listen to them and say, "We think it's 'Mount Fuji' and they say 'Mount Fhuji.'" We think, "Oh, they have such a peculiar accent." They're not pronouncing an [f] at all; it is a voiceless bilabial fricative: [ɸ]. You would think that sounds generally are there in a relationship, and so there's always going to be a significant other. If there's a voiceless [ɸ], then you know that there's going to be [ß]. Romanian has these two sounds; these are central sounds from our chart, so you see this barred *i*: [ɨ]. That is not a bit of smudge on your screen; it is a barred *i*, and the sound is "uhl"—like that, "uhl"—it sounds prettier when someone is making the sound who is Romanian and not me. Then we have the schwa; but the word is [rɨpə]; that's how they say *shore*.

What would the original be? In terms of majority rules, as so often happens, Romanian loses. You know, those central sounds, none of the other Romance languages have [rɨpə], so apparently that's derived; that came later. Then, in deciding between Spanish and Sardinian—whether it was [rißa] or [ripa]—the relationship is once again one of these where we've got voiceless and we've got voiced. Therefore, it seems that [*ripa] would be our original sound. Doing that with hundreds and hundreds of words, we could reconstruct a whole Proto-Romance vocabulary, and it's just a matter of these kinds of deductions.

In any case, this Proto-Romance one is kind of a test drive, because we do have Latin to allow us to check up on ourselves and to make sure that our methodology is appropriate and actually corresponds to reality. But there are cases where we can reconstruct a language that is truly lost. For example, the Polynesian islands were settled starting at about 1500 B.C. We can assume that it was a small group and that they spoke a single language; this would be a language in the Austronesian family. They did not write, and because they didn't write, the language died with them, and so we can't know what their language was. But there are many Polynesian islands and many Polynesian languages today. We can compare them, and we can reconstruct what these original people—apparently in small boats with a very close relationship to beating bark—would have done. For example, there's Maori from New Zealand; Hawaiian, I'm not sure what island that's spoken on; Samoan; and Fijian, which is spoken on Fiji.

If we look at the words for concepts in all of those languages, we can figure out what words people were using while they were in those little boats. For example, in Maori, the word for *post* is [pou], and it's that word in

Hawaiian and Samoan as well. Then, in Fijian, it's [bou]. This is a pretty easy one: majority rules. In the case of [bou], a consonant happened to go voiced. They do that, but that means that it hadn't done it originally. If you look at the word for *forbidden*—as in taboo—in Maori, it's [tapu]; and then in Hawaiian it's [kapu]; Samoan [tapu]; and Fijian [tabu]. As soon as you see the [b] you can kick that out, because once again we know that that wasn't the original situation; [p] is what a [b] so often starts as.

For *cry*, we have our engma; so [taŋi] and then in Hawaiian it's [kani]; then in Samoan it's [taŋi]; and Fijian it's [taŋi]. We might think, "Anything with this engma—this [ŋ]—that must have been later, because [ŋ] is this strange sound. It must have originally been [n]." But no, there is nothing strange about [ŋ]; it's just that English doesn't happen to have a letter for the sound [ŋ]. But, as we talked about, it is a sound; it's the difference between a *singer* and a *finger*. If in *singer* you're pronouncing an [n] and a [g], then how come you don't say "sing-ger"; "singer"? Now strip away the rest of it, and you're pronouncing a consonant that is [ŋ], and that's what this engma is. Apparently, it was first: majority rules. We don't want to discriminate against engma.

Then, when we have stay, we have [hono], [hono], [fono], and [vono]. In this case, we have to stand back. The first consonant seems to be [h], and so naturally we think majority rules. However, sometimes we do have to discriminate, because [h] is a peculiar sound. [h] is very often what some other sound becomes; it's kind of this hand-me-down sound. [h] kind of couldn't keep up in the schoolyard. For example, in Latin, *to make* or *to do* is *facere* ([fakare]). That word means *to make* or *to do*, not what it sounds like. In Spanish—for those of you who know Spanish—you know that *facere*, *to make* or *to do*, is *hacer*, spelled with an *h*, which of course used to be pronounced: The [f] became an [h]. Sounds tend to kind of go back in the throat and get all puffy. [h]'s tend to disappear like "'enry 'iggins" in *Pygmalion*, and so on. Here, the [h] has to tip us off; something turned into [h]. Rarely is it going to be [h] is majority rules, unless they're all [h]'s; so [h] is second class. There actually is an [f] here. Which was first, the [f] or the [v]? We know that because [f] is voiceless and [v] is voiced that voiceless wins; and so [f] was the beginning. We can look at [hono], [hono], [fono], [vono] for *stay*, and we can know that even though there are more [hono]'s, it must have been [*fono]. [f] would have been the first sound.

This is a general principle that we see. To make it clear that it's not just the sorts of things that we usually see in the textbooks or that we might readily think about, you can see that in the Chinese varieties there is immense difference. Mandarin and Cantonese are often talked about as if they were dialects of one another; that's only because they use the same writing system. Mandarin to Cantonese is like Spanish to Italian. There are many other Chinese "dialects," which are actually all completely different languages. When you look at all of them, you're looking at as much variety as you see among the Germanic languages or the Romance languages. The word for *I* in all of them is massively variant; you see all of these different shapes (in the outline, item V.B.). You wonder, what could the original old Chinese form have been? As a matter of fact, we know from old Chinese that the original form was—and here comes engma again—[*ŋag]; and so it was [*ŋag] with a final [g].

It might be counterintuitive that you could get that from all of these forms, but looking at all of them, you see that many of them do begin with [ŋ]—with our engma—and looking at all of them, you see that what some of the other ones begin with is derivable from engma, and so [ŋ] is our velar nasal. Now we have these forms from Min in Fujian and Taiwanese that begin with [g]. There you go; that's velar, too. It just happens to be a stop. There's a relationship. We have this one Min form that begins with an [h]. [h] is that weak sound that could have just come from [ŋ], because [ŋ] beat it up in the schoolyard. You can see that there is a common [a] sound—an "ah" sound—that is used in many of them. In the Gan form that we see near the bottom of this chart, that the actual word for *I* is [a]. This is a tip off that that was our original vowel, and because we see that there are many of them that end in a consonant—not so many, but enough of them—we wonder, "Did a consonant just spring forth? Did all of a sudden people start sticking an engma on the end, or is that originally there was a consonant and in most of these forms—especially with a word like *I* that's used so heavily—the final consonant dropped off?" Obviously it's the latter, and when we wonder what that final consonant was, it would seem that it probably was velar, given that we see these engmas at the end in some cases here. It doesn't surprise us to find that when we go back to old Chinese, we find that even though the form in Mandarin for *I* is [uo] and the form in Cantonese is [ŋo], that the original word was [*ŋag].

These are the techniques of what's called *comparative reconstruction*, and these are the techniques that historical linguists use to figure out what languages were like, which otherwise we have no access to, and also to help to determine what the relationships are in terms of sub-families and sub-sub-families in languages that have long and deep relationships.

# Lecture Thirteen
## Where Grammar Comes From

**Scope:** Languages develop new grammatical features when the meaning of an independent word is gradually reinterpreted as serving to mark grammar rather than to indicate a concrete concept. An example is *going to*, which now marks the future (*I'm going to feel good*), whereas in earlier times it could only refer to literal movement (*I'm going to church*). This process has been studied by linguists only over the past few decades.

## Outline

I. If you found yourself having to make up a language, like Adam and Eve, it's hard to imagine making up a word for *from* or *about*.

    **A.** Historical linguists over about the past 30 years have been giving more attention to where such things come from.

    **B.** This process of how languages develop material to mark grammar is called *grammaticalization*.

II. In order to understand this process, we differentiate between the concrete and the abstract.

    **A.** There are *concrete* words that stand for an object, action, quality, or concept, such as *apple, run, blue, elation, despair*.

    **B.** There are also *grammatical* words that have no independent meaning but function as parts of a language's grammar, such as *as, for, until, such*.

    **C.** In grammaticalization, a concrete word becomes a grammatical item.

III. Some early thinkers on language intuited that grammatical words are historical developments from concrete ones.

    **A.** Political reformer John Horne Tooke (1736–1812) was one.

        **1.** Cast as a dialogue between himself and others, Tooke's *The Diversions of Purley* (1786) included passages such as this one:

> The French peculiar preposition CHEZ is no other than the Italian substantive CASA or CA. … I am persuaded

that Door and Through have one and the same Gothic origin *dauro*, mean one and the same thing; and are in fact one and the same word.

    **2.** Tooke was wrong about the derivation of *through* but correct about French's *chez*, and his intuition was sound. However, his work had no lasting influence.

**B.** Antoine Meillet (1866–1936) was an Indo-Europeanist who wrote the first article on grammaticalization in 1912.

    **1.** In his time, Neogrammarians thought that the way grammar developed was through analogy, as we saw in Lecture Eleven, when English developed the plural marking -ee- in *feet*.

    **2.** Meillet argued that the main way grammars develop is through concrete words being reinterpreted as grammatical ones. He referred to evidence of this within modern languages, such as in French's various uses of *être* ("to be").

> *Je **suis** ton père.* "I am your father."
> *Je **suis** sous la table.* "I am under the table."
> *Je **suis** malade.* "I am sick."
> *Je me **suis** lavé les mains.* "I washed my hands."

    **3.** The notion of *being* is clearly and literally indicated in the first sentence, is somewhat less literal in marking a location (one does not "be" the fact of huddling under a table), even less so with an adjective in the third, and quite abstract in a sentence where *suis* marks the concept as past and is a mechanical requirement when the reflexive *se* is used.

**C.** It was not until the 1980s, however, that linguists began examining grammaticalization on a sustained basis.

**IV.** Grammaticalization is now well understood, as we can see from examples.

**A.** *Going to*: In Old English, there was no such thing as using the word for *go* to put a verb in the future, as in "I'm going to think about that."

    **1.** Even as late as the 1590s, in Shakespeare's *Two Gentlemen of Verona*, the Duke asks Valentine "Sir Valentine, whither away so fast?" and Valentine answers "Please it your Grace, there is a messenger that stays to bear my letters to my friends, and I am *going to* deliver them."

2. Valentine means that he is literally going in order to deliver the letters.

3. However, Valentine's statement could be taken as meaning that his delivery of the letters will occur in the future—that is, that he *will* deliver the letters. Because of that implication, *going to* started to actually mean the future rather than actual going.

4. About 50 years after *Two Gentlemen*, England's King Charles I rallied the gentry of Yorkshire, saying, "You see that My Magazine is going to be taken from Me," which could not have, in a literal sense, referred to movement.

5. The casual rendition of *going to*, *gonna*, can be seen as a subsequent stage. *Gonna* is shorter than *going to*, which is typical of grammaticalization, in which items tend to become shorter due to heavy use.

B. The *-mente* ending in Romance languages began as Latin for *mind*, used as in *clara mente*: "with clear mind."

1. Gradually it became an adverbial ending, used in cases in which "mind" would make no sense, such as French's *L'eau coule doucement* ("The water flows sweetly").

2. There is still a clue that *-mente* began as a separate word, in that when two adjectives are used in French and Spanish, only the final one is marked with *-ment/-mente*, as if the ending were still a separate noun that happened to be modified by two adjectives: *clara y concisamente* ("clearly and concisely").

V. Grammaticalization is the source of the tables of endings typical in Indo-European languages.

A. For example, Polish has past-tense endings that began as the verb "to be," which attached itself to the verb. See the "be" forms from an earlier stage of Polish and what the past tense endings are now:

| | | | |
|---|---|---|---|
| *pisalem* | "I wrote" | *jeśm* | "I am" |
| *pisales* | "you wrote" | *jes* | "you are" |
| *pisalismy* | "we wrote" | *jesmy* | "we are" |
| *pisaliscie* | "you (pl.) wrote" | *jeśće* | "you (pl.) are" |

**B.** A clue that the past endings began as separate words for "to be" is that, even today, the endings can occur either on the verb or on another word in the sentence.

    **1.** That is, it retains a bit of its original freedom as a word that can get around, rather than an ending stuck on to a verb.

    **2.** For example, *Where have you been?* in Polish can be either of the following:

> *Gdzie byliscie?*
> *Gdziescie byli?*

**VI.** Many of the things we hear as "slang" in English are grammaticalization on the march.

    **A.** Another modern example is the use of *all* as a *quotative marker*, as in *She's all "I don't know!"*

    **B.** *All* has gone from its literal meaning to serving as a piece of grammar, just as *that* is used in standard English as a quotative marker (*She said that she didn't know*).

**Essential Reading:**

Hopper and Traugott, *Grammaticalization*.

**Supplemental Reading:**

Traugott and Heine, *Approaches to Grammaticalization*.

**Questions to Consider:**

**1.** "We're in a hurry—tsgo!" A Martian writing a description of English based only on hearing it would include a prefix *ts-*, used by speakers to suggest that they and another person (or people) do something. This prefix is the result of a process of grammaticalization. Can you describe what the steps in that process were?

**2.** Let's get some IPA practice and get one more look at grammaticalization too. Here is a sentence in natural, colloquial English:

> [hi ʃʊdə told ju ðæt ajv gaʔ θri ænd ajl gɪv hɪm wʌn]

Find the three examples in this sentence of a grammaticalization: grammatical morphemes that began as content words.

# Lecture Thirteen—Transcript
## Where Grammar Comes From

You are naked, you are sitting under a tree, it's with someone else in an equally denuded state, and you are going to make up a language; for some reason, you have to make up a language. It's easy to imagine that you would first make up a word for *coconut*—we imagine for some reason that this is on an island, so let's go with that—then you're probably going to make up some word for *give*. You're going to make up a word for *rain*. If you think about it, you could keep doing that for years, and still, if it were a matter of pointing to things and making up a word—that kind of Adam and Eve thing—you would not have a language in the sense that we know it. The reason is because it's much harder to imagine making up a word for *from*; you're going to want to express that concept. How would you make up a word for *from*? *From* doesn't bark; *from* doesn't smell like anything. It would be quite a challenge. It's hard to imagine how you would decide how to make up a word for, say, *about*, because you're going to talk *about* things. What's your word for *about*? It's hard to imagine just how you would manage that kind of thing. One wonders in a language, where do those words come from? How do those words arise?

We have already seen how sounds change in a language, but of course phonology is just one level of language. There are many other aspects of language. For example, there's the morphological level, and that includes affixes, prefixes, and suffixes and the concept that they convey, especially in languages that are familiar to us, such as placing things in time via tense. Our question is: Where do those things come from in a language? Because they don't just come out of nowhere; no one decrees that our past-tense marker is going to be what is spelled *-ed*. These things happen, but the question is exactly how. That is a question which did not concern the Neogrammarians very much but has concerned historical linguists more over about the past 30 years. It is a study which is called the study of *grammaticalization*. Where does grammar come from?

In order to understand it, we have to first make a differentiation between the *concrete* and the *abstract*. There are concrete words that stand for an object, or an action, or a quality, or a concept. There's *apple*; that's a good Wonder-Bread noun. There is *run*; that is a verb. It refers to a concept; this is very concrete. There is *blue*; we know what *blue* is. It's the kind of thing we can imagine making up a word for when we're naked on that island.

What are we going to call the things that happen to be this color? There is *elation*; that is a concept, but it's something that we can put into our minds. It's possible that one might have a word for *elation*. Probably, you would start with *happiness*; but *elation* is something. There is *despair*; etc.

But then there are not concrete words, but *grammatical* words. They don't have an independent meaning; they're part of a language's grammar. For example, you have a word like *as*. That's not a concrete concept. What's an *as*? Imagine a foreigner asking you, "What does *as* mean?" You'd have to think for a minute, and then you'd say, "Well, *as* means like." Then they'd say, "What does *like* mean?" Then you'd have to keep on thinking. It's really a matter of conveying grammar. Or *for*; what does *for* mean? The first thing you think is, "Well, it means for." Because actually, it is a grammatical word that indicates that something is benefactive, as a linguist would put it. Or *until*, or *such*: These are grammatical words. A language has concrete words, and a language has grammatical words.

In grammaticalization, what happens is a concrete word gradually evolves into a grammatical word. Where grammatical words come from is what start out as concrete words. Words' meanings change over time, and that's not only in the sense that, for example, the word *bird* in English used to mean *a small bird*—like little dickey bird—and now it means all birds, it's that words can change in meaning from being concrete to being words that don't have a concrete meaning but serve as a part of grammar. The first person who actually seemed to engage with this concept—because it's something that's not precisely unclear to somebody who has a certain kind of head and looks at the word in a language carefully—the first person was John Horne Tooke. Most of his life was in the 1700s. He was mostly a political reformer, but he was one of these Renaissance men of the period who could do quite few things and did quite a few of them well. He actually first noted what we would consider the concept of grammaticalization in a book where he cast it as a dialogue. The expectations were different in this era, and he was not the only person who, in writing what he thought of as a scholarly treatise, cast it as a conversation between people. There is still a kind of orality to writing in this period that led him to do something like this. He had a work called *The Diversions of Purley*, and he had a passage like this one: Beadon says, "But of what real object is THROUGH the name?" Then Tooke—he cast himself in the book—says:

> Of a very common one indeed. For as the French peculiar preposition CHEZ is no other than the Italian substantive CASA or CA, so is the English preposition THOROUGH no other than the

Gothic substantive *dauro*, or the Teutonic substantive *thuruh*: and like them, means door, gate, passage. I am persuaded that Door and Through have one in the same Gothic origin *dauro*, mean one and the same thing; and are in fact one in the same word.

That's 1786; *The Diversions of Purley*. What he is saying is that *through* and *thorough* are derivants of the word *door*—the word that meant *door* in earlier Germanic languages. You can see how that would work, because a door is something that you go through. His idea is that that's where we get the word *through* and that's where we get the word *thorough*. His idea is even—and this is very innovative—that actually *through* and *door* are the same word, that the sounds have changed, and we don't really know it, but we're actually still just saying, "door." His comparison is with the French *chez*, as in *chez moi* means that you're at my house. This *chez* is the French sound development of what begins as a word for *house*, which is still *casa* in Italian. His idea is that when you say, "*chez*," you're really still saying, "house." He didn't call this grammaticalization, but he was looking at language with the fundamental insight that words that are grammatical must come from words that are concrete. The idea that they are words that are concrete is a leap that few people would take after him, but that was his idea.

Tooke was wrong about *through*—*through* was not the word for *door*—but he did have the basic idea. Subsequent research has revealed actually that if you trace *through* back, then the original Proto-Indo-European root was something like *tera*—that was the original—and what *tera* meant was *to cross over* or *to pass through*, and it was a verb. Now we have *through*, which is no longer a verb—it is a grammatical item—and so something that starts out as concrete has become a grammatical concept. It's interesting what happened to *tera*. All sorts of things can happen via grammaticalization or semantic change. For example, if you are crossing through something—if you are passing through something—then you might be overcoming it; that might be a victory. As a result, the word *thrill* actually comes from that original *tera* root. In addition, the *trans-* prefix from Latin that we have in so many words such as *transfer* is originally from that *tera*. First, you're talking about passing through; the next thing you know, you've got a prefix that refers to transfer, for example. That did happen; that was a grammaticalization. Actually, as a matter of fact, the word *nostril* begins as "nose thrill," and the *thrill* is referring to the through-ness of the hole in your nose. It's kind of a "nose through"; that *tera* root actually fell into English in that way too.

Tooke was wrong specifically, but he definitely had the right idea. The idea is that if you see a grammatical word that looks similar to a concrete word, then there probably is a relationship. For example, how we express the future in English: *I will see about that*. What's *will*? In our minds, we're just saying that the *seeing about that* is going to take place in the future, rather than in the past. But the fact is we do have more concrete versions of the word *will*. *Will* has to do with the desire to do something. You can have free will; as a matter of fact, that relationship is very much there. There was a time in English when you did not express the future in that way. We use *will* in that way because it's a grammaticalization of what began as a matter of your will to do something, which naturally entails that in the future you were more likely to do it than not.

Grammaticalization is everywhere. The person who actually nailed this—the person who actually gave terminology to it—was Antoine Meillet. He was an Indo-Europeanist, and he wrote the first recognizable article on grammaticalization in 1912. He was a person of French-ness, and therefore his example that has come down through the years because it was so good is a French one. He noticed that the way French uses its verb *être* is one which can be seen as on a climb of grammaticalization from the concrete to the abstract. For example, *suis* is the first-person singular form of *être* in French. "I am your father." I'm not going to do the Star Wars joke. *Je suis ton père*; "I am your father." That's the core of being; that is the concrete being. "I am your father. Your father is what I am." Then, you can also say, "I am under the table": *Je suis sous la table*. That's being, too. But if you think about it, that's a more abstract kind of being: "I am your father"; "I am under the table." Do you embody the state of being under the table? Maybe in some philosophical way you do, but it's actually a bit of a stretch from the more neutral and concrete meaning of *to be*.

You can say, "I am sick": *Je suis malade*. "I am illness forever," when you know that you're not always going to be sick? Rather unusual. It seems very normal to we Indo-European speakers, but in a great many languages, adjectives are expressed in different ways; they're very often verbs. In many languages, to say, "He is sick," you'd say, "He sicks." The idea being that "he sicks" only right now, not that he embodies the state of being sick or "I am sick." That's more abstract.

Then in French there is a bit of grammar that is a nuisance to English speakers where you have to use the verb *to be* when you are using the past tense—the *passé composé*—with reflexive verbs. If you say, "I ate," you say, "I have eaten"—*J'ai mangé*—and you use the verb "to have," and so that's *avoir*. That's easy. But if you want to say that you washed your hands where it's reflexive and you did something to yourself, then you have to say, "I am washed me the hands." That's a kink in French and some Romance languages. So: *Je me suis lavé les mains.* Now, that's just weird; there is no reason that we can process in this present time slice why you would use the verb *to be* in that particular context. That's very grammaticalized. You just have to know that when you're using a verb that involves doing something to yourself and it took place in the past, then the way that you render it in the past involves yanking in the verb *to be*, whereas if you didn't do it to yourself, then you use the verb *to have*. Grammars are a nuisance; you just have to know. This represents the grammaticalization of the verb "to be." You have the concrete concept of being somebody's father; there's nobody else who could be that person's father. Then you have it used as just a chunk of stuff when you're talking about washing your hands. That is an example of grammaticalization. That was Antoine Meillet, and he was the first person who really broke it down. It wasn't until the '80s, though, that this became something people had conferences about and that there were books about and the like. Now it is pretty well understood.

Here's a classic example of grammaticalization in the language that most of us are familiar with. In Old English, if you were going to talk about the future, there was no such thing as using *go* to do that. You did not say, "I'm going to think about that." Or, if you did, it meant that you were going to remove yourself from this location to another location to go cogitate. But the idea of using *going to* or *gonna* to express the future, that just hadn't happened yet. Even as late as Shakespeare in *Two Gentlemen of Verona*, the Duke asks Valentine, "Sir Valentine, whither away so fast?" Valentine answers, "Please it your Grace, there is a messenger that stays to bear my letters to my friends, and I am going to deliver them." We hear that and we think, "Oh, he's delivering them in the future." But what that meant in Shakespeare's time is *I am going to hie myself to deliver these letters*—it was meant literally. There was *will*—will future—but not this business of *going to*. So he's actually going to deliver the letters.

When he says that he is moving to deliver the letters, of course it does contain an implication. The implication is that the delivery of the letters will occur in the future. That means that he will deliver the letters. That kind of implication has a way of hanging around. It's kind of like between couples: There are these unsaid things that hang around, and then when you drink a little too much, it all kind of comes out. Implications like that hang in a language. If there's this implication when you talk about you're "going to"—you're going to move yourself to do something, that it's going to happen in the future—that may start to color the meaning of what people are actually saying. It's in the late 1640s, when Charles I is about to have his body removed from his head. He rallied the gentry of Yorkshire, and he said, "You see that My Magazine is going to be taken from Me." By magazine, he didn't mean his *Atlantic Monthly*; he was talking about magazine in the army, weapon sense. But he said, "You see that My Magazine is going to be taken from Me." That's an interesting example, because that couldn't have referred to movement—neither the *Atlantic Monthly* nor a munitions type of magazine can go to do anything—he meant this in the future. That is something that he probably would not have said even 50 years before. Language is always changing, and it had been then.

Then there is something else about going to use in the future, which is that as often as not, it is pronounced as "gonna." We think of that as slangy and casual, but gosh, that really is the way you almost have to say it much of the time, unless you're "gonna" sound kind of like Hyacinth Bouquet on *Keeping Up Appearances*. The word is *gonna*. That is typical of the fact that there is a shortening that happens in grammaticalization very often. You'll start with a concrete word that is of a certain substance, and this concrete word will take on this new grammatical meaning which is different from that concrete one—of a different nature. Because it is no longer the word that it used to be, phonetic erosion has a way of beating it up, and it tends to become shorter. It's a symptom of grammaticalization. For example, when you say, "I will go," that's the clearest way to say it, but really, just as often you'll say, "I'll go." Nobody thinks of "I'll go" as bad grammar; it's just what happens, which means that the future marker can be *will* or it can be *ll*. If a Martian came down and listened, the Martian would say, "There are two future markers: [wɪl], then there is also sometimes the pronunciation [l]," because the Martian doesn't know how we write. It doesn't think about things like that; so there's that.

Or, even "shoulda," like, for example, "I should have told her"; "I shoulda told her." That's "Oh, I shoulda told her." It starts as *have* and that puts it in the past, but when we use that expression—when we use that construction—really often we just say "uh" ([ə]). An example of that that shows just how really ingrained in English that is: Think about Journey. Remember that song, "Oh Sherrie"? You know, that was one wonderful pop song; remember it? It starts with silence. Well, no, there is this thing done on the synthesizer—very '80s. I think the song was from the '80s. Then it's silent, and then the singer sang, "You shoulda been gone, knowing how you made me feel." I forget who the singer was; he had that vocal quality. "You shoulda been gone." He couldn't have said, "Well, you should have been"; he said, "shoulda." That's the English language; that is actually how we speak. The [ə] in there—what the Martian would hear—the [ə] puts it in the past. It's short because it's grammaticalized. That's something that happens in grammaticalization: Not only does the meaning change, but generally there's a phonetic erosion.

Another example of grammaticalization is *-mente* in Spanish, or *-ment* in French. There was a word that meant *mind* in Latin. For example, you would say, "*clara mente*": "clear mind." The concrete meaning of *mind* changed, and gradually it became an adverbial ending, like *-ly—l, y—*in English. After a while, it began to be used in cases where *mind* itself would make no sense. For example, here, in French, we have "The water flows sweetly": "*L'eau coule doucement.*" That's pretty French, but water can't flow with a sweet mind because most water doesn't have a mind. Clearly, we're no longer in the concrete sense of it being about a mind. It's just an adverbial ending; it conveys manner. The concrete aspect of it being a mind is completely gone.

There are often hints that something began as a concrete item. For example, in Spanish, to say, "clearly and concisely" you could say, "*claramente y concisamente,*" but really the elegant way to say it is "*clara y concisamente.*" You only need to have the *-mente* once. What this actually channels is that there was a time when *-mente* really was just a noun, and so it was "with a clear and a concise mind." That is evidence that a grammaticalization has happened of something that was originally concrete.

What this all means is that when you look at a table of endings in a language—for example, a European language—what you're seeing is the result of the grammaticalization of something else. Chances are that those endings used to be free-floating words, and now they have glommed onto the root. Like you can look at Polish. (This table is in the outline, section V.A.) Let's look at the past tense in Polish. You've got, "I wrote," "you wrote," "we wrote," and "y'all wrote" (you in the plural wrote). What we have here is *pisałem*, *pisałes*—I am not talking like Elmer Fudd in pronouncing this *l* as a [w]; that's actually the way they pronounce it. I know because I asked somebody—*pisałem*, *pisałes* and then *pisalismy*, *pisaliscie*. Polish is really hard to pronounce. It's one of those languages where either you've got to be born to it, obsessive, or marry somebody who speaks it. I am speaking Polish with a thick accent here, but that is approximately how those are pronounced. What's important is that we have these endings: the *-em*, the *-es*, the *-smy*, and the *-scie*. It's the *-scie* that's hard; I think it's like the click in those click languages: You've got to be born to it. Polish people, in my experience, never indulge you with the idea that you're saying it right. You go "*-scie*," and they'll kind of smile, "No, it's *-scie*," and there's something they can do. Languages are delicious. But here are these endings.

Those didn't just happen. Imagine naked Polish people sitting under a tree trying to give a name to borscht, or whatever Polish people eat. How are you going to decide what the endings are? Of course, you might come up with some word for *to write*—who knows what it is; it might be *pisał*. But how are you going to decide what the ending is going to be for the first-person singular? Nobody decides that. There is reason to believe that when a language is created, nobody wants there to be endings for the first-person singular and the second person. I certainly wouldn't; that stuff is hard, especially when you're trying to teach it to somebody else. It happens by accident because of the grammaticalization of other things.

The clue is if we look at forms of "to be." For example, we have these here: "I am" is *jeśm*; and "you are" is *jes*; and then "we are" is *jesmy*; and then "you are" is *jeśće*, approximately. These are old Polish forms, so you Polish listeners and viewers don't worry that these seem incorrect; they would have been a long time ago when this grammaticalization happened. The similarity in shape is obvious and, in fact, where these past-tense endings in Polish came from was these forms of the verb "to be" glomming on to the end of what used to be just, approximately, *pisał*. They used to have this concrete meaning of *being*—just as *être/suis* did in French—and now they also serve as these appendages, and next thing you know, you've got a list of endings. So, a list of endings is not something that has to be; it's something that arises by accident because grammaticalization is always happening below the radar but creating new material in the language. Just as *-mente* can occur on one adjective but not the other one—which shows that it used to be a noun where you would not have to repeat the noun twice— you have these endings which can occur either on the verb or they can occur on some other part of the sentence, which shows that it used to be a free item. "Where have you been?" is *Gdzie byliscie?* That makes sense to us; "Where were you being?" So, "*gdzie*," *where*, and then "*byliscie*," *were you being*. But you can also say, "*Gdziescie byli?*" You can take the ending and put it on *where*. That just shows that there's still a certain amount of freedom; it used to be something free. Now it is part of these verb roots, and it indicates the past tense, but there's an extent to which it still has a little bit of independent spirit because it used to be a free item on its own. It means that in Polish there was a time when, to put a verb into the past, you would use this verb "to be." It would be kind of like saying, "I was write," if you were talking about writing. Now that means *I wrote*.

This is the way these sorts of things happen. Even in English, for example, our past-tense marker: It is likely that that past-tense marker that we spell *-ed* came from something which meant *did*. It used to be, "I walk did," which makes a certain sense because it had to come from somewhere. This did not happen in English itself. Already the endings are there in Old English, but when you look at other Germanic languages, you see something similar. In German, for example: "*Ich sage*," I say; "*Ich sagte*," I said. The word for *did* in that language is "*tat*", and so it seems as if something's going on. If you notice, there's a relationship between our [d] in our past ending and the [t] in German's. They are not just the fourth letter of the alphabet and the seventh one back from the end; [t] is a voiceless stop and [d] is a voiced stop. There's some relationship there, and it's thought that probably in the Proto-Germanic ancestors somewhere, the past ending originally began as something meaning *did* and ended up sticking on the end of verbs. That was a grammaticalization. Doing is a concrete concept in the beginning, but then it can be yanked into indicating something that's just grammatical that you wouldn't make up under a tree. It's just something that happens as the language moves along: One goes from concrete to the abstract.

Many of the things that we hear as noisome developments in English are just grammaticalization on the march. For example, "She's all, 'I don't know.' And then he's all, 'Well, give me a pencil.' Then she's all, 'Well, I want to watch *The Simpsons*.'" Many of us listen to that *all*, and we think somehow that's just wrong. But actually, that *all* is a grammaticalization. I am old enough to remember in about the '70s when people were using *all*. *All* was very literal; it was, "She's all, 'Well, get out of my face.' And he's all, 'Well I'm going downstairs.'" The *all* had a kind of exclamatory quality to it; it was about things that were remarkable. Now you can listen to teenagers using that *all* in a blank way to talk about people walking down the street, pulling a pencil out of a bag, looking at the sky; there's no emotion to it. Now it's what the Martian would just call a *quotative construction*. When you are talking about how people are doing things—what people are doing—and you're quoting them, there is a construction where you say, "He is all," "I was all." It doesn't have any kind of emotive effect; it's just a quotative construction. There are many in many languages; there are all sorts of ways to do it. English has developed this one with *all*. It looks like slang to us, but really that's just one more example of how what begins as something relatively concrete can become something which is highly abstract and grammatical. And that is how grammar is born.

# Lecture Fourteen
## Language Change from Old English to Now

**Scope:** The processes of language change that I have described in the previous three lectures are not mere abstractions but what made the difference between Old and modern English. In this lecture, we examine a passage of Old English and see how regular processes of change in sound pattern, how words are formed, and how these grammatical patterns changed a language into a new one, which we now speak.

## Outline

I. Languages tend to take words from other languages, often in large quantity as English did from the French of the Normans. It is less apparent that the pathway from Old English to modern English also involves precisely the kinds of language change that we have seen in the past three lectures.

A. Old English was not the "Olde Englishe" that features in parodies, with *thou, ye, wouldst fain*, and so on. That English is closer to Middle English, which began in about 1100.

B. Old English would be entirely incomprehensible to us spoken and virtually is on the page. It was much more like German than modern English is.

C. Consider a sample of Old English, with translation, from Bede's *Ecclesiastical History*, and you can see that we would not understand this if spoken, and we do not understand it on the page unless we have training.

> *Oft in gebeorscipe, þonne þær wæs blisse intinga gedemed,*
> often in banquet, then there was joyous occasion decided,
>
> *þonne se mon geseah þa hearpan him nealecan,*
> then the man saw the harp him approach,
>
> *þonne aras he for scome from þæm symble ond cwæð*
> then arose he for shame from the feast and said
>
> *"Ne con ic noht singan!" for þon ic naht singan ne cuðe.*
> not can I not sing for that I nothing sing not could.

> Bede, *Ecclesiastical History* (Book 4, chap. 24)

**D.** It took many things to bring us from the now-foreign language of Old English to the language that we speak today.

**II.** The sounds of the language changed.

**A.** Old English had a high front unrounded vowel like French's in *lune*: [y], as in *symble* ("feast"), and also a velar fricative: [x], indicated as h (*noht*).

**B.** There are cases where sounds that were just allophones of a phoneme in Old English—variations on a sound that happened only under certain conditions—are separate phonemes today.

**1.** In modern English, /ð/ is a phoneme but it is uncommon as the first sound in a word. Notice that the only words in which it comes first are these mostly "little" words: *the, this, that, these, those, they, then, there, then, thus, thence, though.*

**2.** This is a remnant of the fact that in Old English, [ð] was not a "real sound" yet. Rather, it was an allophone of /θ/ used only when /θ/ came between vowels, as we see in the word *cuðe* in the sample from Bede.

**3.** In Old English writing, the symbols for θ and ð were used interchangeably; neither meant exclusively [θ] or [ð].

**4.** Over time, words like *this* and *them* were used so often that the sound change process that weakens voiceless stops into voiced ones changed [θ] into [ð] at the beginning of those words—but only in heavily used words of this kind.

**5.** There is no regular rule anymore as to where [ð] appears instead of [θ]. For example, *this* [ðɪs] and *that* [ðæt] but *thick* [θɪk] and *thin* [θɪn]. [ð] is no longer a "kind of /θ/" but is its own sound.

**III.** How to make words, which is the territory of morphology, also changed.

**A.** Old English had many more affixes than modern English, marking case more exactly. This included forms of the definite article.

**1.** Note in the sample that the form is *se* in the nominative but *þa* in the accusative:

> *þonne se mon geseah þa hearpan him nealecan*
> then the man saw the harp him approach

**2.** The definite article was marked for three genders plus a plural, in five cases!

|  | masculine | feminine | neuter | plural |
|---|---|---|---|---|
| nominative | sē | sēo | þæt | þā |
| genitive | þæs | þǣre | þæs | þāra |
| dative | þǣm | þǣre | þǣm | þǣm |
| accusative | þone | þā | þæt | þā |
| instrumental | þȳ | þǣre | þȳ | |

**3.** This means that in terms of morphological typology of languages, Old English was even more fusional than English, in which the definite article has only two allomorphs, whose occurrence depends on sound rather than gender or number or case: *the* [ði] *apple*, *the* [ðə] *pear*. In Old English, *þǣm* conveyed the definite, the dative, and the masculine or neuter all at the same time.

**B.** *Nealecan* in the sample is an example of words developing through compounding: It is composed of the words for *near* (*neah*) and *rise* (*lǣcan*). This is like the Vietnamese example in Lecture Five, where the word for *begin* is composed of the words for *take* and *start*.

**IV.** Grammatical change from Old English to now has often been quite dramatic.

**A.** We see grammaticalization of the sort that we saw in Lecture Thirteen. Something that started in Old English as two words becomes one.

**1.** The negative construction in Old English had not grammaticalized as much as the word *not* has in modern English.

**2.** *Ne con ic noht singan* actually translated as "I can not sing nothing." *Noht* comes down in modern English as *naught*.

**3.** Over time, the *ne* dropped out, and only the *noht* remained. Now it was no longer a word with concrete meaning; it was a piece of grammar. Grammaticalization occurred from Old to modern English.

**B.** Old English usually kept verbs at the end of sentences. Its syntactic tree, then, was different from modern English's.

**C.** One thing that has happened to Old English syntax that has really turned it upside down and that is still debated by scholars of the subject today is called *do-support*.

    **1.** There is no use of *do* in questions and negative sentences in Old English along the lines of: *Do you sing? I don't sing.*

    **2.** We only start seeing this in Middle English documents, and it is familiar to us in Shakespeare's English, where it was also used in neutral affirmative sentences: "My pulse as yours **doth** temperately keep time" (*Hamlet* 3.4.147).

    **3.** However, *do* is not used this way this regularly in any other Germanic language, or even in most of the world's languages, except in the Celtic languages like Welsh and Cornish:

Welsh:

| Did I open? | *Nes i agor?* |
|---|---|
| I did *not* open. | *Nes i* ddim *agor.* |
| I opened. | *Nes i agor.* |

Cornish:

| *Mi a wra cara.* | *Gwra cara?* |
|---|---|
| I at do love | do-you love |
| "I love" | "Do you love?" |

    **4.** It is likely that English uses *do* in this way because Old English was learned by so many Celtic speakers.

**D.** The development from Old English to modern English included a great deal of *affixal loss*.

    **1.** Nouns were marked for case, such as *symble*, the bare form of which was *symbel*.

    **2.** Verbs still had an inflectional suffix in Old English, *-an*, and a participial prefix, *ge-*.

    **3.** English has lost more of this affixal machinery than any other Germanic language.

        **a.** This is likely because of contact with Norse invaders; the endings fell off most quickly where they settled.

        **b.** As late as the late 1800s, gender persisted in Cornwall in demonstratives, which had "personal" as well as "impersonal" forms: *theäse* as well as *this*; *thik* as well as *that*.

**Essential Reading:**

Bryson, *The Mother Tongue.*

Crystal, *The Cambridge Encyclopedia of the English Language.*

**Supplemental Reading:**

Baugh and Cable, *A History of the English Language.*

**Questions to Consider:**

1. A friend of mine once envied the Germans for having a language with so much less basic vocabulary than other languages, such that their word stock is "purer." Old English was much like this, while modern English's vocabulary is mostly French, Latin, and Old Norse in origin. In his translation of *Beowulf*, poet Seamus Heaney even translated some Old English compounds with English words in order to convey the archaic "feel" of the poem ("whale road" for "sea"). If you could wave a magic wand, would you prefer English to be the "melting pot" that it is or the more uniform, "Germanic" entity it once was?

2. Many students of linguistics find wrapping their heads around the concept of phoneme versus allophone the trickiest concept in the whole field. If you by chance have found this concept a bit of a challenge, then please review this outline (especially II.B) and the corresponding portion of this lecture. If you fully comprehend what happened to the sounds [θ] and [ð] from Old English to modern English, then whether you know it or not, you understand what a phoneme is!

# Lecture Fourteen—Transcript
# Language Change from Old English to Now

We all know that there was something called Old English, and we know that modern English is very different from it. But too often when Old English is discussed in terms of the development from Old English to modern English, what we hear about is just words. It's just all about words. We hear the Norman French ran England for a while, and they lent a lot of words to the language. Then there's a list of the words, and it's supposed to be so wonderful that there are all these words. Frankly, is that really that interesting? I mean, of course the French were there and so the French had some words, and so of course the people who were already in England started using some of their words. That's fine, but it's kind of listy, really. I want to show in this lecture that the development from Old English to modern English was about more than "Oh, look at this word." It's about the processes of language change that we've seen over these past few lectures happening from Old English to modern English, just as all languages are the product of these sorts of processes. This is to exemplify the sorts of things that we've been seeing and to see how, basically, one language can turn into another because of the slow movement of changes on the phonological level, on the morphological level, and on the syntactic level.

Just to be clear: Old English is not the kind of "Olde Englishe" of parodies with the "thou wouldst fain" and the "ye" and all of that; we're talking about something that is much more different. The "thou wouldst fain"—that is more like Middle English; that stage of English begins in about 1100. We're talking about Old English, which would have been completely incomprehensible to us and is a language very much like German. Let's look at a sample of Old English. No one knows exactly how Old English was pronounced. We can't be quite sure what the vowels were like; nobody was there to record it, and nobody ever will be. There are all sorts of questions. We can only approximate; nobody knows whether Old English was spoken with a cute lilt or whether it was spoken in a different way. I'm going to try my version; I don't know how it's going to come out.

This is a passage of Old English, and we're going to keep referring to this passage throughout the lecture. This is just a little scene from Bede's *Ecclesiastical History*: "*Oft in gebeorscipe*"—"often in a banquet"; "often during a feast"—"*Oft in gebeorscipe, þonne þær wæs blisse intinga gedemed.*" I don't know what accent this is, but somehow I'm just sliding into it; they may have sounded like this: "*þonne þær wæs blisse intinga gedemed*"—"then there was joyous occasion decided." Basically, everybody said, "Let's party": "*þonne þær wæs blisse intinga gedemed*." "*þonne se mon geseah þa hearpan him nealecan*"—"then the man saw the harp coming to him"; "the harp being given to him": "*þonne se mon*," "then the man"; "*geseah þa hearpan*," "saw the harp"; "*him nealecan*," "him approaching." "*þonne aras he for scome from þæm symble*"—"then arose he from shame from the feast"—"*þonne aras he for scome from þæm symble ond cwæð*"—"and said"—"'*Ne con ic noht singan!*'"—"'not can I not sing'"; "'I can't sing anything'": "'*Ne con ic noht singan!*'"; then, "*for þon ic naht singan ne cuðe*"—"because I couldn't sing anything."

That's a passage of Old English. It's this poor guy who doesn't happen to have musical talent, and they try to give him a harp. So he shouts out, with a rather quizzical urgency, "Oh dear, I can't sing. I don't have anything to sing for you." But that is this passage of Old English. What is that language? For one thing, you can see that it's not really English at all. This is something which we wouldn't understand spoken. We don't understand it on the page unless we have training. This is a different language altogether. Gradually, step by step over time, this English that we speak came along. What brought us from this foreign thing to the language that we speak today? It was a bunch of things.

One thing that happened was sound change. For example, Old English had some sounds that we no longer have in English. One thing that makes this language exotic to us, for example, is a word like *symble*. This is when he arose for shame from the feast, and so "*þonne aras he for scome from þæm symble*." *Symble* was the word for "feast." What it had is what we've seen before as a high front rounded vowel; and so it's the cute *lune* sound in French: *symble*. So it wasn't *soombul*; it was *symble*; that was the word for "feast." That was a different sound; we do not have that sound in English anymore, and so that's part of what gives Old English a different sound.

There was also a nice velar fricative ([x]); it's the sound in "Bach," except we English speakers are really more inclined to say, "Bock" because we don't have a—*cccch*—velar fricative. There was one in Old English, just as there is today in German. For example, "I can't sing anything"—"*Ne con ic noht singan*"—so [x] was still there. Today we see remnants in the spelling of what used to be velar fricatives in words like *night*—either night time or knights in shining armor—but we no longer have the sound. That was still present in Old English.

More to the point, in Old English we can see the development of new phonemes in modern English. An example of that is our friends, the interdental fricatives. We have our voiceless interdental fricative—[θ], as in *thin*—and then we have our voiced interdental fricative—[ð], as in *this*. Those are different phonemes in our language. In Old English, however—and this will help us to review and get across the notion of phoneme and allophone—in Old English, [ð] was only something that happened to /θ/ in a certain context. [ð] was an allophone of /θ/; there was a grand concept of θ-ness, so to speak. You could have [θ], and sometimes it would come out as [ð]. As you might predict, that happened—the voiced version happened—when this element came between vowels. Vowels have voices, and so /θ/, when it came between, say, two *o*'s," came out as [ð]. So [ð] was just a kind of /θ/ in Old English.

In the written language, the symbols for [θ] and [ð]—which are called "thorn" (þ) and "eth" (ð)—were used interchangeably. Nobody really cared; it was not highly codified. But in terms of the actual sound, [ð] was something that only happened in between vowels. Now, as time went by, something happened to [θ] in some other places. When [θ] came at the beginning of a word, because of rapid pronunciation and heavy use—when it came at the beginning of little, heavily-used words—it started being pronounced [ð]; this only happened on certain words. If you think about it, even in modern English, although /θ/ and /ð/ are separate phonemes today, [ð] only comes at the beginning of a certain small collection of mostly little words: *the*, *this*, *that*, *these*, *those*, *they*, *then*, *there*, *thus*, *thence*, *though*. If you think about it, if there was going to be a new word, it wouldn't begin with [ð]. Let's say that you saw a bird walk into your yard with three wings and it camouflages against anything that it walks past, so you can never see it, because if it's plaid, it looks like a bush, it looks like a person. So there's this weird bird. We have to give it a name, and let's say that the name is going to begin with what we spell as *th*. You might call it "Thaddeus" ([θadiʌs]), you might call it "Thocal" ([θokəl]), but you wouldn't call it "Thinkum" ([ðinkəm]) or "Thalley" ([ðali]); that would not feel like English. The [ð] sound is not really something that occurs at the beginning of a word, except in a very few. Nevertheless, that does mean that in the modern language, [ð] has become a real sound, because you can't predict. There are words like *this* and *that* where you have it at the beginning, but then there's *thick* and *thin* where you have the voiceless version coming at the beginning. Now they are completely different sounds. In Old English, [ð] was just something that happened to /θ/ in one particular context. We have developed a phoneme in our language. To an Old English speaker the, [ð] was not anything; it was just what happened when the /θ/ was in between two vowels.

That's some sound change from Old English to modern English. Then there's the issue of how to make words; there's the issue of Old English morphology. Old English had a lot more affixal morphology than modern English. Old English indicated grammatical gender—so not just biological gender as to whether something is a man or a woman or a rooster or a hen. But there were things allotted into grammatical genders rather arbitrarily, just like in French we have *le bateau* as if a boat is a man, and then *la lune*—the moon is a woman for some reason. This was a language where morphology was yoked to indicate that kind of thing much more than in English. Even with the word *the*, we can see that we're dealing with a very different language. Just as German has *der, die, das* for masculine, feminine, and neuter definite articles, in Old English things were very similar.

You can see (in the outline, III.A.2) that there was a masculine, a feminine, and a neuter definite article and then a whole different one—*þā*—for the plural. Then all of this changed according to whether we were in the genitive—that is, the possessive case, and so, "The boy's ball"—or the dative—and that indicates to-ness and so giving something to your grandmother, that's the dative—and the accusative, i.e., when something is an object. Then even in the instrumental, in terms of, "Fred Flintstone hit Barney with a hammer." That's the instrumental; I don't know why I thought of that. But here, you see that in terms of the morphological typology of languages—where we saw that there are analytic languages, where basically morphemes are separate, like say Vietnamese; and then agglutinative languages, like Swahili; fusional languages, like English; and polysynthetic languages, like, for example, Chinook—we saw that in a fusional language an ending can often mean two things. For example, the *-s* in the third-person singular in English means both third-person singular and present tense. Here, in Old English, we see that that kind of fusionality was much richer. For example, if we go back to our sentence with the feast— "*þonne aras he*"—"then arose he" or "he rose up"—"*for scome from þæm symble*"—the *þæm* is the word for *the*, but it's connoting, all at the same time, the definite, the dative, and the masculine or the neuter; all of that is on that one item. In Old English, we're dealing with heavy, heavy fusion of a type that, for example, our definite article in Modern English does not have. We just have [ðʌ] and we do have [ði]; technically, we do have two allomorphs of it: "the apple" ([ðiæpl]), that's before a vowel, and then "the peacock" ([ðʌpʰikak]) that's before a consonant. That is much less of a load than something like *þæm* in Old English.

We can see word building in Old English. For example, we have this word "*nealecan*." So the man saw the harp approaching him: "*þonne se mon geseah þa hearpan him nealecan*." Notice how if I keep saying it, you kind of start to understand it? At least I'm beginning to understand it. "*þonne se mon geseah þa hearpan him nealecan*": then the man saw the harp coming to him. *Nealecan* was actually originally a compound word: It was *neah*, which was *near*; and then there was *lǽcan*, which was *rise*. It "rose near"; so *nealecan* was a compound word. This is something that happens in all languages all the time—kind of like in the earlier lecture where in Vietnamese we saw how the word for *begin* is actually a compound of *take* and *start*. That's a process that is foreign to no language, and we see a bit of it here.

In Old English, we also see grammatical change. The grammatical change is often quite dramatic. For one thing, we see the grammaticalization of the sort that we saw in the previous lecture. When our man is pleading that he is incapable of singing a song, he uses two forms—actually two alternates of the negative. First, he says, "*Ne con ic noht singan*," "I can *noht singen*"; then, " *for þon*"—"because"—"*ic naht singan ne cuðe*." At first in Old English—although we don't see this stage, but we can presume that in an earlier stage of English, you could say just "*ne*." Your negative marker would have been, for example, "*Ic ne con singan*": "I can't sing." As it happens a lot in languages—something similar has happened in French with *pas*, which used to mean *step*—you emphasize the negation by putting something after. Now, *ne wiht* comes together, and you have this item *naht*; and so this now is the source of *naught* for one thing—it comes down to us as *naught*, but that's a rather rarified word—but more to the point, it ends up becoming what we now know as *not*. As time went by, the original *ne* eroded; and so we no longer have that *ne*, we just have the *naht*. For us, the word *not*—n, o, t—is our negator; that's how you do it. But to somebody who spoke an earlier form of English, that was just a kind of decoration that you added afterwards when you had used the original negator, which was the word *ne* that we no longer have. That is a grammaticalization.

Another thing that we see in terms of grammatical change is that Old English liked to keep verbs at the end of sentences. For example, in our first phrase here—"*Oft in gebeorscipe*"—"often during a banquet, then there was joyous occasion decided"—"*þonne þær wæs blisse intinga gedemed*." So here it is at the end. Or "Then the man saw the harp him approach": "*þonne se mon geseah þa hearpan him nealecan*"; here it is at the end. Or "because I couldn't sing anything": "*for þon ic naht singan ne cuðe*"; and so the *cuðe* is *could*, and that's at the end. That is something that is common in Germanic languages to some extent in all of those grammars; Old English used to be that way. That means that if we were going to make a syntactic tree for Old English, it would be quite different from the one for modern English; I would have introduced the phrase-structure rules in a completely different way. For us, the notion that a language would have its verbs at the ends—such as in Japanese, or even sometimes as in German—seems very counterintuitive and peculiar. To an Old English speaker, that was just the sort of thing that happened every day.

But there have been some things that have happened to Old English syntax that have really turned it upside down, and they are still debated by scholars of the subject today. One thing that you do not see here in our passage, and which does not exist in Old English, is something called *do-support*. What I mean by do-support is the way we use that peculiar little word *do* in contexts like "Do you sing?"; "I sing."; "Do you sing?" Of course, all of us say that a million times a day—use that construction a million times a day—but actually it's rather peculiar. "I sing." "Do you sing?" Think about any other language that you've learned. Did it have that? If anything you have to unlearn that; you have to unlearn that the way that you make a question is to stick *do* in. Or to negate a sentence: "I sing."; "I do not sing." What's the *do* doing in there? Shouldn't it be "I sing not"? What's wrong with that? That's the way it used to be in Old English, but for some reason, we have to say, "I do." What are you doing? Why do you have to put that in? That is something which linguists call do-support. One has to wonder, how did that start? Why is that there? We talked about grammaticalization, and so maybe there's this notion that because doing is doing, there's going to have to be this abstract contribution of the verb *to do* to every single negative and question in a sentence that we utter. Obviously, that is a very peculiar development.

The fact of the matter is we see it developing in Middle English documents; it's not in Old English documents. It's something familiar to us in Shakespeare's English, where it's used even in a context we don't use it in. It's used in the affirmative as well; in *Hamlet*, Gertrude says, "Alas, how is't with you, / That you do bend your eye on vacancy, / And with th' incorporal air do hold discourse?" Then Hamlet answers, and he uses it in an affirmative sentence: "My pulse as yours doth temperately keep time, / And makes as healthful music."

These are these *do*'s. It becomes very well established; eventually; you have to use *do* when you are negating a sentence and when you are questioning a sentence. It's very odd; even most linguists don't realize how odd this is. But you think, "It's just a grammaticalization." But where else has that happened? I personally am aware of that kind of usage of *do* in exactly three places. One is that there's a language where *be* is used in a similar way. It's not obligatory, but it's similar. It's a language called Nanai—it's spoken by about two-and-a-half people in Siberia—and that's one of 6,000 languages. You look all over the place, and you just find these people kind of herding their yaks in this one place, so it's extremely rare. They're not even doing it with the verb *to do*; they're doing it with *to be*. Then there are a couple of dialects, spoken by about four-and-a-half people, of Italian, way up in the mountains. These are nonstandard dialects of Italian where only in questions—not in the negative and not in the affirmative—only in questions, they use *do* in this way. For the record, this is documented particularly in the Monese dialect of Italian; only there.

Other than that, you can go all over the world—imagine yourself in a little plane (I don't know why it's little), and you're flying all over the world—all the languages people speak (Japanese, and Tagalog, and Klingon, and Pig Latin, and everything that people are speaking), there's nothing like this *do*. There are things that are kind of like it, but nothing just like this, except in one place—the third place. That is the Celtic languages that are also spoken in Great Britain—or have been—alongside English. Welsh is a Celtic language; it's in the Celtic family of Indo-European. Cornish is no longer natively spoken, but that was a closely related Celtic language spoken there before people who spoke early English came to the island. In these languages, you have something that is very much like the way do-support works in English. For example, here in Welsh we have, "I opened." The way you say it is with the *do* verb: *Nes*; so "*Nes i agor?*" *Did I open?* uses their *do* verb. *I did not open* uses a *do* verb. In Welsh, it's not obligatory; nevertheless, the way they do it is exactly the way it was done, for example, in Shakespeare's time.

Then in Cornish—Cornish is now dead. There's a revival movement, but in terms of somebody being spoken Cornish to in the cradle and learning it as their main language, that is a thing of the past. But we have ample documentation of it; there was something very similar. You would use your do verb—and it was optional, but very commonly used—to say, "I love" and you would use your *do* verb to make it into a question. Only places in the world where it's this similar to what goes on English—only languages on Earth—and they were present on the island when English was brought to the island.

Nevertheless, there is this whole industry of describing how do-support arose in English, where supposedly it just happened by itself. The fact that the only languages in the world that do it very much like English were spoken on that very island—and the island is like the size of a parking lot; these people were jammed together—that they happened to be there, somehow that's irrelevant. It's just an accident or, I swear to God, for many of them, it somehow is not interesting. They're more interested in saying, "*Do* would have happened through this series, and here we see in these documents …" and they just kind of go on and on and on. Somebody will point out—and that somebody might be me—did you ever notice that Welsh and Cornish have the exact same thing and that they actually were there? If you look in early documents about how [England] was run, it's clear that there were many Celts hanging around permeating society and people were marrying Celts. Don't you think that there's some kind of causal relationship? People just say, "Well, maybe." That really won't do. I think the case is painfully clear, and there are more and more linguists who are thinking in the way that I do. I didn't even start this; I joined them. There is what's called a *Celtic Hypothesis* and, I'm sorry, it's correct. The reason that English has this do-support is because it was learned as a second language by millions and billions of people whose languages had do-support a long time ago. This was not happening in written documentation in Old English because it was considered nonstandard. It starts appearing in documentation, almost ominously suddenly, in Middle English. One of our syntactic changes was a result of contact with other languages. That is as important in how a language changes as anything else.

Finally, one thing that we see in the development from Old English to modern English is just an awful lot of loss of affixation. For example, we saw how the definite article is a much less complex business in the modern language than it was in the earlier language. In general, you had case marking on nouns in Old English. So our word for "feast," *symble*, the actual word is *symbel*. Our form, *symble*, is a case marker. That's actually a dative case marker; *þæm symble*, and so *þæm* is our dative definite article. There was an inflectional suffix. We say, "sing"; they said, "*singan*." We say, "to sing" to replace that, in a sense. They had *singan*, just like in German you would say, "*singen*." Just like in the typical European language, you have an infinitive ending. English, mysteriously, does not have one. You had the participial prefix, *ge-*, and so "*Oft in gebeorscipe*"—

"often during banquets, then there was joyous occasion decided"—"*þær wæs blisse intinga gedemed*": *ge-*. That has become our word *deemed*; we don't have to *ge-* any more. Off goes the affix.

That has happened to such an extent in English that it's rather peculiar. Germanic is a relatively compact group; it consists of Icelandic, Faroese, Swedish, Norwegian, Danish, Dutch, Frisian, German, Yiddish, English, Afrikaans. It's a relatively compact group, and it's interesting that only English has lost that much affixation. Something very peculiar happened in the history of the English language it seems. There are some people who seem to think that this was just an accident, but I think that they lack imagination. It seems that in the history of English, something peculiar happened that left it a language strangely denuded of what the typical Germanic language has. If you learn German, you have to master three grammatical genders; you have to deal with many words varying according to whether they are a nominative, accusative, dative, or genitive. Suddenly, in English, you don't.

It was the Vikings. The Vikings invaded Great Britain starting in 787 according to most documentation. They were Danes; they were what we would now call Norwegians. They invaded; they married into society. Certainly, they learned Old English. There were a great many of them; their invasion shows up vibrantly in the genetic blueprint of Britons today. It seems clear that they learned a kind of schoolboy Old English. They got things across, but they ended up doing the sorts of things to the language that all of us do to a language when we're learning it in a classroom. There were so many of them, and so many of them were daddies, exposing their children to their way of speaking English, that that way of speaking English affected what English actually was throughout the island.

That this happened seems especially clear in that the Vikings settled mostly in what, if you look on the map, is northeasterly of the line, the "Dane Law" line. The agreement was that they would run things up there and everybody would be left alone on the other side of the line. That is where the endings start falling away most quickly. Whereas down in the southwest, old-fashioned things—the sorts of things that you expect English to have as a good card-carrying Germanic language—persist as late as 1886; that's when the book came out (*A Glossary of the Dorset Dialect* by William Barnes). We're talking about when there were presidents like Grover Cleveland and Benjamin Harrison and there was electricity—a relatively modern era, except that it wasn't. Way down in Cornwall in the southwest, you still had some indication of grammatical gender.

For example, in as late as the late 19th century, in the English of Cornwall, if you were talking about something that's inanimate like a rock or a blanket or a hangnail or something like that, then you would talk about "this blanket" or "that blanket." But if you were talking about something that you could call personal—and that is usually animate things, but also things that are dear to you; for some reason it was, with them, tools, or, I presume, if it were Linus, it would be his blanket—then you would say, "*theäse*" for *this* and you would say, "*thik*" for *that*. You had a different gender; so *theäse dog thik cat*. That still persisted down there where Vikings had never settled.

Old English to modern English was a very dynamic process. We've seen how the things that we have seen in the previous lectures, as well as some that we have seen less of that are equally important, have made the difference between then and now.

# Lecture Fifteen
## What Is an Impossible Language?

**Scope:** There are various features in a language that are only present if another type of feature is, and features often occur in chains of this kind: Some features are "core" to the essence of a language, while others are more optional and occur only when the core ones do. This is a distinction known as markedness, and it also shapes which features occur together in a language over time.

## Outline

I.  While there is a great deal of diversity in structures among the world's languages, the diversity is not a simple matter of "anything goes."

   **A.** There are strong tendencies in how languages are configured. Certain features in a language only occur if others ones have.

   **B.** In this lecture, we explore the concept of *markedness*, which refers to things that are present in only a subset of the languages of the world and then only if certain other things have already happened to the language.

   **1.** We see what are called *implicational hierarchies* or *markedness hierarchies*.

   **2.** Markedness hierarchies will be important in understanding topics of later lectures, such as how language is learned.

   **3.** Markedness hierarchies will seem familiar from the world of syntactic Parameters that we saw in Lecture Eight; what is new is that the concept of nestedness goes far beyond those particular hypothesized, syntactic Parameters.

II. Some language universals do not involve nested hierarchies.

   **A.** Almost all languages have at least /a/, /i/, and /u/ vowels; about half have /a/, /e/, /i/, /o/, and /u/.

   **B.** Most of the world's languages place the subject before the object.

   **1.** This can occur in various permutations of subject, verb, and object, such as Japanese's SOV, English's SVO, and Welsh's VSO.

   **2.** Languages that place the object before the subject are more rare, with OVS especially rare, as in the Amazonian language of Hixkaryana.

**III.** However, universals often manifest themselves in nested hierarchies, where they are known as *implicational universals*.

    **A.** For example, all languages have stops, usually /p/, /t/, and /k/. The other kinds of consonant *imply* the presence of stops, i.e., occur only if there are also stops, although there can be stops without the occurrence of these other sounds.

        **1.** If there are fricatives, there are also stops.

        **2.** If there are affricates, there are also fricatives.

        **3.** Hawaiian, for example, has very few consonant sounds, but they include stops:

|  | bilabial | alveolar | velar | glottal |
|---|---|---|---|---|
| voiceless stops | p |  | k | ʔ |
| voiceless fricative |  |  |  | h |
| nasals | m | n |  |  |
| lateral liquid |  | l |  |  |
| glides | w |  |  |  |

    **B.** Consonants therefore occur in languages in a markedness hierarchy. Fricatives are more *marked* than stops; for example, a uvular fricative like the *r* in French ([ʁ]) is more *marked* than a voiceless alveolar fricative ([s]).

**IV.** There are also markedness hierarchies in morphology.

    **A.** Morphology includes two kinds of affix.

        **1.** *Derivational* ones change a root into a new word entirely: *happy, happiness*.

        **2.** *Inflectional* ones merely modify a root in a way relating to grammatical "traffic rules" but do not create a "new word": *pig, pigs*.

    **B.** Often, derivational affixes change the part of speech: *Happy* is an adjective; *happiness* is a noun. This is not always the case, however: *Do* and *redo* are both verbs.

    **C.** Inflectional affixes imply derivational ones.

        **1.** There are languages with neither, such as Lahu, an analytic language spoken in parts of Southeast Asia; there, an expression for *mislead* is to use the verb for "lead" and then the word for "fault."

2. There are languages with only derivational affixes, such as Fongbe, spoken in West Africa, which distinguishes "singer" from "sing" but lacks inflectional affixes such as plurals or past tense.

3. There are languages, like English (fusional) or Turkish (agglutinative), with both kinds of affixes.

4. But there are no languages with only inflectional affixes. Inflectional affixes are more *marked* than derivational ones and occur within a nested hierarchy in which derivational affixes are higher.

**D.** Marking of number also happens, though in ways less familiar from English.

1. The plural is not the only way that languages mark that there is more than one of something. Many languages can also mark the *dual*—that there are only two of something.

2. However, the dual is more marked than the plural. A language that marks the dual also marks the plural.

3. The dual in Kharia, spoken in eastern India, is typical in being marked on (or along with) the plural, rather than by itself as the plural can occur. The plural for "cats" is *biloi-ki*; the dual for "two cats" is *biloi-ki-yar*.

4. Very often, the dual only occurs with pronouns or is marked only on a small collection of nouns. For example, in Hebrew there are dual forms only of certain nouns that often occur in pairs, such as body parts, as well as some units of time, such as days or years, but not for the vast majority of nouns. It is very common that the dual is slightly impoverished compared to the plural because the dual is more marked than the plural.

**V.** There are also markedness hierarchies in syntax. These differ from the ways we discussed Parameters. There is a hierarchy of how a language handles its complement phrases, called the *relativization hierarchy*.

**A.** In English, one can relativize subjects, objects, indirect objects, and beyond (a grab-bag category called *oblique*).

**B.** However, languages vary in this, and in an implicational way. Some languages can only relativize the subject, as in the Sumatran language Toba Batak.

**C.** There are none that can relativize the object but not the subject; those that can relativize the indirect object can also relativize the subject and object, and so on. Relativization is manifested in an implicational hierarchy, in which relativizing the oblique is the most marked:

subject < direct object < indirect object < oblique

**VI.** Markedness hierarchies constrain how language can change over time.

**A.** Joseph Greenberg (1915–2001) demonstrated a certain implicational hierarchy involving word order: If a language places its verb before the subject (as in Welsh, a VSO language), then it also places nouns before adjectives, places nouns before genitives (that is, possessives), and has prepositions rather than postpositions.

**1.** In other words, it is a Head-First language: a language where you will say, "cat black" rather than "black cat" and "crown of Gold" (noun-genitive), rather than "Gold's crown" (genitive-noun).

**2.** If a language places its verb at the end (SOV), then all of these things are opposite.

**B.** Greenberg noticed something off among the languages of Ethiopia. Some of them, like the ancestral Ge'ez, behaved like a "proper" VSO language. Also, Harari, an SOV language, was a proper example of the other order.

**C.** But there are also Ethiopian languages that depart from the template. Amharic is SOV but "slips" in having prepositions.

**D.** Interestingly, there is no language with postpositions but still with noun-genitive order. It would appear that these languages shift to the ideal SOV template in an implicational fashion. Supporting this is that it is possible, although not required, to express postpositions in Amharic.

**E.** The basic concept of markedness and implicational hierarchies will occur elsewhere in the course and is a fundamental insight into how language is structured and evolves. (The subfield investigating the tendency for languages to hone to certain types where features tend to cluster together is called *typology*.)

**Essential Reading:**

Comrie, *Language Universals*.

**Supplemental Reading:**

Croft, *Typology and Universals*.

**Questions to Consider:**

1. Some languages contain massive numbers of marked features: They have huge sound inventories; they have markers for concepts like dual and other ones that only occur if less marked markers occur as well; they exhibit mixed word orders. Some languages are less marked in the general sense. Is a language with ample markedness "more of a language" than one with less? Recall that it used to be thought that Latin and Greek were the "best" languages for reasons like this. What's your take on that view today?

2. As word-order correlations go, English is, in fact, somewhat off-pattern, i.e., marked. Based on the discussion of Ethiopian languages, identify what is "off" about English's word-order patterns.

# Lecture Fifteen—Transcript
# What Is an Impossible Language?

We've been looking at the way language changes over time, and we've seen that it can be quite stunning: how different a language can look at point B, as opposed to how it looked at point A. However, there are constraints on the process. There are ways that a language can change; then there are ways that a language does not change. There are things that do not happen. Language change is constrained in a particular way. What it's constrained by, to a large extent, is something called *markedness*. We're going to examine markedness in this lecture.

What I mean by that is that there are some things which are quite ordinary, present in virtually all the languages of the world. Then there are some that are present in only a subset of the languages of the world, and then only if certain other things have already happened to the language. There is the universal—or the almost universal—and then the more particular, which is highly contingent on what had happened before. We see what are called *implicational hierarchies* or *markedness hierarchies*, and it's important to understand them, because markedness hierarchies are also important in how language is learned—as well as some other processes—in what is considered to be the field of linguistics. But particularly in terms of how languages change and how languages are learned, markedness is an important concept. It'll seem familiar from the world of syntactic Parameters that we saw in Lecture Eight: That basic concept of implication—that basic concept of nestedness—is something that goes far beyond those particular hypothesized, syntactic Parameters. That's what we're going to look at in this lecture.

What do I mean by *language universals*? One thing that I mean by language universals is something like this: There are 6,000 languages in the world; almost all languages have the vowels /a/, /i/, /u/. There are languages that have a great many more vowels than that; there are languages that don't have many vowels at all; but almost all of them have /i/, /u/, /a/. About half have /a/, /e/, /i/, /o/, /u/, among others. But with about half, you have that classic set. There are plenty of languages that really do just make do with /a/, /i/, /u/. One of them, actually, is classical Arabic. That is why sometimes, for example, in the spelling of Osama bin Laden's name, you'll see his name spelled "Usama" and you'll see it spelled "bin Ladin," where you have this *u* substituting for the *o*, and the *i* substituting for the *e* that we often see. That's because in the classical language it would be "Usama," because the classical language vowel system does not properly have /e/ and /o/. Or, in terms that we now know, it doesn't have mid vowels. The fact of the matter is that in practice, in actual spoken Arabic, allophonically—in terms of what vowels are surrounded by—you might get mid vowels. Also, Arabic is actually a cover term for what is possibly even two dozen different languages. Moroccan Arabic and the Arabic spoken by Palestinians are really completely different languages, just like French and Spanish. In the different Arabic varieties—they're called dialects, but really, like the Chinese varieties, they're separate languages—there certainly are mid vowels. But in the classical language there wasn't, because classical Arabic happened to be one of those languages with a very compact set of vowels.

Or most of the world's languages—this is something that is very typical—put the subject before the object. There are different ways of doing that, but the vast preference is for putting the subject before the object. You can do that in various ways. *Taroo bought a book* in Japanese is "*Taroo ga hon o katta*." The subject is before the object—the verb is at the end—but just like in our SVO (subject, verb, object) language, the subject is before the object. Or there are languages that are verb, subject, object. Even there, however, the subject is before the object. Welsh is a language like this, and it may seem peculiar to us in putting the verb up front. Here is a Welsh sentence: *The dragon killed the man*: "*Lladdodd y ddraig y dyn*." We see that it's *killed the dragon the man*. Still, as peculiar as that looks to us, the subject is still before the object.

A language that places the object before the subject is much rarer; languages seem to resist that happening. That is very much an anti-universal. In fact, until not very long ago, it was thought that that kind of language was completely impossible; there was no such thing as putting the object before the subject. It was actually only discovered in a chance way. An Englishman who just worked a rather gray desk job—his name was Desmond Derbyshire—was visiting the Guyanese jungle, and he got lost. He got lost enough that the Sun went down, and he spent the night lost in the jungle. I swear this is the story: He sat down on a log, and he thought to himself, "If I come out of this alive—if I do not starve to death or get eaten by something—I will devote the rest of my life to the service of God." Wouldn't you know, the next morning he was discovered by a tribe, and they took care of him and they got him back to the road. He actually followed through: He joined the Summer Institute of Linguistics, which actually operates year round and is a missionary organization to indigenous groups, trying to convert them to Christianity and using their languages as one of the conduits. The language that he ended up studying was an Amazonian language called Hixkaryana. Hixkaryana, of all things, is actually a language with the word order object, verb, subject. You can see in this sentence for *The boy caught a fish*, the way they say it in Hixkaryana is *Fish caught boy* ("*Kana yanɨmno bɨryekomo*"). Really what this is is a head-final language. The verb comes at the end of the VP—O, V—and then you have the S, the subject, appended. But this is a language where the subject placement is different. As a matter of fact, it's been thought that subject placement might be a Parameter. In this case, one of them is very much default. The unmarked case is the subject coming before the object.

In general, universals often manifest themselves in this kind of nested hierarchy, and this is beyond syntax. For example, all languages have stops. Usually, there is /p/, /t/, /k/; that's your standard, basic kit. Other kinds of consonants imply the presence of stops; that is, they only occur if there are stops, although there can be stops without any other kind of consonants. If they're fricatives, then there are stops. If they're affricates—like [tʃ]—then there are definitely fricatives. For example, look at Hawaiian's consonant grid here: [p], [k], [ʔ], [h], [m], [n], [l], [w]. Hawaiian actually has very few phonemes. It is typical of Polynesian languages, which often have fewer phonemes than we can even imagine. That's just typical of their group. You can see here that it has very few consonants. One thing it does have, however, is stops. There's no such thing as a language with this hypothetical consonant grid, where what you have is a nice line of fricatives and a scattering of other things, but there are no stops. No language is like that. Stops are the beginning; stops are the unmarked case. Fricatives are more marked than stops. A uvular fricative like [ʁ] in French is more marked than an ordinary vanilla voiceless alveolar like [s]. There's a markedness hierarchy. Sounds don't just occur willy-nilly. There are some sounds that are very basic and others that are more optional. They are either rarer or they only occur if your more basic sounds are there. Sounds occur in a markedness hierarchy. This is something that's not only typical of sounds, but you can see it in morphology as well.

Now a little terminology here: There are two kinds of affix. There is what's called a *derivational affix*, and there is what's called an *inflectional affix*. This is the difference: Derivational affixes are the ones that create a whole new word. *Happy*: That's one word. *Happiness*: Nobody would say that *happiness* and *happy* are the same word. There's clearly the relationship, but this *-ness* created a whole different word. Inflectional affixes just change things in terms of grammatical traffic rules, and they don't create what you would think of as a new word to the same extent. There's *pig*, and then there's *pigs*. *Pig* and *pigs* can be thought of as the same word; *pigs* is the plural form of *pig*. You don't think of *happiness* as the *-ness* form of *happy*; you think of it as a separate word. One rule of thumb in order to think about the difference is that derivational affixes, as often as not, change a word's part of speech; and so *happy* is an adjective, *happiness* is a noun. That's not always the case, because *do* is a verb and *redo* is still a verb, yet *redo* is a different word from *do*, and so *re-* is a derivational affix. But it's a good rule of thumb: The derivational affixes are the ones that create a new word, often changing the part of speech. Inflectional affixes are ones that are just fitting the word into the grammar: making it plural, making it past, or something like that. In terms of a markedness hierarchy, inflectional affixes imply derivational ones. That means there are languages that don't have any affixes at all. We've seen these: the analytic languages or isolating languages.

Here is one called Lahu. Lahu is spoken in parts of China and Burma, Laos, and also Thailand. Lahu is a very analytic, isolating language. If you *lead* somebody, you've done one thing; if you *mislead* somebody, well, in English we have a derivational affix, *mis-*. Obviously, *mislead* and *lead* are separate words. *Mis-* is a derivational affix. Lahu just doesn't have anything of that kind, and so *to mislead* is to use the verb for *lead* and then to use the word for *fault*. You end up with this compound, and that's how they express *mislead*. There are languages like that. Then there are also languages that have derivational affixes only. They don't have the inflections. For example, Fongbe is a language spoken in Togo and Benin on the west coast of Africa, and as a matter of fact, many slaves were taken from that area. You can find remnants of Fongbe still spoken among dark-skinned populations in Brazil today; it's interesting. But in the language, as it is spoken in full in Togo and Benin, you can see in this sentence [*Túkpén àtón hù xódó-tó*] that you do have a derivational affix; for example, *-er* in *singer*. There's the word *sing*, and there's the word *singer*—that's a different word; *-er* is a derivational affix that connotes what we call *agentivity*. You have this: *xódó-tó*; the *-tó* is a derivational affix meaning *singer*. But you can also see in this sentence that there are no inflections. For example, there is no plural marker on the word *bullets*: "Three bullets killed the singer." But what Fongbe actually has is *bullet three*. Note also that you say, "Three bullets killed the singer." You don't have any past tense affix, and that would be another inflection. Fongbe has affixation, but it only has derivational affixation.

Then, of course, there are languages like—for example—ours, where you have both kinds of affixes: You have the derivational affixes and the inflectional affixes. We would say in English *work-er-s*, and the *-er* is derivational and the *-s* is inflectional. In Turkish, that would be [iʃ-tʃi-ler]. Turkish is a nice, agglutinative language, and so you have the morphemes nicely distinguished. That's derivational and inflectional. But the fact of the matter is that there's no such thing as a language that only has inflectional affixes but no derivational affixes. Before you have inflectional affixes, you have to have derivational ones. In terms of how a language develops through time, the derivational ones are the ones that are going to come first. That's how language moves along.

We might go back to that old movie analogy where the root here is the *All About Eve*, the inflection is the *Fog Over Frisco*, and then the derivation is the *Now, Voyager*. If you've seen *Fog Over Frisco*, you have seen *Now, Voyager*. If you have seen *Now, Voyager*, you might not have seen *Fog Over Frisco*, and you probably haven't. That is, if you've seen *Now, Voyager*, you might not have any inflections. There is a markedness relationship here. Inflectional affixes are more marked than derivational ones, and they occur within a nested hierarchy in which derivational affixes are higher.

This also happens with the marking of number in ways that are less familiar from English. The plural isn't the only way that you can mark number. There are many languages—many, many languages—in the world where there's also a particular way to mark if there's exactly two of something, and that's called the *dual*. But the dual, as you might guess being an English speaker because it sounds so peculiar, is more marked than the plural. For example, if a language marks the dual, it also marks the plural. There's no such thing as a language that can mark that there's two of something but then doesn't care if there's more than that.

For example, this is the Kharia language, which is spoken in eastern India. When they're talking about cats in Kharia land, a *cat* is a *biloi*, and then the plural—*cats*—is *biloi-ki*. If that musical played there, it would be called *Biloi-ki*; never mind. Then, if you have a dual, then you have this marker *-yar*, and so it would be *biloi-ki-yar*. Notice that the dual is marked on the plural, which is one indication that the dual is a stage that comes after the plural. It's more marked; it's something that happens less in a language, and when it does happen in a language, it's often parasitic, to an extent, on the plural. You can't say in Kharia, "*biloi-yar*." It's kind of like you're saying, "cats two." That's how they mark the dual; so the plural still has the juice.

Another thing about the dual is that when a language has the dual, often it only uses the dual with a small set of nouns, so you can't talk about there being two of everything with an ending. For example, in Hebrew the *day* is *yom*, like Yom Kippur. *Days* is *yomim*; that's one of the plural affixes in Hebrew: -*im*. You can say, "a couple of days": *yomayim*; it's a nice thing about Hebrew that you can do that. But you can only do that with some things: You can do it with body parts that happen to come in two; you can do it with some times such as years and things like that; but you can't just do it with anything. A cat is a *khatul*; that's the word for *cat*. If you want to talk about *cats*, it's *khatulim*; that's plural for *cats*. There's no such thing as *khatulayim*; there is no dual for *cats*. There is no way of saying, "Oh, look, two Sylvesters." You just have to say, "two cats," like in what we think of as any normal language; that is, the plural can be applied to anything; you can talk about several anything in Hebrew. But in terms of having an ending to mark that it's two, in Hebrew that's only with certain words. That is very common in languages: that the dual is slightly impoverished compared to the plural. That's because the dual is more marked. Often, you'll only get it with some pronouns and things like that; so that's how that works.

This is something that you can also see in terms of syntax, but in ways different from the way we discussed Parameters. You can see something like what's called the *relativization hierarchy*. This is how a language handles its complement phrases, as we saw in an earlier lecture. What I mean by relativization is how can you handle the subject, or the object, or something else of a relative clause? When you front it and you leave a gap, is that grammatical or not? For example, look here: We can say, "The man that left the house." Now, who left the house is *the man*; **the man** *left the house*. That is relativizing a subject: **The man that** *left the house*. We can also relativize an object, though. If I say, "The book that I read," what I read was *the book*. *The book* has been put up front, and so we relativize the object. We can also relativize the indirect object, and so, "The woman that I sent the report to." To who? *The woman*. *The woman* has been put up front, and we've got a trace there at the end, so: **The woman that** *I sent the report to*.

We can also do it with other prepositions, and we can call this the *oblique*. That is often used to indicate a kind of grab-bag category, once you've gotten beyond subject, object, and indirect object. And so the oblique: **The** *person* that I went to the party *with*. You can feel it, that, underlyingly, the person—underlyingly—*the person* that I went to the party *with*: that person. You went with that person, and so it's been fronted: *The person that I went to the party with*. That is not the way it goes in all languages, that you can relativize subjects, objects, indirect objects, and obliques. English is actually pretty loosey-goosey in this. Also, I know that for the indirect object for some people it's not *The woman that I sent the report to*, but *The woman to whom I sent the report*. I know you can say that; well, I said that. Anyway, English is loosey-goosey in this way. There are many languages that are much less permissive about it.

For example, this is the Toba Batak language, and it is spoken in Sumatra, that big beautiful island that is in Southeast Asia, except it's in the water because it's an island. In Toba Batak, you can only relativize the subject. *The woman who is washing the clothes*; you can take woman—*boru-boru*—and put that up front: *The woman who is washing the clothes*. But if you want to say, "The clothes that the woman is washing," you have to use a different construction. You cannot just take *clothes* and put it up front. In Toba Batak, you can only relativize the subject.

What's important is there is no language that can only relativize the object but not the subject. They can only relativize the indirect object and say, "The woman to whom I was speaking," but not the subject or the object. Or it can do that and the subject but not the object. It's implicational. There are languages that can relativize the subject and the object, and then stop at the indirect object. There are languages that can do subject, object, indirect object; but you couldn't say, "The man who I went to the party with." This is a nested hierarchy. The oblique is the most marked locus here; the subject is the least marked.

When I say that this issue of markedness is one that has to do with how language changes, what I mean is that what a language does, in terms of what new constructions arise or how constructions change, is constrained by these issues of what is most normal, what is least normal, what things go together, and what things do not. For example, you can see this in the languages of Ethiopia. The languages of Ethiopia that I'm talking about are Semitic languages. Semitic is a subfamily, technically, of a larger family, but, we'll call it—in shorthand—a family of languages. Its shop-window representatives, these days, are Arabic and Hebrew. There are others, of course. One of them is Amharic, which is the main language of Ethiopia. It might seem almost counterintuitive culturally that the language that is spoken in Tel Aviv is very closely related to the language that is spoken across the Red Sea in Addis Ababa, but it very much is. There is more than one Semitic language in Ethiopia. Amharic is the one that has the most influence, but there is also Tigrinya, Tigre, and there are a group of languages called the Gurage languages, which kind of teeter between being different languages and different dialects. All of these are descended from a single Proto-Semitic root.

It's interesting how they have been changing. Joseph Greenberg was a linguist who did a great deal to uncover these markedness hierarchies. He spent most of his career at Stanford, and he is most famous, actually, for his classification of the languages of Africa into four families, which was a massive undertaking. Also, he's famous for his proposition of a Proto-World first language based on reconstructing from roots and languages around the world, which is very controversial but a very ambitious idea. He demonstrated something involving word order: He showed that if a language is one where it places its verb before the subject, and so that's a language like Welsh—you can look at this sentence from Welsh again about the dragon; the verb comes first—then there is an implication: If it places the verb before, then it also puts nouns before adjectives, it puts nouns before genitives, and it has prepositions rather than postpositions. What those three things meant is it's a Head-First language. It's a language where you will say, "cat black" rather than "black cat." You will say, "crown of Gold"—noun-genitive—rather than "Gold's crown." You will have prepositions.

If a language is SOV, Greenberg noticed, then all of those things are opposite; it will be completely different. Now you might be thinking about Head-First and the fact that in English the nouns actually come at the end. Think about a Romance language in order to actually have a sense of what sort of language we're thinking about in terms of Head-First. You will have "a black cat": In Spanish, it's "*un gato negro*"; that's the way it would be. If you are going to talk about, in French, "skin of silk," then you would say, "*peau*," "skin"; "*de soie*," "of silk," and your genitive is after. I happen to have kind of soft skin on the back of my hands. I remember one time in college, one of the most annoying things was that this woman was caressing my hand and saying, "Oh, he has *peau de soie*" (she was speaking French). But then she ended up dating my roommate instead of me. Anyway: *peau de soie*.

Greenberg noticed something about the languages of Ethiopia. The ancestral language—Semitic language—in Ethiopia is called Ge'ez. In documents of Ge'ez, he noticed that Ge'ez—the kind of a Latin of

Ethiopia—was a nice, well-behaved Ethiopian Semitic language. It has its verb coming before the subject, and it does have noun-adjective. It has noun-genitive. We can see the "crown of Gold" is *ʔäklil zä wärq*, and that's how it goes. It is a language with prepositions, as you can see, because "of Gold" is *zä wärq*, and *zä* is a *pre*-position. Then, on the other hand, he saw that in Harari—which is another one of these languages, and it's SOV—you do have the opposite. You have adjective-noun, and so you have "big market," not "market big." You have genitive-noun, and so you say, "of the boy house," to say, "the boy's house," just like we can in English, instead of saying, "the house of the boy." You have "with me," and the way you say that is by putting *with* afterwards; so the word for *with* is *be*; "with me" is *a:n-be*. That's the way it's supposed to be; you look around the world, and those are the correlations.

The problem is Amharic, itself, does not behave. Amharic is SOV like Harari: It has the adjective-noun and it has the genitive-noun, but the problem is it has prepositions. It's kind of not doing it right. It's got the nice genitive-noun—"of me house," instead of "house of me"—but then it just has *bä bet* for "in the house." That's not the way it's supposed to be; if it's SOV, then you're supposed to have this general correlation that you see worldwide where it has postpositions (and recall that Japanese has postpositions). Amharic, for some reason, has prepositions.

That looked like a hair out of place, but Greenberg thought maybe it's a matter of Amharic being an intermediate step between the development from an early Ethio-Semitic language—that's what he called them—language like Ge'ez with its VSO, and then a perfect SOV language like Harari. His idea was that maybe these languages can be put on a scale, and the way they change is constrained by this markedness hierarchy. He predicted that if that were true, then there must be signs in Amharic that it's trying to be like Harari, that it wants to be maximally unmarked in terms of these correlations. I remember, not too long before he died—well, actually, it was a long time before he died; it was just the last time that I saw him because I took a class from him. Greenberg—at this point, he was very, very old—he talked about how he had been frustrated by this lack of correlation in Amharic, and he talked like this, and he was saying, "I was just looking for something that would make it more like Harari." He still spoke with great joy about finding that it is possible in Amharic to say, "*bä bet wəst*"—to say, "in the house"— where the *wəst* is a postposition. He found in that and other cases that there is evidence that Amharic wants to be a language where everything is correlating perfectly in terms of what a good VSO language does and what a good SOV language does. I can still hear him, "*Bä bet wəst*; we were so happy when we finally found *bä bet wəst*." That's how he talked; *bä bet wəst* is in my mind. That is how it seems to occur that these languages are constrained. There is, as far as anyone knows, no such thing as one of these languages that has postpositions but then has messed something else up like noun-genitive order. It seems that the change happens in order down our list. Of course, nobody who speaks these languages is aware of this sort of thing, but the language change is constrained by these concerns of markedness. It's as if Amharic knows that it's supposed to be head-final in some way.

In any case, now that you understand the basic notion of some things being marked compared to others, then you'll be in a position to understand how it is that children learn language and in what way they do it. Follow me to the next lecture, and we'll take a look at that.

# Lecture Sixteen
# How Children Learn to Speak

**Scope:** Children acquire language spontaneously without being explicitly taught how. Their mastery of sounds passes through stages determined by a progression from unmarked (ontologically primary) to more marked sounds, unmarked ones also being those most commonly found in languages and least likely to erode over time, as discovered by founding linguist Roman Jakobson. Their mastery of other aspects of grammar proceeds along with their ability to master rules, rather than simply memorize.

## Outline

I. It was once thought that children learned to speak simply by imitating adults: They hear adults saying words, and then they pick up words. However, modern linguists have found that it is something apparently innate to the species, and thus it proceeds according to basic aspects of linguistic structure that we have seen in this course.

    **A.** Children do not just master a basket of words and expressions. There's something more constrained and systematic going on.

        **1.** Speaking ability merges without teaching, like fish swimming. Many cultures do not "teach" language, and much of language is not taught (one might correct *The cat's hands are dirty* but not *Where kitty go?*).

        **2.** In general, we only teach so much, and we cannot correct everything. Children often insist that what they are saying is right and eventually learn to speak correctly on their own.

    **B.** Babbling is universal: The first stage of language acquisition is spontaneous vocalizing.

        **1.** Children worldwide do this.

        **2.** Even deaf kids do it, and kids with throat blockages do it after their throats are unblocked.

**II.** Learning to make sounds comes before learning to make words, and the order in which sounds are learned follows a pattern.

    **A.** At first, voiced stops and nasals predominate; fricatives and liquids are rare. That is, children learn the most *unmarked* sounds first.

    **B.** By age two, a child has all consonants except /j/ and /ŋ/.

    **C.** Children's first renditions of sounds are unmarked substitutions.

        **1.** Rendering fricatives as stops: *sing* as *ting*, *zebra* as *dibra*.

        **2.** Fronting, e.g., alveopalatal to alveolar: *shoes* becomes *sooz*, velar to alveolar: *goat* becomes *doat*.

        **3.** Voicing, e.g., of stops before vowels (*pot* to *baht*).

        **4.** Denasalization (*jam* to *dab*, *room* to *woob*). (Note the effects piling on one another, which is what makes children hard to understand.)

**III.** Roman Jakobson and other scholars who developed the concept of markedness are known as the *Prague School*.

    **A.** Roman Jakobson (1896–1982) was a Russian thinker who observed, during a series of exchanges with fellow linguist Nikolai Trubetskoy (1890–1938), that the order in which children learn sounds demonstrates that sounds are related to one another in a hierarchy based on markedness.

    **B.** All children, learning all languages, acquire the vowel /a/ first, then stop consonants, and then nasal consonants before others.

    **C.** This implies that there is something developmentally primary about those sounds. Babies do not master them first because they are the easiest to make, given that during the initial babbling stage, children make all sounds. Rather, /a/ and stops and nasals are the easiest for the brain to *perceive* as distinct sounds.

    **D.** These sounds are the least marked. Bilabial fricatives like /ß/ or /ɸ/ or vowels like /ə/ are more marked compared to these. No child masters the latter sounds first.

    **E.** That some sounds are especially unmarked is supported by the fact that while some languages have very small inventories of phonemes, even the ones with the fewest sounds have stops and /a/. No languages have, instead, only nasals and glides.

**1.** For example, in the Pirahã language of the Amazon, there are only 11 sounds, including these 8 consonants:

|  | bilabial | labio-dental | inter-dental | alveolar | alveo-palatal | velar | glottal |
|---|---|---|---|---|---|---|---|
| voiceless stops | p |  |  | t |  | k | ʔ |
| voiced stops | b |  |  |  |  | g |  |
| voiceless fricative |  |  |  | s |  |  | h |

    **2.** Note, this small collection includes stops.

   **F.** Also, marked sounds are more likely to disappear as languages change than unmarked ones. /θ/, for example, is rendered as [d] in many colloquial varieties of English and is absent in a great many languages. Languages do not, in contrast, lose their /t/ sound.

   **G.** The concept of markedness will arise again in Lecture Seventeen; it crucially affects processes such as language change, language acquisition, and what happens when languages come into contact.

**IV.** How children acquire morphology shows something else that is interesting.

   **A.** First, children retain fossilized memorization of irregular forms: *came, men.*

   **B.** Then children pass through a stage of processing that there are rules in the language but of overgeneralization, in which they produce forms like *feets* and *mouses*, which—ironically—shows that they are internalizing rules. Then the exceptions are "relearned."

**V.** The process of acquiring syntax is much more gradual than for morphology.

   **A.** One-word stage (at one year old): At first, children use single words to refer to entire propositions: "dada" means *Here comes Daddy* or *This shoe is Daddy's*, etc.

   **B.** Two-word stage (at one year and eight months): children refer to an entity and a predicate ("dada chair," "hit doggie"), which is the heart of the configuration of the syntactic trees we encountered in earlier lectures.

**C.** Telegraphic stage (between two- and two-and-a-half years old): word order is accurate, but no grammatical items such as definite articles and the verb *to be*: "Daddy like this book," "I good boy."

    **1.** They first understand the concrete, rather than the words that express abstract concepts.

    **2.** This correlates with how in our adult consciousness concrete words become grammatical ones "under the radar," such as *going to* in the literal sense of movement becoming a marker of futurity as in *I am going to think about that someday*.

**VI.** How children acquire vocabulary also follows an orderly progression.

    **A.** *Overextension* is very common—*fly* may refer to dirt, dust, small bugs, toes, crumbs; *quack* to birds, flies, even coins; *dog* to any animal. *Underextension* occurs as well, such as *kitty* referring only to the cat in the house.

    **B.** By one year and eight months old, children typically know about 50 words. By age five, children are learning about 15 or 20 words per day (about a word every two hours), and by age eight they know about 18,000 basic words.

    **C.** It is often said that a child's basic acquisition of a language is largely complete at six or seven.

        **1.** That certainly seems to be true of children mastering European languages such as English, French, and German.

        **2.** However, there are anecdotal reports that children do take a little bit longer to learn languages that are extremely complex.

        **3.** The Cree Native American language, which is spoken in Canada, is massively complex, and it has been said that children are not competent in even the basic language until they are about 10 years old.

**Essential Reading:**

O'Grady, *How Children Learn Language*.

**Supplemental Reading:**

Lust and Foley, *First Language Acquisition*.

Slobin, *The Crosslinguistic Study of Language Acquisition*.

**Questions to Consider:**

1. Imagine someone saying, "He actually thinks I meant that." Do you imagine the person learning how to say this by matching words to objects and actions?

2. Elmer Fudd says he wants "west and wewaxation." Children go through a stage where this substitution happens. However, it is hard to imagine someone, even with a speech impediment, saying, "Rell, rax ron't rork" for *Well, wax won't work*. What does this suggest about glides versus liquids in terms of markedness?

# Lecture Sixteen—Transcript
## How Children Learn to Speak

It seems relatively simple, in its way: How do children learn to speak? They imitate adults; they hear an adult saying a word, and they pick up that word. Then they hear adults saying other words, and they pick up those words. But the fact is that there's more to it than that in how children learn language. It's not simply that children learn language the way they might learn how to swim or they might learn how to stack blocks or what have you; there is a great deal of evidence that the ability to learn how to use fluent, natural language is innate.

We've talked about the innate language competence. There are linguists who study language acquisition with the aim of seeing if the way children learn language seems to confirm that there actually is some sort of innate configuration in the syntactic fashion in our brains for learning language. There are linguists who examine the way children learn language with a view toward seeing if our ideas about markedness that we have seen recently are valid. Those things have been borne out in various ways.

What has certainly been seen is that children learning language is much more than children just mastering a basket of words and expressions; there's something more constrained and systematic going on. The important thing to realize is that speaking ability happens mostly without teaching. We might try to burnish the way our children speak or learn to speak—we may correct their mistakes—but the ability largely emerges by itself, as many parents have probably observed. It's like fish swimming. It's important that there are many cultures where there is not any effort made on any level to "teach" children how to speak. There are cultures where children really are not spoken to very much out of a sense that they don't understand and/or they don't have anything interesting to say (we're talking about very young children). Yet the people who are these children become adults who speak confidently and fluently, just like anything else.

In general, we only teach so much. If a child says, "Where kitty go?" chances are we're going to let it go because, of course, everything that a small child says—for the most part—is wrong; you can't correct everything. Of course, when you do try to correct a child, very often the child will tell you that he or she is correct, because the child has a sense of language that can be very confident. I talked about how I thought "gots" was the way to express *have* in the first-person singular when I was small, and when my mother told me that was wrong, I insisted otherwise. This is something that language-acquisition specialists are finding all the time: that children are quite insistent that what they're saying is correct. It's very hard to correct a child; it's something that the child seems to do on its own.

Using language is so spontaneous that all children around the world babble spontaneously before they can even utter words. This is not something that only kids who live in the suburbs in the United States do or something like that; it is children around the world in any culture. There seems to be this innate predisposition to vocalizing for no particular reason—not to say, "ouch"; not to say, "I'm hungry"—but just *ga-ga-ga-ga-ga-ga*; all children just do that. What's interesting is that even deaf kids do this, so kids who can't even hear themselves doing it spontaneously will do this random babbling. Even more, if the deaf child is lucky enough to be raised in a home with parents who sign, then deaf children babble in sign; they babble with their hands, just randomly, before they can actually make signs. It seems to be something that is very much programmed for us to do. If a child is born with a throat blockage, take out the throat blockage and they start babbling right away. That is the first stage of language: just exercising the articulatory organs in a random or playful way. That's universal.

Then there's the matter of learning sounds. Words is one thing, but first children have to learn how to simply make sounds. At first what predominates are nasals—/n/, /m/, /ŋ/—and voiced stops, actually. It's not the voiceless stops at the top of our chart; it's the voiced ones: so /b/, /d/, and /g/. Intuitively, you see that those are baby sounds. What this means is that we're seeing markedness in action again, in that children learn the most unmarked sounds first (fricatives and liquids at the early stage are very rare—when you go low down on our consonant chart, that is). First, you have voiced stops and nasals. By two, the child usually has all the consonants except maybe /j/ (the glide) and /ŋ/ (engma). But in the beginning, it is the unmarked sounds that are first. In between those two stages, what children do is they render words—or words that they're trying to enunciate—by making substitutions based on unmarkedness. You can see this rather systematically. If you get the consonant chart in your head, it can often be easier to understand what a child is saying if you understand that they're really just making a certain systematic series of substitutions.

For example, children will render fricatives as stops. They don't have fricatives yet, and so they'll use the stop that is most similar to the fricative. They want to say, "sing," and so they'll say, "ting" because they don't have the alveolar fricative, and so they use an alveolar stop. Notice they make it something that actually corresponds in what's actually a predictable way. They just take it up a notch—so to speak—on the chart, and they use a stop. A *zebra* might be a *dibra*, and that's because they don't have their voiced alveolar fricative, and so they end up using this stop, which is the equivalent.

There is something else children do, which is that they tend to move things to the front. For example: alveopalatal sound—/ʃ/—that does not happen early. They'll use a substitution—they'll take it forward to the alveolar region—and they'll use [s]; *shoes* becomes *sooz*. Or when a *goat* becomes a *doat*—I don't know how often most kids talk about goats, but apparently some do—so where *goat* becomes *doat*, then that's where the velar moves forward to the alveolar region; that's common, too. The back is more of a forbidden zone than the front. There's changing things to stops; there's moving things to the front; and there's also voicing, especially before vowels. A *pot* might be a *baht* because, for the child, the voiced consonants are the unmarked equivalent.

Then there's also denasalization—before the children have nasals yet—when they want to express something. For example, *jam* might be pronounced as *dab*; so /m/ is a bilabial nasal, /b/ is bilabial stop, and so there is this substitution. The child hears it; it cannot do it yet, and so you'll have /b/. Or a *room* might be a *woob*, and the child is trying to say, "room." It can hear "room," but it cannot do that yet, and so the next best thing is to at least have a bilabial stop. That's what children do. Basically, what we see is a kind of substitution, which is constrained by things that the children can and cannot do yet.

A good example of this—we even have an intuition of this when we imitate a child—is what Tweety says: "I tawt I taw a puddy tat." That is actually not random. When Mel Blanc came up with that way of speaking, what he was doing was recapitulating what a child does in terms of rendering things unmarked. For example, "I tawt": The first consonant in *tawt*, what that's supposed to be is an interdental fricative—/θ/—but the interdental fricatives come in relatively late for a child, just like your alveopalatals do. What's the next best thing? If you look on the chart, the alveolar region is just behind. Instead of your interdental fricative, you go to stops—which the child is more comfortable with—and it's going to be an alveolar stop; and so: "I tawt." Then, for, "I taw a puddy tat": If you don't have a fricative yet, then you just jump up and you go to your stop. Then, notice that it's *puddy tat*, and so what the child is already doing is assimilating. It should be *pussycat*, and then the /s/ becomes a /t/; but it's not *putty tat*, it's *puddy tat*. A child very plausibly would do that because it's in between two vowel sounds, not to mention that the voiced sounds are already more unmarked for the child. Then you have instead of *cat*—which in spelling begins with a *c*, but of course in the IPA begins with a /k/—and that becomes "tat." What that is, is our velar stop moving frontward and becoming an alveolar stop. All of that is very plausible as the way a child might move.

We are looking at how markedness affects how children learn language. This is something that is based on a synthesis that was created by Roman Jakobson. Roman Jakobson was a Russian linguist. The revolution in Russia made things uncomfortable for him, and so he moved first to what is now the Czech Republic—Czechoslovakia—to Prague. He and other linguists and linguistically minded people formed what was known as the *Prague School*, where they hatched up a lot of foundational concepts to linguistics now. Much of our conception of what phonemes are was cast in stone by—not created by, but cast in stone by—the Prague School. They, especially Jakobson and his kind of boon companion Nikolai Trubetskoy, were the ones that came up with this notion that there are marked sounds in language—marked elements in language—and that this determines how language changes, and it determines, also, how language is acquired. Jakoboson noticed that the order that children learn sounds in is based on a markedness hierarchy.

For example, in learning all languages, Jakobson observed that children all acquire the vowel /a/ first, and then stop consonants before others, and then comes the nasals. That implies that there is something developmentally primary about those sounds. What's interesting—this is an important detail—is that it's not that the babies can't make the sounds, technically. They don't, but it's not that they can't. Actually, in the initial babbling stage, babies make all possible sounds. What learning the sound system of a language consists of is narrowing down the range of sounds that you make into the ones that are native to your language. It seems that /a/—the vowel /a/—plus stops, and then to a lesser extent nasals, are the easiest for the baby to perceive. The things that you can perceive easiest are the ones that you are going to narrow down to the fastest. For example, a child is not going to narrow down to bilabial fricatives; this is the /ß/ sound that you often learn in Spanish, or the /ɸ/ sound, which is the *f* in *Fuji* in Japanese. Those sounds aren't going to be the ones; schwa is not going to be the one. It's going to be the ones that are easiest to perceive amidst the great soup of sounds that there is.

The fact is—and this is what Jakobson and the Prague School noticed—the fact that these sounds are especially unmarked and the fact that babies zero in upon them so quickly is supported by the fact that in languages that have very small inventories of phonemes, even the ones with the fewest sounds have stops and also the vowel /a/. There's no such thing as a language with only nasals and glides. For example, the Pirahã language of the Amazon is spoken today by about 150 people, and it has an unusually small consonant and vowel inventory. As a matter of fact, it only has eight consonants and three vowels. You can see these consonants here: [p], [t], [k], [ʔ], [b], [g], [s], [h]. What's important about this is that there are the stops; this is just as we saw in the lecture with Hawaiian. Even when you get down this low, you find that you actually have your stops. These are the things that are important, and also one of the vowels is [a]. It has [i], [o], and [a].

Pirahã actually has gotten a lot of attention in the media lately because it is a language which seems to have less machinery for encoding some basic concepts than we would ever expect a human language to have. This includes that it has for numbers a word for *one* and a word for *two* and then nothing else. After that, you just say, "a lot of"; that's it. It has two words for color: One of them means *light*; one of them means *dark*. If you want to say that something is pink, you've got to really kind of talk around it and really just compare it to something that happens to be pink. They don't have a word for *pink* or *green* or *blue*. It's *light* and *dark*; that's it. There is not a separate word for *father* and *mother*; there's just one word for *parent*—you don't distinguish, so if you're talking about your mother, it's your [màíʔì]. If you're talking about your father, it's also your [màíʔì]. It's a very generalizing language. Another one little thing about Pirahã is that in terms of phonemes and allophones, it's interesting: There are only a certain amount of phonemes in Pirahã, but then some of the allophones—some of what happens to a phoneme in a certain environment—can be quite bizarre. For example, there is a phoneme—/b/—which is just a nice voiced stop, and when it comes before [o], /b/ is pronounced like this: *bhfrrp*, literally. When it comes before "oh," it's *bhfrrp*; that's an allophone of /b/ in this language. Language can be very different.

But in any case, marked sounds are also more likely to disappear as languages change than unmarked ones. For example, /θ/ is our interdental fricative. Children zero on in it late. /θ/ is also, as languages change, a fragile sound. Think, for example, about the fact that if you've learned some other language, chances are it didn't have a /θ/. You're going to nativize a sense that where we would expect a /θ/, they have a [t] or something like that. Even in many dialects of English, /θ/ is actually pronounced more like [d], and so "dem," "dese," and "dose"—this is both [θ] and [ð] as a matter of fact—it's a fragile sound; it is one that foreigners often fail to acquire. For example, French people who might say, "zis" instead of, "this"; it is very much a marked sound. The idea is that it's a sound that children will learn late; it's a sound that's fragile as languages change, relatively uncommon in the languages of the world. This is a marked sound, and its marked status is reflected both in its distribution in languages of the world and in how children treat it when they are learning it in a language that it happens to be in. That is what Jakobson and the gang worked out, and that's why they have a certain status in linguistics.

There's something else about kids that's interesting when it comes to how they learn morphology: Morphology is first learned almost ominously well and then unlearned. What I mean by that is that we have various words in English where morphology, instead of being an affix, is a matter of just changing a vowel. That's irregular. And so *walk*; and then you put *walk* in the past, and it's *walked*. But if you *come* to the party, then talking about that in the past, you can't "comed" to the party; you *came* to the party, and so the past marker is that vowel change. It's not predictable. There are different kinds of vowel changes; *think* and *thought* is a different kind. These are things that are part of the complexity of morphology in English.

Actually, children learn those forms very quickly at first. At first, children are very happily saying, "men" instead of, "mans"; they say, "came." You often think, "Boy, my child is articulate. He or she already knows the irregular forms." Then what's interesting is that all of the sudden they unlearn them. Suddenly they're saying things like, "feets," and they are saying, "mouses" instead of, "mice." Things they were doing right a few months ago, suddenly they're doing wrong. But in fact, what this is, is the beginnings of the child actually processing that there are rules in the language. People who study language acquisition think of this as the stage where the language-processing apparatus that is part of the human genetic blueprint starts to kick in and starts to be usable. At first, the children were just learning *came* and *men* by rote; they heard the word and they imitated it. It's kind of the way it's easy to think that all of language acquisition is. Then they realize that there is a rule in English where you add what we write as *s* to a noun, and so they start applying that rule, and they over-generalize it. They think that there's such thing as "foots"; they think that there's such thing as "mouses." Then, as time goes by, they learn that there is a rule and then that there are exceptions to the rule.

Some adults actually stay a little bit in the dark; it can be eccentric. I have a friend who just went to India. In India, the mongoose is a common creature. We see squirrels here in America; there, you'll see a mongoose running by. In all seriousness, he kept on talking about the "mongeese," and he wasn't kidding. I said, "Sheldon, wouldn't you want to say, 'mongooses?'" He said, "No, 'mongeese' sounds right to me." I remember thinking, "That's vaguely infantile of a 38-year-old man," but he kept saying, "mongeese," and so I let him. In any case, morphology is something where we get to see the magic window of children actually learning how to apply rules.

In terms of acquiring syntax, the process is much more gradual. There are no abrupt signposts the way there are in morphology. At first, it's hard to say that there's syntax, because it's a one-word stage where children just use one word at a time. Often that word can be something made up. Children have a predilection for applying a random label to something that they want, or something that they've seen, or maybe they've picked up a bit of the shape of the word but not all of it. Often a child will insist that that is the word. One can imagine a hypothetical child who thinks that a lollipop is called a "loo" and keeps on asking for it. When I was a child, I thought crayons were called "luslus." I don't know where I got that, but I would ask for them by going "luslus" and pointing. If I couldn't have them, I kept yelling, "Luslus, luslus, luslus!" That was a word to me, apparently. It wasn't the correct label, but I had a sense that labels apply to things. But that, of course, is not syntax; that's just beginning to master vocabulary.

But then children start using single words to apply to whole propositions. Saying, "Daddy" might mean *Here comes Daddy*; it might mean *This is Daddy's shoe*; it might mean *This shoe is daddy*; or what have you. But there's only one word. As time goes by, there is the two-word stage, and the two words tend to represent an entity and a predication. In a way, the two words seem to represent the beginnings of working with our basic tree that we saw when we looked at syntax. This stage generally starts at about a year and eight months. There'll be something like "Dada chair," and that will have something to do with the father sitting down or wanting the father to put you in a chair. There'll be "Hit doggie," and you can imagine what that is. I am watching a child learn to talk who lives next door right now, and it really is a magical process. Two months ago, you could not communicate with him in any meaningful way. The thing that he enjoyed most was if I would imitate Dino. If I go, "Abararararara!" he thinks that's wonderful; that was our communication. Just the other day, he walked into my gate, and he started swinging the gate, and he actually said, "Open door. Open door." At first I didn't listen because I just assumed that he's this child who only understands Hannah Barbara cartoon voices. Then he's saying, "open door," and I forgot to notice. Then, about a minute later, I said, "Wait a minute, Gabe, were you just talking?" Of course, that's too much for him, but he's at the two-word phase. Now it wasn't a door, it was a gate, but you can imagine that they must do that in his house next door. He's learned "open." To him, opening is just kind of swinging it back and forth; but I got the point, and then he has this door thing. He's at his two-word phase. It was the first thing that resembled a sentence that I ever heard that child utter, and it was quite marvelous because he doesn't know anything yet. He still falls down, he's still in diapers, etc.—and yet: "open door."

Then around two—in between two, two and a half—there is what's known as the *telegraphic stage*. The telegraphic stage means that you start having what is identifiable as sentences. The word order is correct, but what are missing from the sentence are grammatical items. You have concrete words—"Daddy like this book" or "I good boy"—but you don't have the grammatical items such as definite articles and the uses of verb *to be* such as, "I am a good boy," where *am* is actually a rather grammatical and abstract concept. These things don't happen yet because children first grasp, or are inclined to express, the concrete terms. We see a mirroring of that difference between the concrete and the grammatical that determines how language changes. You have concrete items, which gradually develop into abstract meanings that can be only fitfully related to what the original concrete meaning was. Children perceive words according to that classification, as well. For them, the concrete is more important, as naturally you can communicate quite a bit leaving out grammatical words. Children tend to do this just fine.

In terms of vocabulary, what Gabe was doing in terms of calling my gate a door is actually very common. There is a lot of overextension. A child might learn a word for fly, and then that will refer to dirt or dust or bugs or toes or crumbs. *Quack* is something that a child will learn, and they won't know that it only refers to a particular kind of bird that you actually rarely encounter alive anyway. It'll be birds or flies, because flies fly like birds. There was one child who actually though that *quack* also applied to coins for some reason. A dog might be any animal; kitty might refer only to the cat in the house. That sort of thing is very common. As time goes by, children learn to make finer distinctions. Generally, by about a year and eight months, the typical child knows about 50 words. By age five, it's said that kids are learning 15–20 words per day. That means that they're learning a word about every two hours. By age eight, they know around 18,000 words, depending on how you are counting words.

It's often said that child acquisition of a language is largely complete in terms of the basic things—as opposed to the more outer reaches of the vocabulary—at six or seven, depending on what you mean by complete acquisition. That may not actually be true. That certainly seems to be true of children mastering European languages; especially, it seems to be true of children mastering, say, English and French and German. But there are anecdotal reports, at this point—but they should definitely be put out there—that with languages that are extremely complex, that as you might expect, children do take a little bit longer to learn them. The typical idea is that children's brains are programmed to master any language of any degree of complexity, and there's just this amazing degree of plasticity to the human mind at that age, so that language of any degree of baroqueness can be taken in within a certain period of time. Maybe not, because the more isolated a language has been or is, the more complex it tends to be.

For example, the Cree Native American language—which is spoken in Canada, for one thing—is massively complex. You can go through a grammatical description of Cree—or at least I can—and wonder again and again, "Does anybody really speak this?" Having to attend to all of this in every sentence that you utter, how in the world do human beings actually speak this language? Clearly, adults do, and they do it with no effort. But it's said by one person who did a lot of fieldwork on Cree that children are not competent in even the basic language until they're about 10. Adults will lovingly laugh at things that even an eight- or a nine-year-old will say, which shows that they have not mastered this very complex grammar yet. This has not been studied in detail, but I've heard that said by two people who are studying languages of this kind. It may be that the process is not always over by six or seven, and that is something which is more typical of we speakers of a language like English, which has been beaten down—so to speak—in terms of complexity by things like the Viking invasion. English may not be typical.

In any case, the language-learning process is a thing that can occasion great marvel. It is certainly more than a matter of learning just words. Little Gabe has a sister, and to an extent I have watched her learn to talk, too. I had a party, and I had those people over, and I had a friend of mine over, and my friend noted that Molly was a beautiful little girl. I said, "Well, okay." The next day when I saw them, I said to her mother, "By the way, Zander thinks that Molly is a beautiful little girl." Molly buried her face in her mother's skirt and said, "Mommy, I don't want to be beautiful." I didn't know that she could even understand what I was saying. I certainly didn't know that she was going to say, "Mommy, I don't want to be beautiful," partly because that's a rather profound thing for a girl that age to say—she was three; I still don't quite know what she meant by that—but also the fact that she had mastered the syntax of English. How did she know to render the *to be* in that infinitive form, rather than saying, "I don't want that I am beautiful" or something like that? How did she know to put the words in that proper order? Where was the mistake? Suddenly, she wasn't making any; she had acquired language. In this lecture, I've tried to shed some light on what linguists know about how that happens.

# Lecture Seventeen
## How We Learn Languages as Adults

**Scope:** Learning a second language after our brains have already acquired a first one often involves a certain amount of bleeding from the structure of the first language into the second. However, this happens to a greater degree in some aspects of language than others, and it is also constrained by one's level of exposure to the language and one's orientation to learning it. If learners of a new language speak more to one another in that language than to native speakers, the result may be a new language entirely.

## Outline

I. First-language acquisition is virtually always successful, while second-language acquisition is a slippery slope.

    **A.** We are surrounded by people who have achieved varying degrees of mastery of English, some with imperfect syntax or morphology and many with just accents, which, pleasant though they are, are technically incomplete acquisition of English phonology.

    **B.** While first-language acquisition involves learning language for the first time, building up grammatical competence itself, second-language acquisition is mediated by various factors.

II. One of the things that happen when we learn a second language is that we end up transporting features from our native language into our rendition of that second language. Linguists call that *transfer*, and it happens on all levels of the language.

    **A.** Transfer in terms of vocabulary is most salient to most of us.

        **1.** Russian speakers may say, "by my watches" instead of, "by my watch" because *watch* in Russian is a plural word (meaning *hours*).

        **2.** In French, English learners often express *my hair* as *mon cheveux* instead of *mes cheveux*, because *hair* is not rendered regularly as a plural in English.

**B.** Transfer in the realm of phonology is easier to understand now that we know about classes of sounds.

   **1.** In phonology, we see this in how voiced consonants in German are pronounced as their voiceless equivalents. Thus [v] is pronounced as [f] in the English word *have* and, in German, *Hand* is pronounced [hant].

   **2.** Spanish does not allow word-initial consonant clusters beginning with [s], and thus *Spanish* can come out as "Espanish."

   **3.** Phonology is the hardest aspect of one's native language to "unlearn," and this is why someone may speak a second language with perfect syntax and rich vocabulary but with phonology still affected by their native language. This is why, in other words, people have foreign accents.

**C.** In syntax we see transfer in the adverb placement we saw in Lecture Eight: French has *Il boît d'habitude de la bière*, while we have *He usually drinks beer*. French speakers often say, "He drinks usually beer."

**III.** Markedness (e.g., how Parameters are hierarchically organized) plays a large role in how we internalize the syntax of another language via negative evidence.

**A.** Learning a first language is a matter of first learning the basics of grammar and then mastering the marked—more complicated, exceptional—aspects. For example, as we saw in the previous lecture, children learning English learn that the plural marker is *-s*, and then they learn that some nouns' plurals are irregular (marked): One must say, "feet" rather than "foots."

**B.** Learning a second language requires learning that some aspects of the grammar of the new language are unmarked, whereas they are marked in the native language.

   **1.** For example, in Spanish one can omit subject pronouns: for *I speak*, one can say just, "*Hablo*" rather than, "*Yo hablo*."

   **2.** This means there are two possibilities in Spanish, whereas there is just one in English. The Spanish situation is more marked than the English one.

   **3.** The Spanish speaker uses a marked construction natively and has to learn the unmarked English construction. This is harder for them than for an English speaker learning the marked construction of Spanish.

4. English speakers have little trouble learning to just say, "*Hablo*," whereas Spanish speakers often take a while before learning that in English the pronoun must be used.

5. This is because one learns the Pro-Drop Parameter from *positive* evidence: The English speaker sees that Spanish has a feature they have never encountered and has a discrete new construction to learn. On the other hand, to learn that pronouns must be used is based on *negative* evidence. The Spanish speaker hears English speakers using the pronoun, just as they can in their native language, but this is not, in itself, evidence that one *must* use the pronoun.

C. Thus second-language acquisition is often the mirror of first-language acquisition: One must unlearn the *marked* traits of one's native grammar.

D. Second-language learning is not a matter of just plugging in the structures of your language with the words from the other one.

1. One would never hear a German speaker render *I gave him a broom* with the German sentence's word order:

   *Ihmm habe ich einen Besen gegeben.*
   To him have I a broom given.

2. Word-order habits are relatively easy to change.

3. Similarly, Japanese people do not say, "I a book bought."

4. In other words, the Head-First Parameter can be reset pretty easily.

IV. Level of exposure shapes what features are transferred into the rendition of a second language.

A. If level of exposure is extremely low and second-language learners speak more to each other than to first-language speakers, then even things like word order are indeed often transferred.

B. If adults are required to learn a new language quickly and use it for everyday communication, then they acquire a simplified version of the new language, filled out with grammatical structures (and many words) from their native language: a new language entirely.

C. This is a *creole* language. Creoles are a particular kind of second-language acquisition.

1. This happened, for example, on plantations among African slaves.

2. In Surinam, in the Saramaccan language that we saw in Lecture Ten, *under the table* is "the table under" because that is the word order in the Fongbe language of Togo and Benin that the creole's creators spoke:

| English | under the **table** |
|---|---|
| Saramaccan | *a **táfa** básu* |
| Fongbe | ***távò** glúwὲ* |

**D.** African immigrants to the United States today do not say, "the house under," because their level of exposure to, and contact with, English speakers is much greater than the slaves' was.

**E.** In a picture-book version of the Bible regularly used by missionaries among Saramaccan speakers, although the words are from English and Portuguese, the grammar is highly simplified compared to those languages or Fongbe.

  **1.** When Eve says, "*Womi o, luku aki*," *luku* ("look") occurs only in this form; there are no conjugational endings.

  **2.** Adam says, "*Gadu ta-du bunu*," "God does goodness." There is no conjugational suffix on *du* ("do") and *bunu* can mean *good* or *goodness*.

**F.** Saramaccan grammar is also filled out with Fongbe grammatical patterns. When Eve says, "*Womi o*," the *o* conveys a solicitation of agreement or participation—it is a pragmatic marker. It is modeled on a similar Fongbe pragmatic marker that comes after, rather than before:

| Saramaccan | *Womi **o**!* | "**My dear** man!" |
|---|---|---|
|  | man, oh |  |
| Fongbe | *Dù nú **bó**!* | "**(Go ahead and)** eat!" |
|  | eat thing |  |

**V.** *Affective factors* also modify second-language acquisition.

**A.** There are two types of motivation to learn a new language.

  **1.** *Instrumental* motivation means learning a language because one wants to achieve a concrete goal like getting a graduate degree or a government job.

2. *Integrative* motivation involves wanting to enter a fascinating culture or other personal, emotionally connected goals. It is generally more effective. For example, people who learn a language in the context of a romantic relationship tend to learn the language well.

B. Instrumental learners often achieve good accuracy but less fluency than integrative learners.

**Essential Reading:**

Gass and Selinker, *Second Language Acquisition.*

**Supplemental Reading:**

Farber, *How To Learn Any Language.*

**Questions to Consider:**

1. How would you rate yourself as a learner of second languages? Have you found that you had more success learning one with an integrative orientation than with an instrumental one or that results for you were the same in both situations? (A classroom is a typical instrumental context, while seeking to communicate with an intimate is a typical integrative one.)

2. Speakers of languages without articles (*the*, *a*) tend to have a hard time mastering the ones in English and often fossilize at an incomplete point (this is especially common with Russian and Chinese speakers). To get a sense of why this happens, try explaining to a hypothetical foreigner how *the* and *a* are used—and make sure that your explanation can account for *Fishing is a hard thing to do* and *We're looking for the only sushi place in town.* Lucky to have learned English as infants, aren't we?

# Lecture Seventeen—Transcript
## How We Learn Languages as Adults

In the last lecture, we looked at how children acquire language; that is, we looked at how humans acquire the capacity for language for the first time. First-language acquisition, for the most part, is always successful. Unless there is some kind of congenital brain damage, one learns one's first language in a competent way. Of course, some people happen to be more articulate than others, but in terms of basic capacity, you notice that no one—except, say, a foreigner—would say, "thinked" instead of, "thought." Everybody masters the basic irregular verbs. This includes, for example, people who are in some sort of advanced state of narcotic impairment. This would even include, for example, people with Down's syndrome; notice that there's no problem with irregular verbs. First-language acquisition is successful.

Second-language acquisition, however, is a more slippery matter. Some people are better at it than others. It is almost impossible after a certain age—that age generally being the mid-to-late teens—to learn a second language absolutely perfectly; it is a different business. It is a matter of a partial acquisition of the levels of language that we've seen in this course so far. So a partial acquisition of syntax, a partial acquisition of morphology—we can remember the long lists of conjugational endings and case endings in languages like Latin or Spanish that we've dealt with—and also phonology. When you incorporate phonology only partially, then what we call it in lay terms is "you have an accent." That accent may be very pleasant for native speakers to listen to, but technically it represents an incomplete mastery of the sound system of that language.

While first-language acquisition is learning language for the first time, second-language acquisition is mediated by various factors and is rarely what we would call completely successful. One of the things that happen when we learn a second language is that we end up transporting features from our native language into our rendition of that second language. Linguists call that *transfer*, and this happens on all levels of the language. Of course first—and I think most saliently to most of us, if we are learning a second language or listening to someone else learn ours—is transfer in terms of vocabulary. Languages have different ways of expressing concepts in words. In Russian, for example, the way that you refer to a *watch* is with a word meaning *hours*: [chasi̇́] (часы). As a result, for a Russian the watch is something plural; you've got the hours on your wrist. I remember once hearing a Russian who spoke competent, but still flawed, English. One thing she said to me is, I said, "I like dinosaurs," and she said, "I like dinosaurs, either." I thought, "That's cute." Then another thing she said was, "By my watches, it's 2 pm." That made perfect sense from Russian, although of course from an English perspective you think, "You're only wearing one watch." That's something that people do.

To take it the other way, in French you refer to your *hairs*—and so *mes cheveux*—and the hairs are in the plural. In English, that sounds vaguely clinical that you would refer to *hairs* in the plural; we just say, "my hair," just like you talk about *water* or *corn*. It's what you call a mass noun. Very easy, it is, if you are a student of French, to—instead of saying, "*mes cheveux*," *my hairs*—to say, "*mon cheveux*," thinking that it will be a singular word. Things like that happen all the time. I remember once I had—I actually still have—a Bulgarian friend. His English was about at the stage of this Russian person's I was mentioning. He was trying to say, "early riser," but you don't put it that way in Bulgarian. He said, "Well, you are the one who is the early-waking-up person." The reason why he said that was because in a Slavic language, that is the way that you would put it. These are things that happen.

But we can also go to other levels of the language. For example, there's also transfer in the realm of phonology. We can understand this in terms rather cleaner than what we might be used to thinking, because now we know about classes of sounds. For example, Germans will often, when they're first learning English or if they happen to never shed a strong accent, pronounce the word *have* as [hæf]. That sounds kind of maybe severe or funny to us, but what it actually is, is it's a regular process: What they're doing is they're rendering a voiced sound—in this case [v]—as voiceless. [f] is the voiceless correspondent of [v], which is voiced. There's a rule in German, which is that when underlyingly you have a voiced consonant at the end of the word, then when you actually pronounce it on the surface it comes out as voiceless. In writing, the German word for *Hand* is just like the English word for *hand*. But the way they pronounce it in German is not [hænd] but [hant], and that's because the voiced [d] becomes a voiceless [t]. That is a phonological rule in German, which they will often transfer into English; it's their habit of tongue, and so that's what's more comfortable to them.

Or, for example, a Spanish-speaking person might say, "Espanish" instead of, "Spanish." The reason that that initial *e* sound is there is because Spanish does not tolerate—as we say—word-initial consonant clusters beginning with [s]; that's just something that isn't done. We say, "Spanish"; we say, "stir." In Spanish, that's not allowed, and so the extra vowel is put on to the beginning so that you end up having the first *s* sucked into the syllable the *e* is part of, and then the *p* is sucked into the syllable that is "pan"; and so, "Espanish." That's a way of taking care of that consonant cluster, which it doesn't want. That's how that kind of thing can work.

Phonology is the hardest aspect of language to unlearn. How sounds are rendered in a language is, for one thing, very deeply ingrained. It's the first thing, as we've seen, that babies start rendering before they of course know any endings, or any words, or certainly any aspects of word order. These things are very idiosyncratic. One language's rendition of /a/ is different from another language's rendition of /a/. One language's rendition of what we're thinking of as /t/ is different from another one's. For example, let's take /p/. If I see the word spelled *p-o-t*, I say, [pʰat]; and so the /p/ is [pʰ]. But if a French person sees the word *p-a-r-l-e—speak* or *speaks*—on the page, then what they say is [parl]. They don't say [pʰaɹl]; that's how we sound in French class. It's [parl]; it's unaspirated. So there are different kinds of /p/'s. Very idiosyncratic; very hard to lose that habit.

For example, in New York City there are many Slavic-speaking immigrants. If somebody has a really thick accent and is running around saying things like, "early-waking-up persons," that is somebody who came at something like 40 or 50 when it is very hard to undo your native phonology. If it's a Slavic immigrant who sounds just like I sound now, chances are they came to the United States when they were six or seven when they still had their fluid, plastic, language-learning abilities.

Then there's an intermediate variety: people who speak perfectly idiomatic English, don't make any mistakes with morphology or syntax—or maybe they do about every two weeks when they're really tired—but basically they speak perfect English, but with an accent. It's not a Boris and Natasha accent but a light accent that you catch after about two minutes, like in one of the previous lectures I was talking about how somebody had taught me how to pronounce Polish, which is really a nightmare; I'm glad those words were easy. The person who did that was somebody who I don't know very well. I know, really, one thing about her, and it's that she's been in this country for 12 years because she told me that. That's all we've ever discussed. She has that light dusting of an accent, which means you can date it. She must have come here when she was about 16 years old. If she's been here for 12 years, I know her age; she must be 28. Now I'm never going to discuss that with her, but that's how the acquisition of phonology works. There's the phonology.

Then, of course, there is the second-language acquisition of syntax. Various things happen under those conditions. For one thing, remember from our previous lecture about Parameters that we have the issue of the Verb Attraction Parameter where a verb moves to the front—or in terms of our syntactic tree, up to the top—in order to get its tense? This is something that happens in French; it doesn't happen in English. In French, you will say, as we saw, for "He usually drinks beer": "*Il boît*" ("He drinks") "*d'habitude*" ("usually") "*de la bière*" ("beer"). *D'habitude* (the "usually") comes after the "drinks" because the word for *drink* has moved up ahead in order to get its ending, so to speak. In English, because we have so much less of that kind of thing, the verb stays in place. That kind of Verb Attraction Parameter setting is something that can be transferred. It's very common to hear French speakers who've only gotten to a certain point say, "He drinks often beer," because they're transferring their Parameter setting into their rendition of our language, where the setting is actually quite different.

In fact, markedness—we've seen how Parameters are hierarchically organized—markedness plays a large role in how we internalize the syntax of another language. For example, when you learn a first language, what you're doing is first you're learning the basics of grammar, and then you're learning the more marked aspects. You learn, for example, that the plural marker is going to be what we call /s/—although actually as we've seen it has lots of allomorphs—then you learn that there are the irregular plurals. You don't say, "foots" or "feets"; you say, "feet." That's something that a child takes a while to master fully. A child has to learn that, first of all, in most cases, you use a plural /s/ ending. Then there are these other cases like *men* and "mongeese"—mentioning that example from the last lecture—where you have to use the irregular plural.

In a second language, it's different. Often in a second language, what you have to learn is that there are aspects of the grammar you're going into which are unmarked compared to the way that construction works in your language. For example, in Spanish we've seen that there is what we've called the Pro-Drop Parameter. If you say, "I speak," then there are two ways to do it: The kind of basic way—and the one most intuitive for English speakers—is to say, "I speak" and say, "*Yo hablo*." But because the *-o* ending conveys first-personhood, you can also just say, "*Hablo*." That's not seen as clipped language or anything like that; that's an alternative. That means that to say, "I speak," you've got two choices in Spanish—two utterly neutral choices. That is more marked than the English situation, where you just have to say, "I speak." Spanish has more choices; it's got this alternation. Somebody who learns Spanish has to learn these two things.

It's been shown that English-speaking people who learn Spanish have an easier time learning that there's an alternation between "*Yo hablo*" and "*Hablo*" than Spanish speakers have learning that in our language you have to say, "I speak." In what's called Spanish interlanguage—in other words, the intermediate step between being a Spanish speaker and being an English speaker—often the pronoun is left off. This is because learning the more marked setting is a matter of positive evidence. When we learn Spanish, it really stands out to us that you don't always have to use the pronoun, because in our language you always do. As a result, very quickly, you figure out, "Okay, it can either be '*Hablo*' or '*Yo hablo*.'" For the Spanish speaker, they see that we say, "I speak," but then, it's a perfectly rational assumption to think that you can also just say, "Speak." This is especially the case when they're not learning from a textbook and being told about these things, but just learning it on the fly, which is the way a lot of people actually have to learn English from Spanish in the world that we live in.

You hear, "I speak," and you figure, "Okay, that's like my '*Yo hablo*.' Then I figure you can also say, 'Speak' just like I can say, '*Hablo*.'" That, of course, isn't true; but how do you know that it isn't true? No one is going to tell you if you're not in class. It's a matter of hanging around a language long enough for it to occur to you that you have never heard anybody drop the pronoun. That takes a while; that's harder. Even if you do start realizing it, you may not really set the rule. Finding that you have to deal with something that is less marked can be harder.

From the English-speaking perspective, there's actually something similar: It's our sense of present tense. Let's say that you are—actually this is rare, really, that you would be writing a letter, but just for the sake of argument let's assume that anybody still did—that you are sitting there with a quill, and you're writing a letter, and somebody walks in and says, "What are you doing?" Your answer would be: "I'm writing"; that's very simple English. If you think about it, in textbooks it will often be said that English has a past tense, *wrote*; a future tense, *will write*; and a present tense, *I write*. But if you think about it, *I write* is not present tense, because let's say you've got the pen, and you're sitting there and you're writing, and someone walks in and says, "What are you doing?" If you turned to that person and said, "I write," then you are either pretentious, a little bit sick, or foreign. There's just no way you would say, "Well, I write," because you have to say, "I am writing." What *I write* actually means is that you do it on a regular basis. For example, "What do you do too often during the wee hours and not get enough sleep, John?" "I write." That's what I would say; I would not say, "I'm writing" in answer to that; that, again, is a foreigner. "Every Tuesday night I am writing." No. "Every Tuesday night I write." English has a really funny rendition of present tense. If we're talking about something neutral— "What are you doing?"—it's always with this progressive construction. You can't say, "I write." *I write* only means the habitual.

If you think about any other language that you have ever had to learn, that wasn't the case. Let's say that you are holding a quill, and you are a Spanish speaker, and you're doing this and somebody walks in and says, "What are you doing?" (except probably in Spanish). Your answer would be "*Escribo*": *I write*. That would be fine. If you want to emphasize that writing is what you're doing right at that moment, then you can say, "*Yo estoy escribiendo*." That is available, but "*Escribo*" would be perfectly fine to express what you're doing right then. It would also be the way that you express that you do it every Tuesday. Usually languages have a very simple kind of present tense. This progressive is just used when you really want to stress that you're doing something right now.

That's something that we have to learn. It's very easy if we are learning Spanish to overdo the *Yo estoy escribiendo* construction because we figure that's what you have to do when you render the present tense. In fact, no: Spanish is quite unmarked in this way; it's normal. If you're talking about the present tense, whether it's habitual or whether it's right now, you just use a nice, well, present-tense verb. Only here in English do we have this marked choice where we overuse the progressive and the bare verb is used specifically for the habitual. That's weird. It's hard for us to learn the unmarked. That's an aspect of syntax that has been shown in research to apply again and again.

That's the syntactic aspect of it. What we can see is that second-language learning is not, despite how difficult it is on various levels, a matter of just plugging in the structures of your language with the words from the other one. That doesn't happen, and that's because some things are easier than others. In syntax, for example, if you are a German person, then one way you might say—especially colloquially—"I gave him a broom" is "*Ihm habe ich einen Besen gegeben*." You see that on the screen, and so that's how you would say it. No German would come up with something like, "To him have I a broom gaven." Nobody says that. No matter how bad they are at learning languages, that is not something that any German has ever done. That's because the very basics of word order tend to come pretty quickly; it's very salient that a language you're learning does not have a word order that yours has. Word order is easy to perceive. Word-order habits are relatively easy to change. In the same way, even faulty Japanese speakers in the United States don't say, "I a book bought." They learn very quickly that that doesn't happen. I've heard that that happens in classrooms in Japan, during like the first 10 minutes that they're in class, but by the time they're coming here and standing on their two feet and using the language to some extent, they'd never say that, because word order comes. Another way that we can put that is that the Head-First Parameter can be reset pretty easily. It's like children; children get that pretty fast.

But there is the issue of level of exposure. If the level of exposure of a person is relatively low, and the people in question end up speaking to each other more than they end up speaking to native speakers of the language, then actually even features like word order can end up being transferred into their rendition of the language. If you take that level—that rudimentary level of second-language acquisition, that is deeply infused with structures from the person's original language, if you take that and make it into a vehicle of everyday communication—if that, for some reason, is the way that you have to talk all the time—then what ends up happening is that there's a simplified version of the language. In order for it to be a full vehicle of communication, it's filled out with lots of structures from the language that is natively spoken by this population.

That kind of language actually has a name: It's called a *creole*. It happened under a very unusual circumstance, which was that during the middle centuries of the last millennium, there were Africans who spoke many languages brought across the ocean, usually to work on plantations where the language of work was one that they had no reason to know. In order to communicate—not only with the masters, but also with one another, because sometimes they spoke as many as a dozen different languages—to speak with one another they needed to communicate, and the natural choice was this language of the new land. But there was no Berlitz; there were no classes—I'm dating myself by always mentioning Berlitz; let me change that because this is now—there was no Rosetta Stone, nothing like that. You just had to pick it up. You picked it up from the air; you learned it orally. But how much were you really going to learn? As a result, these were situations where people who were learning—for example—English as a second language actually ended up transferring so very much of their native language into their rendition that the result was a new language entirely. Creoles are a particular kind of second-language acquisition.

For example, in Surinam, we have seen that there is a creole language called Saramaccan. This is the one that was created by slaves who escaped from the coastal plantations and founded lives in the interior, and their descendents are still there today. Saramaccan mixes English and Portuguese vocabulary for the most part, with a grammar based mostly on the language Fongbe, which is spoken on the west coast of Africa in what is today Togo and Benin; back in the day, Benin was called Dahomey. Saramaccan is spoken there, and in Saramaccan to say, "under the table," you don't say, "under the table"; you say, "table under," as we can see here (section IV.C.2 of the outline). There is no such thing as "under the table"; "table under" is the way it's said, because in Fongbe that's how the words are arranged, too. In other words, these are languages that don't have, as we've seen, prepositions; they have a different kind of adposition called a postposition.

African immigrants today who we meet in the United States do not walk around saying things like, "The table under." That sort of word-order pattern is the sort of thing that you unlearn very quickly if your language has it. Saramaccan speakers do it because they were in a situation where there was so little reinforcement from the language that they were learning and so much interaction between all of them that it made perfect sense to transfer that into the language. I know you've all been waiting for this: This is a comic book. We're looking at Adam and Eve, and they're speaking Saramaccan. Needless to say, there is a certain difference in tint between Saramaccan speakers and the ones in this picture, but we'll pay that no never mind. We can see that Eve is talking to Adam. She says, "*Womi o, luku aki, luku.*" What that is, is "Man, oh"—and we'll get to the "oh"— "look here, look." (*Womi* is *man*; that's from Portuguese *homem*, for whatever it's worth.) She's saying, "Well, look at this." Now you see *luku*. *Luku* in Saramaccan does not come in various forms with different endings; there's no third-person singular -*s*; there's no past-tense ending. That's because in a creole language not only do you have the transfer, but you also have evidence of the fact that a great deal of grammar from the language that was the target language was not incorporated. There's a great deal of simplification in these languages. Here's this *looking*, and there's no conjugations or anything like that. Then Adam's response is, "God does goodness on us"; he says, "*Gadu ta-du bunu.*" *Gadu* means *God*; *du* means *do*; and *ta* is the *ing*-ness, and it kind of shows that there's something that's ongoing. And so: *Gadu ta-du bunu*. *Bunu* is from *bom—good* in Portuguese—like *bueno* in Spanish. "God does goodness." You notice that with *bunu*—this is *goodness*—here it's a noun, but it can also be an adjective, and *bunu* can also be used as an adverb. For example, one way to say, "Goodbye" or "Be well" in Saramaccan is "*Wáka búnu*"; that's *walk good, walk well*. That's what my Saramaccan informant always finishes his emails to me with: "*Wáka búnu*." *Bunu* can take all of those forms. Morphology has nothing to do with that. We have our *happy*, and our *happiness*, and our *happily*; very, very, very little of that in Saramaccan, and that's because of this simplification.

But then Saramaccan is also full of Fongbe grammatical items. For example, notice Eve says, "*Womi o*," *man, oh*. That's not just random; if you think about it, why isn't it "*O womi*"? That would be a perfectly normal thing to say. Why does she put it afterwards? Because certainly nobody who was speaking English or Portuguese said that. We don't say, "Mother, oh"; we say, "Oh, mother." In fact, in just about any language I can think of, there is some word equivalent to "oh" that comes before. This "oh" is actually something different. It's not really "Oh!" This is a marker in Saramaccan that conveys a certain solicitation of agreement or participation. It's kind of like "Isn't it?" or "Yeah," or if you are a person with a certain genuine and vibrant connection to popular culture of this part of the millennium, the way that many people who are about 10 through 30 and usually a color use the word "Yo." And so, you know, "Good food, yo"; that's what the "*o*" means.

Where that comes from is Fongbe; and so Fongbe actually has an interesting marker, and it means the same thing. If in Saramaccan, *womi o* means *my dear man*—kind of, "Look at this, agree with me about this fruit"—in Fongbe, you have a similar marker, and it's of a different phonetic shape, but it has the same function. For example, if you want to tell somebody to eat, but what you really want to convey is *go ahead and eat*—like "You were eating anyway, go ahead and eat, eat on that thing, chomp down on that, go to town, knock yourself out"—then you say, "*Đù nú bó*." Notice what I just did: It's not "do"; it's "*đù*." That is a kind of sound that I didn't bother to tell you about before because it wasn't really necessary, but it's actually what many people would call "cool"—I don't use that word—but it's an implosive sound. There's "do," and then there's "*đù*," and I'm sucking inward. That is normal in Fongbe. "Go ahead and eat that thing"; "*Ɖù nú bó.*" That is Fongbe. That's why Eve says this "*Womi o*" here; it's modeled on particularly a Fongbe construction.

In any case, transfer definitely modifies our acquisition of a second language. We've seen how it's not only transfer that modifies it but issues of markedness. One other thing that modifies it is what are often called *affective factors*. There are two motivations for learning a language. One of them is instrumental; that means that you want to achieve some some kind of concrete goal like getting a graduate degree, or a government job, or being able to expand your clientele, or the like. That's *instrumental motivation*. *Integrative motivation* is something different; it's usually about wanting to enter a fascinating culture or wanting to communicate with another human being. So there's an emotional reason why you want to learn this language if it's integrative. This means that, for example, the adage that languages are learned best on the pillow is very much true. If that's why you're learning the language, because you're trying to connect with someone who you are intimate with in that way, then chances are you're going to get pretty good at it, as opposed to the more Rosetta Stone motivation where you wish to be able to speak Japanese at business meetings. You don't really care about Japanese or like learning languages, but you want to do that. You're probably only going to get so far. Generally, integrative motivation is successful, except it has lots of mistakes in it. Instrumental motivation can be very tidy but is not as fluent.

I remember I had an office mate, 20 years ago now. (If I died, it wouldn't say in the obituary, "Young man killed." That scares me.) But back 20 years ago, I had an office mate. He was a Japanese individual, and his English was perfect. He never made any mistakes, and his accent WAS. ABOUT. LIKE. THIS. HE. SPOKE. AT. THIS. PACE. AND. HE. WAS. NOT. IN. ANY. SOCIAL. SENSE. A. HUMAN. BEING. DURING. THE. ENTIRE. SIX. YEARS. THAT. I. KNEW. HIM. because he was using a very instrumental motivation. I don't think he liked America very much; he got right back to Japan as soon as he could. He didn't want to make any mistakes; it was instrumental. He knew everything, but frankly he wasn't a person. You could tell that he was just waiting to get back to his Japanese roommates. Whereas I knew someone else, a friend of mine, who had a very integrative motivation. Her English was fluent— admirably fluent—but full of cute stuff. For example, "Oh, I love corns," and I would say, "Well, actually, it's corn." She never got that. For some reason, she thought that the word *coat* was pronounced "court" and would never stop saying that. Her past-tense ending, she thought that it was pronounced "ud" all the time; and so, "Why you stop-ud the car?" That was very hard. Her English was idiomatically brilliant, but she always had these little sorts of mistakes, and that's because she had an integrative motivation and was allowing herself to let go in a way that my office mate did not.

In any case, this has been a cursory, but hopefully moderately interesting, introduction to the study of how people learn second languages.

# Lecture Eighteen
## How You Talk and How They Talk

**Scope:** There are different ways to say words or render grammatical constructions, and different people are more likely to choose some ways than others. The study of sociolinguistics investigates how the social world affects how people express themselves, and this lecture examines variables: different renditions of the same sound or construction, which often correlate with social factors such as class.

## Outline

**I.** We have examined language as it exists now and as it changes through time. Now we will proceed to examining language on another dimension: the social one. First, we will see that phonology, morphology, and syntax differ according to sociological factors in systematic ways; later, we will analyze how people use language as a part of functioning as a social animal.

**II.** In this lecture, we will begin examining one subarea of *sociolinguistics*, the study of *variables* in language use.

   **A.** In some languages, the difference between formal and casual speech is so vast that the two levels are essentially, or are in actuality, different languages, such as standard versus Egyptian Arabic for *He saw a shoe*:

   | Modern Standard Arabic | [raʔā ħiðāʔun] |
   | Egyptian Arabic | [šāf gazma] |

   **B.** In English, there is no gap so vast. However, there is an analogous difference between formal and casual English, and the variation between the two is more systematic than it may appear.

**III.** The study of variables, or variation, investigates individuals' alternative usage of words or constructions with the same meaning.

   **A.** Linguistic variables are composed of *variants* (alternate forms for the same meaning), of which there are two types:
   **1.** *Indicators* have no social significance (for example, [ra] fish, as many Americans currently pronounce *raw*).

**2.** *Markers* have social significance (*singin'* is felt to be less dignified than *singing*).

**B.** Markers are most interesting to variationists because they are the harbingers of change, a crucial concern among scholars of variation.

**IV.** The founder of the study of societal factors in linguistic variation is William Labov of the University of Pennsylvania.

    **A.** Labov has correlated linguistic variables with societal ones such as class, age, gender, and race.

    **B.** Class is assigned according to factors such as occupation, education, residence, and salary.

        **1.** For example, in 1966, Labov described socioeconomic categories from 0 to 9 as follows:

| | |
|---|---|
| 0–1: | lower: grade-school education, laborers, hard time making ends meet |
| 2–4: | working: some high school education, blue collar workers, own cars |
| 5–8: | lower middle: completed high school, semiprofessional/white collar, send kids to college |
| 9: | upper middle: educated, professional. |

        **2.** In America in 1966, the split was 10 percent lower, 40 percent working, 40 percent lower middle, 10 percent upper middle.

    **C.** Class is a difficult and slippery concept; social space is multidimensional. However, in broad terms it is useful to the study of variation and has yielded consistent results.

**V.** Eliciting and recording the *vernacular* can be very difficult.

    **A.** There is an *observer's paradox*: It is impossible for the interviewer not to affect the results by their sheer presence.

    **B.** The vernacular is the object of attention, as it is considered to be the locus of change. The vernacular is the language passed on via ordinary communication, be this standard or otherwise.

    **C.** Labov created the *sociolinguistic interview*, which consists of five segments:

        **1.** *Casual speech* can be elicited by seeking a narration of a dangerous situation, or it can be yielded unconsciously by the interviewee in asides to people other than the interviewer.

2. *Careful speech* will characterize most of the interview.
3. *Reading a passage* will have a certain "upness" (formality).
4. *Word lists* containing the variants investigated are read aloud: For example, to investigate the pronunciation of [ð] as [d], the word list would include words such as *these*, *those*, and *then*.
5. The interviewee is asked to read *minimal pairs*, words that differ in precisely the variable investigated: *those* ([θoz]) versus *doze* ([doz]), or *raw* ([rɔ]) versus *rah*! ([ra]).

VI. Labov's 1966 department store study showed that dropping the [r] at the end of syllables ("caw-nuh" [kɔnə] for corner [korn̩r]) gradually fell out of favor among New Yorkers after World War II.

A. Saks, Macy's, and Klein's were investigated; investigators asked the location of items they knew were on the fourth floor and then pretended not to have heard in order to get a clearer repetition.

B. There was more [r] usage the higher the class; variations in the realization of [θ] as [t] show the class correlations in more detail.

C. Macy's speakers used more [r] the older they were, despite older people generally using less [r]. This suggests that middle-class speakers move to prestige forms as they get older, as part of their aspirations. This has been replicated since in other studies.

D. Lower-middle-class speakers used more [r] in reading word lists and minimal pairs than upper-middle-class speakers, indicating *hypercorrection* to prestige forms. This finding has been replicated enough, not only in the United States but also in other countries, to be considered real.

E. It is among the people who are not upper class, not upper middle class, and not middle class that we can generally see where the language is going.

## Essential Reading:

Labov, *Language in the Inner City.*

## Supplemental Reading:

Labov, *The Social Stratification of English.*

**Questions to Consider:**

1. For many people, their vernacular speech differs rather extensively from the standard variety of the language. For others, their vernacular is quite close to the standard. Where would your own vernacular variety fall according to its difference from the standard—in terms of accent or grammatical constructions?

2. One can say, "He isn't a doctor" and contract *is* and *not*, or one can say, "He's not a doctor" and contract *he* and *is*. Is this variable an indicator or a marker?

# Lecture Eighteen—Transcript
## How You Talk and How They Talk

So far in this course, we have examined language the way it is and we have examined how language changes through time. But our basic perspective has been language as it used by an individual, within an individual's head. In this and the next two lectures, we're going to turn to looking at language from a different dimension, and that's the social one. Namely, we're going to see that phonology, morphology, and syntax, semantics, pragmatics change in systematic ways according to social and sociological factors, because, after all, that's what language was originally for. Now we use language in a solitary way when we, for example, read, but language was actually designed to allow us to act as social animals. We're going to look at how language is quite malleable according to social factors, as well as the grammar-internal factors that we've looked at so far.

In this lecture, we're going to look at one subarea of sociolinguistics, and this is the study of what's called *variables* in language use. To get a sense of what we're looking at—because when it comes to how English is spoken, particularly in first-world contexts like ours, it can be difficult to perceive this; it's a matter of degree—but in, for example, Arabic-speaking societies there is a massive (I mean to us, almost counterintuitively massive) difference between the language that's used on the page and in formal settings and then the way normal people actually talk. For example, let's say that we're dealing with Egypt, and this is the way life is in Egypt for everybody, including Anwar Sadat and Hosni Mubarak. This is not some street phenomenon; this is the way an Egyptian Arabic speaker experiences their language. There is modern standard Arabic, which is pretty much the same across the Arabophone territory, that is derived from the language of the Koran, etc. Then in Egypt there is Egyptian Arabic, which is not just colloquial Arabic; it is really a different language entirely than modern standard Arabic. For example, if you want to say, "He saw a shoe"—if you wanted to say that—then in modern standard Arabic that is [raʔā hiðāʔun]. That is how you say it. You don't have to know Arabic to just see those two words. In Egyptian Arabic, it's [šāf gazma]. Now it's quite different; it's a whole different language. You will often hear in the folk sense Arabic speakers saying, "Well, yes, I have a hard time understanding people from Morocco because I'm from Jordan," or something like that. That's the folk conception. Jordanian Arabic and Moroccan Arabic are as different as

French and Italian. All of the people are united by, say, a Latin. This is the situation where the "high" language and the "low" language—i.e., the formal language and then the way that everybody actually talks—are very different.

In English there is no gap this vast—not in the English that probably those of us who are experiencing this set speak—but there is an analogous difference between formal and casual English, and the variation between the two is more systematic than it might appear. What we're talking about is the study of variables, or variation. This is the investigation of individuals' alternative usage of words or constructions that have the same meaning. There are two kinds of variables or variants, and the difference is crucial in terms of what is significant versus what isn't. One kind of variable is called an *indicator*. An indicator has no social significance; it doesn't convey any particular flavor to use one alternate over another. For example, in modern American English, there are many people who pronounce "aw" ([ɔ]) as [a]; I'm one of the [ɔ] people, and so I would say that sushi is "raw fish." There are other people who would say that sushi is "rah fish." We don't have to caricature—it's not "*Rah*! Fish!"—it's just that they say, "rah fish." I would say, "Don't break the law." They would say, "Don't break the lah." You might be one of these people. Just listen; that's the way a lot of people pronounce it.

When I was teaching linguistics at Berkley, I remember—because this is particularly common in California—that when I was trying to teach the IPA, a lot of the students had trouble with the [ɔ] sound (that lax, rounded, back mid vowel) because they didn't have it. For them, sushi was "rah fish." I was in kind of a clique way, way, way back in California. It was me, John, then there was my friend Dawn, her boyfriend, Sean—don't miss him—and then this other guy named Ron. In my English, it was [dʒan], [ʃɔn], [ran], and [dɔn]. Most people in California said it as [dʒan], [ʃan] [ran], and [dan]. I'm caricaturing a bit, but that is something that is a variation. You might not have thought about it; it is of moderate interest. The fact of the matter is that if somebody says, "I'm going to go to lah school so that I can make lahs," it doesn't seem low class; it doesn't seem ridiculous. You probably don't notice it. It's just a matter of variation.

Then there are *markers*, what are called markers. I'm sorry that these two terms are a little wan and not very indicative, so to speak. There are indicators, and then there are markers. The markers are the ones that have social significance. For example, you can say, "singing" or you can say, "singin'." As I've emphasized, it's not as if a letter's dropped, it's just a difference in sound. One of them ends in an [n]; one of them ends in a [ŋ]. One of them is a matter of alveolar nasal; one of them is a velar nasal. Nevertheless, it is felt that to say, "singin'" is wrong in some way, or kind of six pack in some way. That is something you associate with a garage with shag carpet in it and really kind of kicking back, as opposed to "singing," which is supposed to be proper. That is a marker. The markers are more interesting to sociolinguists because they are the harbingers of a change in the whole language. For example, it might be that over time more American English speakers are saying, "rah fish" instead of "raw fish" and that maybe in 500 years that it'll always be [a]. It could and could not— probably won't be. For example, you can say, "He isn't" or you can say, "He's not." They mean exactly the same thing if you think about it; it's just a matter of how you contract. It could be that one becomes more popular than another, but it never has; so you might see some change from an indicator. But when it comes to a marker where you have that kind of social significance, the fact is that what's going on with the marker is going to tell you where the language is going to go, or would go, under ordinary conditions.

The first person who discovered this and systematized it was William Labov, who was at the University of Pennsylvania. He is regarded as the founder of what is today called *sociolinguistics*, and he is regarded that way because he was. He started doing his foundational work in the 1960s. Before that, there was no such thing as sociolinguistics—certainly nothing called that. It wasn't the kind of thing people were looking at, language in society. Anthropologists might make a stab at it, but the kind of detailed work that's been done over the past 40 years plus would have been quite counterintuitive to earlier linguists, who were looking at just the phonemes and the morphemes, as we saw. This is a relatively new field. It was in the '60s that Labov started correlating linguistic variables with social factors— or societal factors—such as class, age, gender, and race.

The first thing Labov did was he wanted to take a look at the English spoken in New York City; he started looking at various changes in the English of New York City in the '60s. You have to remember, we're talking about the early '60s. It's getting to the point where this research was done long enough ago that we have to understand that there are certain adjustments to make from our time. This is the early '60s; imagine it in black and white. People are still wearing hats. *The Patty Duke Show* is on TV. The first movie to be shown on an airplane was *Inherit the Wind* in

1960; that's still a recent event. People are probably talking about where they were when Kennedy was shot. This is those '60s; it's that world. Imagine the cars going by and stuff like that.

Labov was thinking about class. He interviewed various people, and he assigned them classes. Class is a squishy concept. We don't like to talk about it as Americans; there's a whole university lecture about why we don't. The fact is that even talking about some of Labov's work can be kind of itchy sometimes because we do have to talk a lot about "of the working classes, the lower class." But the fact of the matter is that Labov has gotten at some very systematic variations that are conditioned by this squishy—but nevertheless, I think we all know, real—issue of class. By class, I don't mean whether or not you can identify who Terry Gross is, but there are certain things. Labov looked at it in this way, and I think there'd be slight differences today, but I think we get his gist.

There is the lower-class person, and the way Labov described it is as somebody with a grade-school education and somebody who is a laborer. That to me is a rather obsolete term, "laborer." I think today we'd be more likely to say a blue-collar worker, but still: laborer. Then this is a person for whom it is hard to make ends meet, and they would say this. I would say that the modern equivalent of this is probably somebody who is a casualty of inner-city schools and dropped out and is having a hard time getting a job. That is lower class.

Then there is the working class. The working-class person in this world was somebody who had some high school, was definitely described as blue collar, and probably had a car. I think since those early '60s, this person probably would have finished high school. Nevertheless, it is the realm; if we're going to take TV, this would be *Roseanne* the sitcom. That is working-class people. To be more modern—because this show, I think, will go into syndication forever—*My Name is Earl*. These are working-class people.

Then there is the lower-middle-class person. In Labov's early '60s, these were people who did finish high school. They were semiprofessional or white collar. They sent their kids to college; they didn't go to college, but they sent their kids. Roughly, in terms of families that we're all acquainted with or likely to mostly be acquainted with, this is either *Married with Children* or *The Simpsons*. Marge and Homer did not go to college. You can tell Lisa's going to; Bart will at least make a stab at it. That is the lower middle class.

Then there is the upper middle class. These people are educated, they are professional, they often buy Teaching Company sets, and I think that the television show to refer to would be *Frasier* or—I'm going to look trendy because it's become so trendy to refer to this—the people in the book *The Corrections*, because everybody's read that book—the Jonathan Franzen book.

Anyway, in America in 1966—as far as this class stuff went—10 percent could be seen as lower class, 40 percent could be seen as working, 40 percent could be seen as lower middle, and 10 percent as upper middle. This is what Labov needed to do. Labov was interested in eliciting these markers. He was interested in eliciting, in particular, the markers that were seen as socially pungent or maybe stigmatized in some way. He wanted to elicit real language; in other words, he wanted to elicit what is called the *vernacular*. We look at various levels of language. In Egypt, it would be pretty easy to figure out what the vernacular is. It's Egyptian Arabic, which is something so different from standard Arabic that sometimes you might hear an Egyptian say, "Well, I learned Egyptian at home, and then I learned Arabic in school"; they're that different. For us, it's a little bit less obvious that there's something called a vernacular, which is distinct from the "higher" register that we use. But the idea is to elicit that vernacular, and we're interested in the vernacular because it is the locus of change, which we'll actually get to as we go on. A little preview: It used to be that you wouldn't say, "stacked books," you would say, "stack-ed the books." That's the way this ending was pronounced even as late as the 1700s by some people. To say, "stacked" was seen as a little bit tacky, because you're cutting a sound, and so the way my old Japanese girlfriend would have said, "stack-ed," that was considered correct. Then it got to the point where "stacked," instead of being seen as a vernacular form, was the way everybody spoke. That's a preview of how that kind of thing happened.

What we want to do is elicit the vernacular; we want to record it. We want to put a microphone in and record it and analyze its linguistic features. That's hard. That is really, really difficult, because the vernacular is something where there's often a kind of a mixed feeling. There's a sense that many people have that, "Well, you know, when I relax I kind of let my grammar slip. There's a way that I like to talk when I'm in my garage with the shag rug, but that's not to be shared with the rest of the world." That's a feeling that I think a lot of us have; there's this inferiority complex. What this means is that there is what is termed an *observer's paradox* (that's in capital letters or italics). The observer's paradox, which basically means—

and I could spin out some wordy definition, but basically—it means that you cannot put on a suit and walk into somebody's living room with a microphone and say, "Talk the way you only talk when people like me are not around." You're not really going to get it. A normal person's response, if they're being recorded, is to talk "up," is to talk in the way that is seen as somehow better than the regular way that they talk.

How do you get the vernacular when you're trying to record it? You can hear it on the subway; you can hear it on the Metro. How do you get people to keep speaking it when the microphone is on? Labov developed what is called the *sociolinguistic interview*, and it consists of five segments. One of them is to try to elicit the vernacular, and one of the ways that Labov has done this in the classic sense is to ask people whether they've ever been in danger of death. If someone has ever hung from a cliff or something like that, then when they talk about it their heart rate goes up, they start talking faster, and they end up stopping attending to "what is proper grammar." You'll get the vernacular if the person's talking about when they were hanging from the cliff, or when a steamroller ran over them, or something like that. There are other things that you can ask people about. I don't think I've ever been in danger of death. I think in terms of when I would have been that excited, it was before the first time I ever had to give a lecture. I was sweating bullets. I was a grad student, and I didn't sleep the night before. I'm going to openly admit this: I actually had a shot of gin before I got up in front of the class. I was scared to death. That would elicit my vernacular. I remember everything about that morning, including falling off my bike afterwards and skinning my knee. What a morning! That was October 1989. Anyway, that is casual speech.

Another way that you get the vernacular—and you see this again and again—is that the person will be sitting there, speaking in their doily way into your microphone, and then the dog will come and lick them, or a child will do something wrong. They'll turn around and talk to the dog or the child—or something like that—in good vernacular English, because that's a very spontaneous utterance. That's another way to get vernacular.

Then Part B of the interview is called *careful speech*, and that's the way the person talks in the microphone when they just talk about general things: "I was born in Poughkeepsie," "I like wide-wale corduroy pants," or whatever they're going to say. Then they are asked in Part C to read. Of course, there's a certain "upness" that one uses when one reads. Then one is asked to read actual lists of words. For example, let's say that you were trying to analyze the pronunciation of a word like "those" as "dose." That is one of these issues: [ð] versus [d]. In this case, that alternation is a marker, because of course "dose" is seen to have a certain meaning in comparison to "those." If you were going to look at that, then Part D is to have the person read words like "these," "those," and "them" to see if even in this particularly formal context they would say, "dese," "dem," and "dose." Finally, there's something called *minimal pairs*. The interviewee is asked to read words that differ precisely in terms of the variable that's being investigated. If you were going to look at "dose" instead of "those," you'd have them read first the word "those" and then the word "doze"—as in snoozing—and see if there's any kind of difference, or something like "raw" and then "Rah, rah, rah!" as in "Go team!" That's the interview format that is used. That's been being done for about 40 years now.

What Labov then did with this was he decided to look at the disappearance of syllable-final [r] in New York City. What I mean by that is that back in the day, what's called "r-less dialect" was very widespread in New York and in many Northeastern cities. What I mean is instead of saying, "corner," you say, "cawnuh." We kind of hear an [r] in there maybe because we think of it as version of *corner*, but in terms of transcribing what "cawnuh" actually is, you see that there are no [r]'s ([kɔnə]). That's because there is a phenomenon in that dialect that you don't have [r]'s at the end of syllables. When we say, "r-less," we don't mean that they call *rabbits* "'abbits." It's specific; it's about syllables. It can't be at the end of the word, because then it would be "cornah." It's "cawnah," so always at the end of a syllable, it's gone. This was not only the cab driver; this was also upper-crusty sorts of people. I actually am no particular fan of Bette Davis. I don't know why I keep bringing her up, but people who used to imitate her back in the day would always say, "Petah, the lettah." Not only does that sound kind of funny, but she had r-less dialect, as she was coached in the schools that she went to. She didn't say, "Peter the letter"; she said, "Petah," and there's no [r] at the end. Now you may recognize that way of speaking from old movies. You may notice that actually starting in the black-and-white, *Camelot*, early '60s you get a sense of it disappearing. The people in the movie *Who's Afraid of Virginia Woolf* do not talk that way. If they had filmed that play in 1946, then it would have been, "I don't want to kiss you, Mahtha," but then it's different because speech had changed. (Martha is his wife.)

Anyway, what Labov did was he did interviews around New York City investigating this. Then he made a kind of a side trip, which was a classic experiment in order to elicit the way people actually talk, rather than the way we present ourselves as talking, in order to get a sense of who was developing r-lessness in terms of class, age, and everything. He looked at three department stores: Saks, Macy's, and Kline's. Saks I think we still know of today as the kind of place where you walk in, you get perfume squirted in your face, and everything is too expensive. Macy's is the middle ground. They always seem to have a sale, and they will let you return things. I wore a coat recently for three months. I decided I didn't like it. I'm a pretty clean person, and so I took it back to Macy's, and I said, "I don't like this." They just took it right back, so I like Macy's. Then there was Kline's. Kline's was kind of a big-box store that was low priced and kind of chaotic. It was the sort of thing where in a '30s cartoon, if Olive Oyl is going to go buy a hat and there are all these hats in the trough, and then all these other women come and everybody starts fighting over the hats, and they have rubbery limbs—I'm assuming everybody has seen that cartoon—that would have been at Kline's. Kline's had linoleum floor, and nobody was squirting anything at you. You have those three levels of department stores.

Labov and his graduate students went into all three of these stores, and this was the trick: They figured out what was on the fourth floor—I don't know what would be on the fourth floor: safety pins, hats, something like that. Then they'd go into the store and they'd ask, "Where can I find safety pins?" Then the person would say, "Fourth floor," however they would say it—often "Fawth flaw." Then they'd ask, "What did you say?" to get it more explicit, because there are people who, when being more explicit, will then use the formal variant and some where the marker is so far advanced that even explicitly they'll still say, "Fawth flaw." The idea was to see those two levels, to see how far this r-lessness had gone and to what extent it was disappearing. They ran around these stores and they did that—"Fourth floor!" "Fourth floor!" They annoyed a lot of people. What they found was that the use of syllable-final [r] and the disappearance of syllable-final [r] correlated very strongly with various sociological factors. It wasn't just random. It wasn't all just kind of fluttering away. There was system to this.

For example, it was found that at Kline's—this is the kind of Popeye store—79 percent of the people who they accosted that way had no syllable-final [r] at all, even when speaking explicitly. "Where did you say the safety pins were?" "Fawth flaw." They just don't have it. That's the way they talk. Then, at Saks, that was only 38 percent of people. So it shows it was a different era; there were people even at Saks who would say those gold-plated safety pins were on the "fawth flaw." For the most part, you'd get either "fawth flaw" and then "I said fourth floor" or very often it would be, "Fourth floor, sir. I said, fourth floor." That was at Saks. This was a matter of class. There was more [r] usage the higher the class. This is an era when the old days when both Bette Davis and the cab driver were r-less, which was the fact way back in the day, was changing. It was the upper classes and the people who were less poor who led in that particular change.

You can see the same sort of thing, actually, in the difference between saying, something like "thing" and "ting" in this chart. That was analyzed as well. Here Labov did the sociolinguistic interviews that I talked about. You can see that in terms of the lower-class people, they said, "ting" instead of "thing" the most in casual speech. But then you see on the graph that everybody is almost the same when it comes to being as explicit as, for example, reading. There were very few people who would look at the word *thing* written on the page and look at you and say, "ting." Then they're going to say, "thing." They're capable of pronouncing the sound. There's a difference between, so to speak, their Egyptian and their Modern Standard, their vernacular and formal language. You can't just ask people about this sort of thing, however. You have to kind of trick it out of them, and that's what a lot of this interview style is about.

Now: Why age? There was something interesting at Macy's, the middle store. Generally, older people had less [r]; they had more r-lessness, because this was an antique feature. But at Macy's, no matter how old the people got, they were more "r-ful," so to speak. That phenomenon was only at Macy's. At Kline's and at Saks, older people tended to reflect the r-less old days. The hypothesis was that middle-class speakers were moving to r-ful forms as they got older as part of having middle-class aspiration. That kind of quirk in terms of the middle-class older person has been found in many studies since, or I should I say was found often after this study, because it was a while ago. That's one way that age had an interesting ripple.

Another interesting ripple in the data is something that you can see in this chart, which is something that the lower-middle-class speakers are doing. You see this ordinary hierarchical progression on the left half of the chart when we're talking about the vernacular speech and even the sort of language that you use within the interview. But suddenly in the middle, something happened: The lower-middle-class speakers suddenly kind of broke out. When it comes to doing something as careful and as exposed as reading a word list or reading minimal pairs, suddenly these people are being even more careful and being even more diligent—if you want to call it that—about using the prestige variant than the people who are of higher class than them. You see how their line breaks upward of everybody-else's.

If Labov had only found that with his particular corpus of speakers of English in New York City in that particular era, then this would qualify as just a kind of a fluke. But in fact, that has been replicated in a great many studies, that you see that lower-middle-class speakers—i.e., Peg Bundy; i.e., Marge Simpson—when they're going through especially Parts D and E of the sociolinguistic interview, end up speaking particularly "properly." This has been found not only in the United States, but this has been found in other countries. It seems that people of that particular stratum in terms of class might have a certain self-consciousness about their speech and whether or not they speak well. If that were true, then it wouldn't be a surprise, given that there's such a witch hunt in our society and in most societies against what is considered bad grammar. As a result, when there is this exposed kind of performance in the language expected, it may be that people who are of that class—and, interestingly, not above or below, but that particular class—have a predisposition toward being particularly attendant to the way that they speak. That phenomenon of course has a jargonistic name; it's called *hypercorrection*. That's something that the study of variables has shown again and again.

The basic insight of this introduction to the notion of variables is that certainly we don't want to stereotype people as all talking one way because they belong to a certain social class. It's hard enough to decide, often, what social class a person belongs to. However, the fact of the matter is that vernacular variance—i.e., ways of speaking that are considered less prestigious than what is often considered good grammar—are used, statistically, more by people who are not upper class and who are not upper middle class. The reason that that ends up being interesting is because it is among the people who are not upper class, not upper middle class, not middle class, that we can see where under ordinary conditions—which is not always the case in a first-world society; that's a different issue we'll talk about—but under ordinary conditions, that would be where the language is going. If you want to know what a language's grammar is going to be like in 500 years, then the place to look is in the speech of the working classes, for example, and not others.

# Timeline

1786 ............................................... Sir William Jones addresses the Bengal Asiatic Society and observes that Sanskrit, Greek, and Latin are similar in grammatical structure to such a degree that they must all trace to a single ancestor, "which, perhaps, no longer exists." This was the first clear acknowledgment that languages exist in an evolutionary relationship to one another.

1822 ............................................... Jacob Grimm proposes what is later termed Grimm's Law, describing the regular contrasts between consonants in cognate words in Germanic languages and others of the Indo-European family (i.e., English's *father* and *fish* are *pater* and *piscis* in Latin). This inaugurates the study of sound change as a regular process, the beginning of what would become modern linguistic science.

1916 ............................................... Ferdinand de Saussure's *Course in General Linguistics* is published posthumously, outlining the analysis of language not from a historical perspective but as it exists at the moment, proposing that grammar consists of a conglomeration of signs of contrasting function. This furnished the basis of modern linguistic description of languages' grammars.

1924 ............................................... The Linguistic Society of America (LSA) is formed. The LSA holds an annual conference, the largest in the linguistics field, and publishes the journal *Language*.

1926 .................................................The Prague School is founded in Czechoslovakia among Czech and Russian expatriate linguists, including Roman Jakobson and Nikolai Trubetzkoy. Among its achievements is a conception of markedness among sounds and its relationship to language production and acquisition, as well as the conception of sounds as characterized by opposing qualities such as voiced and unvoiced. Modern phonology begins here.

1933 .................................................Leonard Bloomfield's *Language* is published. Bloomfield officially imprints the study of unknown languages' grammars from a purely scientific perspective, using the tools developed by de Saussure, the Prague school, and others to describe languages' phonology, morphology, and syntax. This approach has come to be termed structuralist linguistics.

1957 .................................................Noam Chomsky's *Syntactic Structures* is published. In this work and future ones, Chomsky develops a theory that sentences as generated at a deep-structure level and as produced at a surface-structure level are often quite different and that there is an innate universal grammar structure in which all languages, despite their surface differences, are founded. Modern syntactic theory begins here.

1966 ................................................Joseph Greenberg's *Language Universals, With Special Reference to Feature Hierarchies* is published. Greenberg shows that languages do not consist of random conglomerations of grammatical traits but that certain ones are only present when others are, in a nested fashion. This inspires the study of language universals and typology and provides a body of observations that generativists find it useful to attempt to explain in their framework.

1966 ................................................William Labov's *The Social Stratification of English in New York City* is published. Labov shows that language changes at different rates and in different ways among subpopulations according to gender, class, and race and does so with various ingenious systems for eliciting casual (genuine), rather than artificially "polite," speech. This inaugurates the now-vigorous subfield of sociolinguistics.

2001 ................................................The *FOXP2* gene is discovered to play an important role in humans' speech capacity. Specifically, the gene produces a protein that activates other genes; currently, these appear to include genes connected to brain development and motor control. Human *FOXP2* differs from that of chimpanzees by only two amino acids, but it would appear that, in a fashion as yet unknown, this determines that humans are alone among the world's fauna in using full language.

# Glossary

**age grading**: When a variable is used more by younger people than older ones; often evidence that the young's choice is a change happening in the language.

**agent**: A subject that has an effect upon the object (*the boy kicked the ball*) rather than experiencing the object (*the boy liked the ball*) or referring to no object (*the boy slept*).

**agglutinative**: A language that assigns grammatical functions one at a time to discretely separate morphemes that agglutinate together, like Turkish and Swahili (see *fusional*).

**allophone**: One of two or more variant renditions of a basic sound (*phoneme*) in a language, determined by what kinds of sounds it occurs near. The [p] sound is pronounced with a puff of air when initial (*Paul*) but not otherwise (*spat*); these are two allophones of the phoneme /p/.

**alveolar**: Sounds produced by tapping the alveolar ridge, behind the upper teeth, with the tip of the tongue. In English, these include [t], [d], [s], and [n].

**analytic**: A language in which morphemes are generally separate words rather than occurring as prefixes and suffixes; sometimes called *isolating languages*.

**assimilation**: When a sound takes on qualities of a sound it occurs near; the *m* in *impossible* is due to what was once an [n] assimilating to the bilabial articulation of [p].

**code switching**: Using two or more languages within the same sentence or utterance.

**complement phrase**: A relative or subordinate clause, represented in theoretical syntax notation as a subsentence headed by a comp (C) node.

**compound**: A word composed of two content morphemes, such as *blackbird* and *streetcar*.

**consonant weakening**: The tendency for consonants to change into less phonetically robust ones via usage; stops become fricatives, fricatives become glides, and glides disappear: *ripe* is *maturus* in Latin, *mathuro* in Castilian, and *mûr* in French.

**constituent**: An element in a sentence that may consist of a single word, such as a noun or verb, but can also consist of this plus its modifiers: *a small, black cat* is a constituent—namely, a noun phrase.

**conversational implicature**: Conventionalized understandings that set requests and statements presuppose responses that do not correspond literally to what was asked or stated; *Do you have the time?* is not understood as a query as to whether one is wearing a watch.

**covert prestige**: The tacit sense of pride that vernacular speakers have in variables officially considered nonstandard; i.e., "the way we talk in these parts."

**deixis**: A language's mechanisms for placing a statement in time, space, and attitudinal realm.

**derivational**: Morphemes that typically change a root to a different part of speech (*happy, happiness*) or, if not, create a different word (*friend, friendship*).

**diachronic**: A perspective on language addressing its change over time.

**dual marking**: In many languages, one can mark not only the plural but more precisely that there are two of something.

**ergativity**: When a language marks subjects when they are agents of patients with one marker but other subjects with a different marker or not at all. If there is this different marker for nonagents, it is also used on objects. Thus the *ergative* marker marks agents, while the *absolutive* marker marks objects and nonagent subjects.

**experiencer**: A subject that does not affect the object; e.g., *I like Alice*; *I see a snowflake*.

**fricative**: "Hissy" sounds involving letting air flow in an obstructed fashion; in English, examples include [f], [s], and [h].

**fusional**: A language in which grammatical morphemes often indicate two or more functions; e.g., in *walks*, *-s* indicates both present tense and third-person singular.

**given information**: Content in a sentence that is already known via previous exchange and is thus often abridged; A: *Who took my pen?* B: *That man*. A: *Where did he go?* In the final sentence, *he* is an abbreviation of *That man*, possible because it refers to given information.

**glides**: Consonants produced with only passing friction, to the point of being almost like vowels; in English, [w] and the sound of *y* ([j]).

**grammar**: In linguistics, this refers not to "proper" grammar but to the basic workings of sentence structure (as well as, in practice, often phonology).

**head**: The morpheme that determines the syntactic type of phrase (i.e., noun phrase, verb phrase) of which the morpheme is a member; it is the morpheme being modified by the others; in *the bushy old anteater*, the head is the noun *anteater*.

**Head-First Parameter**: A syntactic setting in which heads occur either first (when set "on") or finally (when set "off") in their *constituents* in a more-or-less regular fashion throughout the language.

**historical linguistics**: The study of how language changes over time, as opposed to its state in the here and now.

**hypercorrection**: A tendency to use forms considered standard to such a pronounced extent as to surpass the habits of even the most typically "proper" speakers; often observed among working-class speakers engaging in the reading of word lists.

**illocutionary**: Utterances that constitute, in themselves, the execution of an action, such as *I apologize*.

**implicational universals**: The tendency for certain grammatical structures to occur in a language only if certain others do; e.g., a language has dual marking only if it also has plural marking; many languages have only plural marking, but none have only dual marking.

**indicator**: A variable with no social significance; i.e., *he's not* versus *he isn't*.

**Indo-European**: The language family that most European languages belong to, as well as most of those of Iran and India.

**inflection**: A grammatical morpheme that fulfills a syntactic function but does not change a word's part of speech or meaning; e.g., *-s* in *walks*.

**manner of articulation**: One of several ways of producing consonants; i.e., stops, fricatives, nasals, glides; contrast with *place of articulation*.

**markedness**: This is a multifarious term in linguistics, both over time and across the various subfields. As used in this course, *marked* features are sounds or grammatical features that are less common across all languages than those found most commonly in languages (*unmarked* features). Often the marked rendition is found only when the unmarked rendition is found in a language as well. For example, the final sound in Bach (a voiceless velar fricative) is more marked—meaning less common—than the sound of *a* in father. To take a grammatical example, some languages mark not only plurality but the more specific concept of the dual, indicating that there are two of something. Dual marking, which is less common than plural marking and only occurs in languages that also have plural marking, is more marked than plural marking.

**marker**: A variable that has social significance; i.e., *singing* versus *singin'*.

**minimal pair**: Words that contrast in only a single sound, such as *those* and *doze*; often adduced to determine what constitutes a phoneme.

**morpheme**: A unit of meaning, of which a word may contain several; *hunters* contains three morphemes (*hunt*, *-er*, and *-s*).

**new information**: Content in a sentence or utterance that is novel, marked explicitly as such in many languages with particles or affixes.

**nonproductive**: A derivational morpheme no longer applied to new words, such as *-dom* in *freedom*.

**observer's paradox**: The fact that vernacular speakers tend to switch to standard speech in the presence of investigators from outside of their community.

**patient**: An object that is directly affected by a subject (*the boy kicked the ball*).

**phoneme**: A sound in a language that can make the difference between one word and another (*bat* versus *pat*), as opposed to a sound that is just a variant way of rendering another one (the pronunciation of *l* in *lick* is quite different from its pronunciation in *oil*, yet both are "the same sound," the phoneme /l/).

**place of articulation**: Where in the mouth a consonant is produced (bilabial, alveolar, velar, glottal, etc.); contrast with *manner of articulation*.

**polysynthetic**: A language in which a verb's subject, object, and other associated components must either be compounded with the verb or reflected on the verb in the form of affixes; e.g. in Mohawk, to say, "He likes babies," one must say either, "He baby-likes" or, "He likes them, babies."

**prescriptive**: The perspective on language stipulating that there is a "correct" and an "incorrect" way to speak, as contrasted with the descriptive tradition, which accepts all generalized speech patterns as legitimate.

**Pro-Drop Parameter**: A syntactic setting that, when set "on," allows subject pronouns to be omitted (Spanish *hablo*, "I speak"). Also known as the Null Subject Parameter.

**semantic role**: Classes of meaning that elements of a sentence correspond to independently of their grammatical functions as subjects or objects; e.g., in *the dog bit the man* and *the man was bitten by the dog*, the subject is *dog* in one and *man* in the other, but in both, the agent is *dog* and the patient is *man*.

**sociolinguistics**: The study of how language varies according to social factors such as class, race, and gender and external factors such as bilingualism and culture.

**syllabary**: A writing system in which signs indicate syllables rather than individual sounds.

**synchronic**: The perspective on language analyzing its present state, rather than the *diachronic* perspective, which addresses language as it changes.

**syntax**: In linguistics, this refers not to the exercise of sentence parsing on paper but to the mechanisms ordering words in sentences after the processes of phonology and morphology have been applied.

**topic**: In linguistics, an element serving as the focus of an observation, separate from the syntactic subject of the sentence; in *Me, I like pomegranates*, *me* is the topic.

**trace**: In syntactic theory, a "space" left behind when an element is moved in the pathway from deep structure to surface structure; e.g., in *What did you see?* it is hypothesized that there is a trace after *see*, an empty or "phantom" node (sometimes indicated as T), left behind by *what*.

**transfer**: The use of native language grammatical features in one's rendition of a second language, resulting in, for example, a foreign accent in terms of phonology.

**transformation**: Processes involving the movement of words or constituents in the process of generating a sentence from deep to surface structure, such as the movement of *what* to the front of the sentence in *What did you see?*

**variable**: One of two or more possible renditions of a sound or affix in a language, with one rendition often considered less "proper" than others, such as *singing* versus *singin'*.

**vernacular**: Casual speech learned as a child without explicit tutelage, as opposed to standard forms often learned through teaching and reading.

**Verb Attraction Parameter**: A syntactic setting that brings verbs forward in sentences, hypothesized by some linguists to result from ample verb-conjugation suffixes; thus in French *J'embrasse souvent Marie* but in English *I often kiss Mary*; in English the verb stays after the adverb because there is little conjugational morphology in the language. Sometimes referred to as the Inflection Parameter.

# Biographical Notes

**Noam Chomsky** (1928–): Best known in the wider world as a leading leftist political commentator, he was also the founder of today's most influential school of syntactic analysis. He was born in Philadelphia. While doing his graduate work in linguistics on Hebrew grammar at the University of Pennsylvania, he found that the then-reigning theories of how language is structured could not provide a systematic analysis of Hebrew. In his dissertation, published in 1957 as *Syntactic Structures*, he argued that language is generated in the mind first in a deep-structure rendition, upon which various transformations are applied to yield a surface structure. He took a faculty position at the Massachusetts Institute of Technology (where he is currently a professor emeritus) and has developed the hypothesis that humans are born with a hardwired capacity for language, within a larger cognitivist philosophy of the human mind, notoriously opposed to the behaviorist conceptions of B. F. Skinner.

**Joseph Greenberg** (1915–2001): Trained as an anthropologist at Northwestern University but found himself most interested in linguistics. He spent most of his career teaching at Stanford University. Greenberg noted that languages' grammars are organized according to a flow-chart principle, in which certain features are only present if other ones are; otherwise, these features are never present (i.e., no language has vowels like the *i* sound in *sit* or the *u* sound in *but* that does not also have the basic set [a], [e], [i], [o], [u]) and, in this, founded the subfield of typology. He also grouped the 1,000-plus languages of Africa into four subfamilies and, more controversially, the Native American languages into three subfamilies, as well as grouping Indo-European, Uralic, Eskimo-Aleut, and some other families into a megafamily called Eurasiatic.

**Jacob Grimm** (1785–1863): Collected folktales in his native Prussia with his brother Wilhelm and is thus best known for the legacy of *Grimm's Fairy Tales*. This collecting, however, was one part of a broader interest in the earlier stages of his country's language and culture. After training in law and serving in assorted administrative posts, he took his place as a professor at the University of Göttingen, where he wrote a seminal description of German grammar. (According to the convention of the period, this was actually a treatise on the historical development of the language). Grimm's most important insight was that the sounds in a language change in consistent fashion over time, demonstrated most memorably by the regular differences in how consonants are rendered in cognate words in

Germanic languages and classical ones like Latin and Greek. This is called Grimm's Law. Grimm was also a fervent German nationalist and served briefly in the Frankfurt National Parliament in the wake of the political upheavals of 1848.

**Wilhelm von Humboldt** (1767–1835): During his lifetime, he was most widely known as an accomplished diplomat and ambassador for his native Prussia. He was also a political philosopher, espousing classical liberalism ("The government is best which makes itself unnecessary") in *On the Limits of State Action*, a primary source for the ideas that would later influence the Anglophone world through John Stuart Mill's *On Liberty*. Von Humboldt also established the Prussian educational system as a world-class one; as Minister of Education, he was central to the creation of the University of Berlin. He began researching linguistic issues mainly after retiring from politics in 1819. Besides his typologization of languages, his most influential work included foundational research on the Basque language and its history and an exploration of the relationship between languages and their speakers' world views, which anticipated later work in this vein by Edward Sapir and Benjamin Lee Whorf. Von Humboldt's brother Alexander was a world-renowned naturalist.

**Roman Jakobson** (1896–1982): Born in Russia, he embarked upon the study of linguistics there. After the revolution there, he relocated to Czechoslovakia, where he was part of what came to be known as the Prague Circle. Here Jakobson was central to the formulation—developing the ideas of Ferdinand de Saussure—of conceptions of markedness hierarchies and their relationship to phonology, language acquisition, and typology. After a move to Copenhagen, Jakobson moved to New York City. He then taught at Harvard for the rest of his career, where he collaborated with Morris Halle on a foundational text on markedness theory (*Fundamentals of Language*, 1956). Jakobson's scholarly interests also included the study of communication in the broader sense, as well as poetry and art.

**William Labov** (1927–): The founder of variationist linguistics, which analyzes how language structure differs according to sociological factors such as gender, class, and race. After spending his younger adulthood as a chemist, Labov took his doctorate in linguistics at Columbia University in 1964 and since 1971 has taught at the University of Pennsylvania. His foundational text was his master's thesis, analyzing how the local speech of Martha's Vineyard was changing due to factors of social identity. He followed this with his signature study, *The Social Stratification of English in New York City* (1966), analyzing the gradual disappearance of the once-prevalent local New York accent via innovative methods of eliciting unmonitored speech from strangers. He also pioneered the study of Black English as a systematic speech variety in *Language in the Inner City* (1972).

**Rasmus Christian Rask** (1787–1832): Often cited for his astonishing capacity for learning foreign languages, he reportedly spoke about 25. A Dane, he began as assistant librarian at the University of Copenhagen and was soon supported in a two-year expedition to Iceland, after which he wrote the first grammatical description of the Icelandic language. He went on to do foundational research on the relationships between the languages of Northern Europe, Greek, and Latin and the languages of Iran and India, travelling widely to gather data and learning to speak new languages along the way. In his *An Investigation Concerning the Source of the Old Northern or Icelandic Language* (1818), Rask was the first to observe the systematic difference between Icelandic and Greek consonants, which would soon be developed as Grimm's Law.

**Edward Sapir** (1884–1939): His most tangible legacy to modern linguistics is his 1921 book, *Language*, a readable and lucid introduction to the study of human speech. This book and his other writings include an argument that languages to some extent reflect the thought patterns and cultural outlooks of their speakers, an idea that Sapir's student Benjamin Lee Whorf took further after his death. Sapir was born in Prussia and did his graduate study in anthropology at Columbia University in New York. He taught at the University of Chicago and Yale University. His research focus was on Native American languages of the Pacific coast, especially those of the Athabaskan family; he worked with the last surviving Yahi, Ishi, to document the language. Sapir died at 55 but inspired later prominent followers such as Whorf, Mary Haas, and Zellig Harris.

**Ferdinand de Saussure** (1857–1913): A Geneva-born linguist, he attained his doctorate at the University of Leipzig and specialized in the Indo-European language family. His monograph *Course in General Linguistics*, although actually compiled after his death by two of his students from notes taken from his lectures, was the foundation of the concept of language as composed of signs encoding opposite meanings and thus of the basic framework of modern linguistic analysis. During his lifetime, de Saussure was best known for his hypothesis that the ancestor of all of the Indo-European languages had a trio of laryngeal consonants now extinct in all of its descendants but deducible via tracing backward from certain particularities of cognates in the languages. The discovery of documents in the extinct Indo-European language Hittite proved de Saussure correct, despite the initial rejection of his idea.

**Benjamin Lee Whorf** (1897–1941): Despite his renown as a thinker on linguistic issues today, he was during his lifetime a fire-prevention inspector for the Hartford Fire Insurance Company with a degree in chemical engineering from the Massachusetts Institute of Technology. He pursued linguistics as a hobby, and it was while taking linguistics courses at Yale that he came under the influence of Edward Sapir. As a result, he developed and promulgated the Sapir-Whorf hypothesis, proposing that people's languages channel the way that they perceive the world. Whorf was especially interested in the Hopi language and also studied Mayan and Nahuatl. Whorf, like Sapir, died early (at 44), but the influence of his writings on research in linguistics, anthropology, and psychology continues to this day, gathered in the now-classic anthology *Language, Thought, and Reality*.

# Bibliography

Arlotto, Anthony. *Introduction to Historical Linguistics.* Boston: University Press of America, 1972. An especially clear introduction to comparative reconstruction of protolanguages, often assigned in undergraduate courses some years ago. Newer books in the vein have come along, but this one is worth seeking in a library for its conciseness, as the newer ones cover the historical linguistics field more broadly.

Bailey, Richard W. *Nineteenth-Century English.* Ann Arbor: University of Michigan Press, 1996. This book, pitched to general readers as well as scholars, gives thorough (but not compulsive) coverage of what English was like two centuries ago, and it gives invaluable perspective on the arbitrariness of what is considered "proper speech" from one era to another, revealing English as, like all languages, a vast smudge of variations on a theme.

Baker, Mark C. *The Atoms of Language.* New York: Basic, 2001. This is a clear and engaging presentation of the parameter concept by a leading linguist who is one of today's leading proponents of the hypothesis. A fine job of translating an often highly abstract and jargon-heavy school of thought into terms effective for laymen.

Baugh, A. C., and T. Cable. *A History of the English Language.* Englewood Cliffs, NJ: Prentice-Hall, 1978. One of those deathless staple sources, a standard accessible history of English for those hungry for the details but not the trivia.

Bauman, Richard, and Joel Sherzer. *Explorations in the Ethnography of Speaking.* 2nd ed. London: Cambridge University Press, 1989. Long out of print, this anthology remains a classic source of studies in the ethnography of communication framework. I include it in particular because of one of the most illuminating and accessible articles on language use I am aware of, the one on rural Antigua by Karl Reisman, which I highly recommend.

Bernstein, Basil. *Pedagogy, Symbolic Control, and Identity: Theory, Research, Critique.* Lanham, MD: Rowan & Littlefield, 2000. For those interested in engaging Bernstein more closely, this anthology gathers his most significant work; this is a new edition that includes works that an earlier one did not.

Brown, Penelope, and Stephen C. Levinson. *Politeness: Some Universals in Language Usage.* Cambridge: Cambridge University Press, 1987. This remains the foundational text of the study of politeness and is accessible to people outside of linguistics and psychology. It is still in print and is especially useful in addressing three very distinct cultures: America (and England), the Tzeltal Mayans of Mexico, and the Tamil of India.

Bryson, Bill. *The Mother Tongue: English and How it Got that Way*. New York: William Morrow, 1990. Unsurpassed as a jolly, often laugh-out-loud trip through the history of English. Baugh & Cable will give the details, but this is a great introduction.

Colarusso, John. *A Grammar of the Kabardian Language*. Calgary: University of Calgary Press, 1992. This is the only full-length grammatical description of Kabardian. I chose this language because it is so complex that it almost beggars belief that anyone actually speaks it, and those with a bent for checking out obscure tongues just for the glory of it might enjoy curling up with this grammar (luckily, available in an inexpensive paperback).

Comrie, Bernard. *Language Universals and Linguistic Typology*. Chicago: University of Chicago Press, 1981. The closest thing to a book for interested laypeople on universals and implicational hierarchies; I recall reading this one as a first-year graduate student before I was familiar with many concepts or much terminology, and yet it came through loud and clear.

Croft, William. *Typology and Universals*. Cambridge: Cambridge University Press, 2003. This book, revised from a well-received first edition, covers in detailed fashion the basic concepts applied to by specialists in typology. Not one for the beach, but by no means too dense for anyone but superspecialists, either.

Crystal, David. *The Cambridge Encyclopedia of the English Language*. Cambridge: Cambridge University Press, 1995. A magnificent, almost imposingly rich trip through English, past and present, in all of its facets, as beautifully illustrated as the previous volume. Captures between two covers a magnificent volume of information, much of it otherwise hard to access.

———. *The Cambridge Encyclopedia of Language*. Cambridge: Cambridge University Press, 1997. An invaluable encyclopedia, lavishly illustrated, on anything one might want to know about language and languages. This has been at arm's length from my desk for 10 years now.

———. *The Fight for English: How Language Pundits Ate, Shot, and Left*. Oxford: Oxford University Press, 2007. Linguists' anti-prescriptivist stance summarized in a pointed yet temperate tone in a single book, well keyed to the world we live in today.

Farber, Barry. *How To Learn Any Language: Quickly, Easily, Inexpensively, Enjoyably and on Your Own*. Secaucus, NJ: Citadel, 2001. A pleasant-to-read and spot-on guide to how to learn a foreign language by yourself, showing how to make the crucial step beyond reciting the words and sentences in your self-teaching book and generating the language on your own "for real." Not a scholarly book, but effective in every way.

Fasold, Ralph. *The Sociolinguistics of Language*. Oxford: Basil Blackwell, 1990. Those who want a closer look at how socially conditioned variation in language leads to change in the language will do best to consult the eighth chapter of this textbook on sociolinguistics. It has not become one of the standard ones, which is a shame because the author, a career sociolinguist, is a born teacher and writes engagingly.

Finegan, Edward. *Language: Its Structure and Use*. 5th ed. Boston: Thomas Wadsworth, 2008. A uniquely reader-friendly linguistics textbook and likely the one best suited for people outside of a classroom who simply want an introduction to the subject.

Gass, Susan M., and Larry Selinker. *Second Language Acquisition: An Introductory Course*. New York: Routledge, 2008. A solid, comprehensive survey of the best of what has been thought and said about second-language acquisition; it is especially useful in that this subfield straddles several disciplines and subdisciplines and thus can be challenging to gain a bird's-eye view of.

Gentner, Dedre, and Susan Goldin-Meadow, eds. *Language in Mind: Advances in the Study of Language and Thought*. Cambridge, MA: MIT Press, 2003. An anthology of Neo-Whorfian work, which I recommend especially in that it contains an interesting and readable study by Lera Boroditzky on perceptions of objects as gendered, mentioned in Lecture Twenty-Eight.

Harris, Roy, and Talbot J. Taylor, eds. *Landmarks in Linguistic Thought I: The Western Tradition from Socrates to Saussure*. London: Routledge, 1989. For those interested in explorations of language over the millennia with a philosophical orientation (as well as other explorations), this is a handy, readable survey of thinkers' landmark observations about language from antiquity through to the 19th century. Each thinker is treated in a chapter, in which a text is cited, followed by insightful commentary by the editors.

Heath, Shirley Brice. *Ways with Words: Language, Life and Work in Communities and Classrooms*. Cambridge: Cambridge University Press, 1983. This is a classic study on how language use varies according to social class and its effects on children's development and their prospects in school, based on detailed ethnographic research.

Hill, Jane H., and Kenneth C. Hill. *Speaking Mexicano: Dynamics of Syncretic Language in Central Mexico*. Tucson: University of Arizona Press, 1986. A classic and well-written study of language use by indigenous Mexicans, including the use of both Spanish and the local language Nahuatl, with an orientation in the ethnography of communication perspective. Not in print but available, especially in university libraries.

Hock, Hans Heinrich. *Principles of Historical Linguistics*. Berlin: Mouton de Gruyter, 1991. A standard, wide-ranging coverage of the basic tools of historical linguistics, including detailed sections on Grimm's Law, analogy, and related issues.

Hopper, Paul J., and Elizabeth Closs Traugott. *Grammaticalization*. Cambridge: Cambridge University Press, 2003. The standard introduction in the field to grammaticalization, written by two of the pioneers of its incorporation into mainstream linguistic thought in the 1980s.

Horn, Laurence, and Gregory Ward. *The Handbook of Pragmatics*. Malden, MA: Blackwell, 2005. This rich and hefty collection of articles on pragmatics will answer any questions one might have, or guide one to where to find them, on pragmatics, which is a wide-ranging field with applications to many other disciplines and subdisciplines.

Jackendoff, Ray. *Foundations of Language: Brain, Meaning, Grammar, Evolution*. Oxford: Oxford University Press, 2002. This signature book is written more for academics than laymen, but more in its thoroughness of argument than in being utterly opaque to general readers. Those with a serious interest in current conceptions of what language is and how it could have happened will find this a useful source to curl up with.

Joseph, John E., Nigel Love, and Talbot J. Taylor. *Landmarks in Linguistic Thought II: The Western Tradition in the Twentieth Century*. London: Routledge, 2001. This is a continuation of the Harris and Taylor volume described above, covering the 20th century and equally useful.

Kenneally, Christine. *The First Word: The Search for the Origins of Language*. New York: Viking, 2007. This is, finally, a book for general readers chronicling the burgeoning study of how language emerged in humans. Kenneally does not as a rule present substantial outlines of scholars' work on the subject but instead gives previews, after which readers can consult the original sources themselves.

Labov, William. *Language in the Inner City*. Philadelphia: University of Pennsylvania Press, 1972. This remains the summary statement about variation in language, consisting of various foundational studies by Labov from the 1960s. It also remains timely in addressing the speech of inner-city blacks. It's no accident it's still in print almost 40 years after its appearance.

————. *The Social Stratification of English*. Cambridge: Cambridge University Press, 2006. This second edition of a book originally published in 1966 preserves a detailed account of the research project by Labov described in Lecture Sixteen and adds a summary statement of the progress of this kind of inquiry in the decades since.

Ladefoged, Peter, and Ian Maddieson. *The Sounds of the World's Languages*. Malden, MA: Blackwell, 1996. The standard reference work comparing sounds in a wide range of the world's languages, shedding light on how common or rare various sounds are.

Lakoff, Robin. *Language and Women's Place: Text and Commentaries*. New York: Oxford University Press, 2004. This is an annotated version of a text originally published in 1975, which founded the modern school of linguistics investigating language and gender. This source is the perfect way to engage the foundational ideas of 1975, given how much American society has changed since Lakoff first wrote the book. It includes her own commentaries from the vantage point of our times plus others from a wide range of other specialists, including students of Lakoff's.

Levinson, Stephen C., and John J. Gumperz, eds. *Rethinking Linguistic Relativity*. Cambridge: Cambridge University Press, 1996. A substantial anthology of studies under the neo-Whorfian paradigm, including the one mentioned in Lecture Twenty-Eight on directional concepts among an Australian group.

Lightfoot, David. *How to Set Parameters*. Cambridge, MA: MIT Press, 1991. Mainly written for academic linguists, this book will be useful to those who want a deeper engagement with the parameter idea, as Lightfoot is so clear a writer that nonlinguists will be able to approach a great deal of the text. The book is also suitably short.

Lucy, John A. *Language Diversity and Thought: A Reformulation of the Linguistic Relativity Hypothesis*. Cambridge: Cambridge University Press, 1992. A flinty and insightful survey of the original Whorfian hypothesis and the experiments testing it up to the early 1990s, including some by the author.

Lust, Barbara C., and Claire Foley. *First Language Acquisition: The Essential Readings*. Malden, MA: Blackwell, 2004. A collection of seminal writings on how children acquire language; a perfect way to get a sense of how modern linguists approach the subject.

McWhorter, John. *The Power of Babel: A Natural History of Human Language*. New York: HarperCollins, 2001. A reader-friendly survey of what has happened when the world's languages have proliferated and then met one another, with excessive digressionary footnotes about the author's hobbyist predilections and neuroses. (Anyone who agrees with the "excessive" assessment should have seen the first draft!)

McWhorter, John, and Jeff Good. *Saramaccan Grammar*. This will be the first full-length grammatical description of Saramaccan and will contain ampler descriptions of the constructions discussed in this course and, of course, so much more. As I write, the work is just short of completion and has not yet been submitted to a publisher. But it will be sometime in early 2008, and luckily there is no such thing as linguists writing a grammatical description and being unable to find a publisher. So, depending on how much further in the future you are from when I am writing this, hit Amazon and ye shall find.

Milroy, Lesley, and Pieter Muysken, eds. *One Speaker, Two Languages: Cross-Disciplinary Perspectives on Code-Switching*. Cambridge: Cambridge University Press, 1995. A collection of scholarly articles on code switching from a worldwide perspective and from the point of view of various disciplines.

Myers-Scotton, Carol. *Code-Switching: Evidence from Africa*. Oxford: Clarendon Press, 1993. Why Clarendon Press didn't publish this together with Myers-Scotton's *Duelling Languages* as one book has never been clear to me, but this book covers the sociological motivations for code switching and will likely speak more directly to laypeople than the other book.

————. *Duelling Languages: Grammatical Structure in Code-Switching*. Oxford: Clarendon Press, 1993. This is the book-length exposition of a leading and clear theory on how code switching works in the linguistic sense. The details will mostly interest linguists and psychologists, but the first few chapters will nicely acquaint others with what I consider a finely argued hypothesis.

O'Grady, William D. *How Children Learn Language*. Cambridge: Cambridge University Press, 2005. A perfect compact introduction to findings in first-language acquisition, written in accessible prose, almost as if it were explicitly designed for audiences of The Teaching Company's courses.

O'Grady, William, John Archibald, Mark Aronoff, and Janie Rees-Miller, eds. *Contemporary Linguistics: An Introduction*. New York: St. Martin's, 2004. Generally considered the finest linguistics textbook; those interested in delving further into topics covered in this course, including engaging with the "problem set" format via which linguistics is taught in the classroom, will find this textbook highly useful.

Payne, Thomas E. *Describing Morphosyntax: A Guide for Field Linguists*. Cambridge: Cambridge University Press, 1997. Although this is technically intended as a tool for linguists describing hitherto-undocumented language's grammars, it is also a concise yet comprehensive survey of the various functions that affixes and other forms of morphology have in languages and is a handy summary in general of grammatical concepts fundamental to the study of language.

Pinker, Steven. *The Language Instinct*. New York: Harper Perennial, 1994. This is the now-classic source for laymen to examine the issue of whether there is an innately specified ability to use language in our brains. Pinker writes with hipness and wit.

———. *Word and Rules: The Ingredients of Language*. New York: Basic, 1999. Pinker pulls off the achievement of describing various issues and controversies among linguists studying morphology in an engaging fashion. Those who want a rich survey of the most interesting debates surrounding morphology today will find this book just the ticket.

Pullum, Geoffrey K., and William A. Ladusaw. *Phonetic Symbol Guide*. Chicago: University of Chicago Press, 1986. For those interested in a more detailed look at the International Phonetic Alphabet, including indications of which alternative symbols have been used by which schools of linguists over the years, this is the best guide.

Radford, Andrew. *Syntax: A Minimalist Introduction*. Cambridge: Cambridge University Press, 1997. Radford is a gifted explainer, and this is an introduction to Chomskyan syntax as engaged in since the early 1990s, rather different and less layman-friendly than the earlier rendition mainly presented in this set for practical purposes.

Robinson, Andrew. *The Story of Writing*. London: Thames & Hudson, 2007. This is a solid survey of the origin or writing and the proliferation of writing systems worldwide. Some surveys on this subject seek to make in-house cases of various kinds; this one is admirably just-the-facts.

Sacks, David. *Letter Perfect: the Marvelous History of our Alphabet from A to Z*. New York: Broadway Books, 2003. This is the most readable and most up-to-date survey of how the alphabet came to be. It pulls off the trick of getting in much detail while also being hard to put down. For most who are interested in the history of writing, this, although nominally about the alphabet specifically, is the book to buy.

Sampson, Geoffrey. *Writing Systems: A Linguistic Introduction*. Palo Alto, CA: Stanford University Press, 1990. A detailed and insightful survey of writing systems, written from the perspective of linguistic science by a fine teacher.

Sapir, Edward. *Language: An Introduction to the Study of Speech*. Charleston, SC: BiblioBazaar, 2007. This book is now very old (originally published in 1921), but it remains a concise, elegantly written introduction to the basic tenets of modern linguistics. Today's particular frameworks did not exist in the 1920s, of course, but Sapir's is a classic presentation showing what it is to "think like a linguist."

Saussure, Ferdinand de. *Course in General Linguistics*. Translated by Roy Harris. London: Duckworth, 1983. Strangely enough, de Saussure's foundational work (known as *Cours* in French) was not available in English translation until 1983. Those interested in engaging the original who do not happen to know French will find this translation much more useful than the French original, which was in French.

———. *Writings in General Linguistics*. Translated by Carol Sanders and Matthew Pires. Oxford: Oxford University Press, 2006. In the mid-'90s, a cache of new de Saussure manuscripts was discovered, which clarified many questions that had long reigned unanswered by the interesting but fragmentary notes that the original *Cours* book was based on. This book gathers the newly discovered sources in English translation and is in many ways clearer than the *Cours*.

Saville-Troike, Muriel. *The Ethnography of Communication: An Introduction*. Malden, MA: Blackwell, 2002. The standard book-length introduction to its topic, in a third edition including new chapters. Those interested in ethnography of communication should begin here.

Singh, Simon. *The Code Book: The Evolution of Secrecy from Mary, Queen of Scots to Quantum Cryptography*. New York: Anchor, 2000. This book will interest those whose interest in writing systems includes, as it often seems to, an interest in codes and cryptography. It also has well-written accounts of the decipherment of ancient scripts.

Slobin, Dan. *The Crosslinguistic Study of Language Acquisition.* 5 vols. Hillsdale, NJ: L. Erlbaum and Associates, 1986–1997. These volumes examine how children acquire language in a vast number of different languages, lending insight into how children wrap their heads around a wide variety of constructions in languages around the world. A standard reference for scholars of language acquisition.

Tannen, Deborah. *Conversational Style: Analyzing Talk among Friends.* New York: Oxford, 2005. Hands down the most accessible and engaging presentation of the conversation-analysis perspective, with the "hook" of examining spontaneous conversation over a Thanksgiving dinner.

————. *You Just Don't Understand: Women and Men in Conversation.* New York: William Morrow & Company, 1990. Tannen is the bestselling linguist in America other than Steven Pinker, a fact which began with this first and classic book from her pen for the general public. Her popularity does not mean, however, that this book is not a crucial source of information on how linguists have analyzed how gender differentiates the way humans express themselves through language.

Traugott, Elizabeth Closs, and Bernd Heine. *Approaches to Grammaticalization.* Vols. I and II. Amsterdam: John Benjamins, 1991. Benchmark anthologies on grammaticalization, containing articles on the process in several language families; those seeking detailed coverage of the process around the world and through time will value these two books.

Watkins, Calvert, ed. *The American Heritage Dictionary of Indo-European Roots.* Boston: Houghton Mifflin, 1985. This will serve those who want a brass-tacks look at how Indo-Europeanists do comparative reconstruction. This is a book version of an appendix included in the *American Heritage Dictionary,* aimed at a general readership.

Watts, Richard, Sachiko Ide, and Konrad Ehlich, eds. *Politeness in Language: Studies in Its History, Theory, and Practice.* Berlin: Mouton de Gruyter, 2006. The foundational work on politeness in language (Brown and Levinson's *Politeness,* listed above) has been criticized for assuming a conception of politeness as universal when in fact cultures vary in what is considered polite and not. This collection of articles addresses these issues while still taking Brown and Levinson as a benchmark.

Winford, Donald. *An Introduction to Contact Linguistics.* Malden, MA: Blackwell, 2003. An academic survey of work on language contact, an area of inquiry that has only crystallized over the past 20 years or so in such a way that one could compose a useful book on the subject; Winford has done that.

Wolfram, Walt, and Natalie Schilling-Estes. *Hoi Toide on the Outer Banks: The Story of the Ocracoke Brogue*. Chapel Hill, NC: University of North Carolina Press, 1997. A brisk and readable study of the origin of the interesting dialect of the island of Okracoke off of North Carolina, written by specialists in how socially conditioned language variation leads to language change.

Wooffitt, Robin. *Conversation Analysis and Discourse Analysis: A Comparative and Critical Introduction*. London: Sage, 2005. This book outlines the field of conversational analysis in survey fashion, pitched on an undergraduate level and thus not requiring previous knowledge of jargon and previous studies.

**Internet Resources**

The American Heritage Dictionary of the English Language. www.bartleby.com/61. This dictionary is now online and is the most reliable source on etymologies, including its famous list of Indo-European roots and, more recently, Proto-Semitic ones. Between these features and its submission of usage questions to a panel of linguists and writers, this dictionary is a linguist's friend.

Ethnologue. www.ethnologue.com. This site has an entry on every known language in the world, with data on location, population, names of dialects, etc., as well as detailed language maps of all regions of the world (this last is difficult to find for many areas and online is easily printed out).

Language Hat. www.languagehat.com. This site is more of a "language nerd" site than Language Log, less concerned with the media than with engaging with issues such as translation and the art of writing. Recommended for a nice combination of erudition and spirit.

Language Log. languagelog.ldc.upenn.edu/nll. This is one of the most popular and influential blogsites on language, with daily posts from a stable of academic linguists on topics usually concerning the use of language and claims about language in the media and the light that the science of language sheds on them. Posts are well-written and often substantial, and those by site leaders Geoffrey Pullum and Mark Liberman have been published in book form (*Far From the Madding Gerund*).

**Notes**

# Notes

**Notes**

**Notes**